PROVIDING PROMISE

T0160779

A NAVY WIDOW'S JOURNEY TO HOPE

"I could not put this book down. Kris Rystrom Emmert has painted an unforgettable journal of her journey through the death of her navy pilot husband, Jon Rystrom. This is her story of a wonderful marriage and devastating loss. But the story does not end there. Through this journey from tragedy to triumph, devastation to closure, has emerged one of the most incredible stories of deepest grief to eternal hope that can only be found through Jesus Christ. This story will capture your attention and emotions and will challenge you to see past disappointments and tragedies in life to the eternal comfort and grace of a deep faith in God. Read and be blessed. Believe and be transformed."

—JIMMY DRAPER, President Emeritus of Lifeway

"In the past several years, we have simultaneously seen an uprising of recognition and respect for those who serve the rest of us, and a need for a genuine narrative of hope. Kris Rystrom Emmert's book will knock the wind out of you on both accounts. This is the true story of two heroes; one who did not survive and the other who lived to tell. I believe it is a necessary legacy to share with the next generation. Make it a point to get a copy, gather your family, and experience this story of real American heroism, a mom who rose from the ashes and a new life built on promises that not even death could destroy."

—JOANNA SANDERS, Author of *Fire Women: Sexual Purity & Submission for the Passionate Woman*

"For anyone who has been devastated by the death of a loved one, this book will deliver the truth and encouragement everyone needs to hear while going through the grieving process. The author shares her journey from anguish to peace as she walks a lonely path after her husband's death. Kris Rystrom Emmert shares her story of finding hope as she allows God to guide her through what seemed like an insurmountable mountain of grief. *Providing Promise* is a power-packed book that gives the reader an incredible true story of God's promises of redemption and hope."

—**PENELOPE CARLEVATO**, Award-winning author of *Tea on the Titanic, First Class Etiquette, The Art of Afternoon Tea,* and *The Tea Lover's Journal*

"When the journey of grief is a road you must follow, remember that many have traveled that road before. Learn from their experience. Each journey is unique, but there are shared experiences that can help guide us along the way. Kris's story began decades ago. Her story is a look into the deep recesses of grief. It is a captivating journey, compelling, truthful, and an incredible adventure from grief to hope. It is very instructive for those who are given the privilege to walk with someone in their journey of loss and grief. Read how God traveled with her and shaped the experience. Put *Providing Promise* on your reading list today!"

—**CHAPLAIN DAVID MULLIS**, USN (Ret.)

"When I first heard Kris Rystrom Emmert speak, I was completely in awe of her and how she overcame life's hardest hit. Her book, *Providing Promise*, tells her story of tragedy, fear, grief and her heroic efforts to pull her life together for her two daughters. Kris Rystrom Emmert is a strong, bold woman who took the biggest challenge and found that only her unwavering faith in God would see her through to the promises that He gives us all. If you get a chance to hear her speak, it is memorable and life changing as is her book, *Providing Promise: A Navy Widows Journey to Hope*."

— **JAMIE W. LEWIS**, CRMC, RMM, General Sales Manager WJBZ FM/ Praise 96.3, Knoxville Advertising Hall of Fame 2004, Recipient of the Robert McCabe Silver Medal Award 2019

"This is a great book for anyone that has lost a loved one. It is very well written with a lot of details of military life. It is a great story of support from both the military family and the Lord."

— **LUTHER E. SHELTON**, Staff Sergeant US Marine Corp (Retired), Member of East TN Veterans Honor Guard

Kris will inspire you to trust God's plan for your life, even when it looks nothing like what you expected. Through a tragic event that changed everything, Kris shares her journey and struggle with God in a vulnerable and honest way. Her story is a gift to anyone who has ever wondered, *"Where are you Lord?"*

— **JENNY BUSHKELL**, Christian Talk Radio Host, *Crossroads With Jenny Bushkell*

"I just finished the book *Providing Promise*. I started reading it, and it touched home so much I had to stop. See, in 2018 my oldest son Jacob was murdered on base at Fort Polk Louisiana. Something told me I had to finish this book, so I started at 7 pm yesterday evening and read it until 3 am this morning. I was on chapter 13 when I started breaks in between. I want to say thank you to Kris. Even though our losses are different—hers being her husband and mine being my son—the grieving, the anger, the sadness, the confusion, the unanswered questions, the not knowing, having no closure, no justice, my faith in God, my sadness with God, my wanting answers, my healing, my cries, my never, my firsts. This book touched on every level. I understood what Kris was saying. I could relate as if we were walking in the same shoes, just different paths. I prayed for Jacob as he went to the army. I prayed Psalms 91 all the time. I now realize that prayer wasn't for him—it was for me and what God was getting ready to bring me through. I know it's been 25 years for Kris, and she is at peace. It has been almost a year for me, and I still struggle, but I know I will find my peace one day. I thank Kris from the bottom of my heart and soul for writing this book—not just for herself but for all the other people in the world who are grieving whatever their last maybe. This isn't just a 'dead book'—it's a book to make us alive again. ♥"

—**BOBBI JO MALCOLM**, Army Gold Star Mom

"My faith has been strengthened by this story. Kris' vivid imagery paints a riveting and compelling narrative that you just can't pull away from. I can't help but be inspired by this epic story of love, loss, redemption and hope. I'm looking forward to watching this on the big screen someday!"

—**SOFIA J LYONS**, Film Producer of *The Long Goodbye: The Kara Tippetts Story*

PROVIDING PROMISE

A Navy Widow's Journey to Hope

KRIS RYSTROM EMMERT

with Julie Voudrie
Foreword by Dr. Bob Reccord

Carpenter's Son Publishing

PROVIDING
PROMISE

To my girls, Jordyn and Taylor:

Your light and laughter fill my life with joy. You love me through the storms, and I am forever grateful to have you as my daughters. May you continue to hold onto God's promises throughout your lives and always remember your father deeply loved you.

Love, Mom

In loving memory of my beloved husband,
Commander Jon Alvin Rystrom,
and the crew of VAW-124 Bear Ace 603

Lost but never forgotten

Contents

Foreword

"Since you've never served in the military, what makes you think you could minister to those of us who *are* serving when we suffer tragedy?" The attractive young woman who voiced the penetrating question was the wife of a navy lieutenant commander soon to be deployed. I knew she hadn't meant it harshly but simply out of honest concern and uncertainty.

I was being interviewed by the historic First Baptist Church of Norfolk, Virginia, as its potential new senior pastor. Norfolk is home to arguably the largest concentration of military in the world. While both my biological father and my adoptive father had served in the military, I had not. At that moment, I searched for some amazingly wise and profound response that would satisfactorily answer this piercing question, but nothing brilliant came to mind. I simply knew from experience that when people walk through tragedy, whether they are privileged to be in the military or not, they all transition through the same stages of grief.

Tragedy—regardless of the context—shatters life, never allowing it to be quite the same again. And whenever tragedy is experienced by people anywhere and under any condition, they cry for understanding, empathy, compassion, love, and support. This is the only answer I could offer in that moment. Who but God could have known that only a few months later, I would be officiating her husband's funeral?

As my wife and I came to know Kris in the wake of the disaster, we saw a woman with two young daughters trudging through the muck and the mire that tragedy brings. It is said that heartache and tragedy often can make a person. While this is somewhat true, I have discovered that far more often, it *reveals* the person. For Kris, tragedy ushered in a crisis of belief that continually bombarded her with soul-searching questions: Where is God in this? Why did God let this happen? Why us? Why now? (And that's okay; God was not threatened by her questions.)

Finding no real answers to life's *why* questions, Kris began focusing on two important *what* questions: What is God teaching me in the wake of this tragedy? and What does God desire to change in me through this tragedy? Although drowning in grief, she began taking increasingly significant steps in her faith and deepening her dependence upon God. And then—slowly—she started the long, lonely journey toward healing.

I have found it true that God shapes us far more in the valleys of heartache and loss than on the mountaintops of success and victory. It is not that He causes them, but He redeems them. Recovery is largely dependent upon the choices we make when moving through what feels like the impossible. In 2 Corinthians 1:4, we are told that God "comforts us in all our troubles, so that we can comfort those in any trouble with the comfort we ourselves receive from God." This truth has been fleshed out repeatedly in Kris's life. Having found hope amid heartbreak, she now works tirelessly to support, care, and love those who need it most.

So grab a cup of coffee or a hot tea, find a comfortable and quiet place to relax, and walk through this remarkable journey with Kris. It may reshape your focus on what's really important, offer hope to you for the challenges you face, and persuade you that God is *never* finished with you, regardless of the heartache that might be suffocating you. Don't ever forget the promise He holds out to you during every struggle:

> Do not be afraid, for I have ransomed you.
>   I have called you by name; you are mine.
> When you go through deep waters,
>   I will be with you.

When you go through rivers of difficulty,
    You will not drown.
When you walk through the fire of oppression, you
    will not be burned up;
    the flames will not consume you.
For I am the Lord your God. (Isa. 43:1–3)

—Dr. Robert E. "Bob" Reccord
    Author and Founder, Total Impact Ministries
    Canton, Georgia

A Word from the Co-Author

I remember when Kris handed me small pieces of wreckage from Jon's plane. We were well into the interview process for this book, and she kept bringing in items dating from the tragic mishap. That day, she brought in some special framed letters, various photographs, newspaper clippings, and the like, but the pieces of wreckage impacted me the most. Small, white, ragged pieces of honeycomb metal with sharp edges—no more than three inches wide—one stamped with letters, the other with rivet holes ripped open from the plane's violent impact with the Ionian Sea. I cried as I held them, their weight far exceeding their few grams of mass. I shouldn't be holding these—two pieces from the fractured fuselage of an E-2C Hawkeye that once housed sixty million dollars of technology and the souls of five airmen.

I looked up and met Kris's gaze as she witnessed my initial reaction. "I'm so sorry," I whispered. I didn't know what else to say. For her, the wound was old, well-healed, and softened with grace and time, but I was experiencing the tragedy little by little as Kris unfolded her story. That day, the actuality of her loss, the loss of the other families, and the tragedy of five precious lives cut painfully short became extremely real to me as I held the wreckage in the palm of my hand.

Wreckage. We all have it—perhaps not pieces of a plane but shattered pieces left behind from losses we have suffered. Whether it's a loved one's death, a divorce, chronic disease, a failed business, broken dreams, childhood trauma, or estranged relationships, each of us has suffered or will suffer loss; it's simply a fact of life. We live in a fallen world where bad things happen to good people. The question is not whether we will suffer loss but rather what we will do with the pieces left behind.

Can shattered lives truly be put together again? That is the central question answered in this book as Kris shares her struggle with faith, sorrow, loneliness, and doubt on a journey through grief and into hope. As she bravely shows us—yes, the shattered pieces of a life can be put together again. And though the process is not without pain, tears, and trials, there is joy, life, and peace for anyone who surrenders a broken heart to the only One who can heal it.

I challenge you to consider your own shattered pieces as you read this book and take courage from one who has traveled the road of loss and found life again. Like Kris, you too can find joy after disaster, peace after heartache, and purpose after loss.

Weeping may last through the night,
  but joy comes with the morning. (Ps. 30:5)

—Julie Voudrie
Co-Author

Preface

"Do you know who this is?" I ask as I hold a framed family portrait and point to a man in navy dress blues smiling broadly and standing next to his wife and their two little girls.

Rystrom Family Portrait 1993

"That's Daddy Jon," replies Isabella cheerfully. "And this is you, and this is Taylor, and this is Mommy," she continues, her bright, hazel eyes scanning the other familiar faces. She's seen this picture many times. There I am with shoulder-length, curly, brown hair, dressed in pearls and a white blazer with a lace overlay and shoulder pads typical of early '90s fashion. On my lap is baby Taylor in her pink, ruffled dress and pink headband with a white bow on her nearly bald head. Jordyn's face is framed by curly, dark blond hair—the same color as her father's. A pink bow matches her polka-dot jumper. Her sparkling eyes are a mirror image of Isabella's. Behind us is Jon—his hair neatly trimmed, and his dark blue eyes set off with laugh lines—looking dashing in his navy uniform with his Joint Services Medal and rows of award ribbons under his gold wings. All four of us are smiling—happy, close, and so content.

For as long as she can remember, my granddaughter has seen this picture on the shelf sitting next to other family portraits taken over the years. And while she knows the names and faces—and she giggles at my out-of-style hairdo and how little her aunt and mommy once were—there's so much more she doesn't know about this photograph. There's so much *I* didn't know in 1993 when I donned my Sunday best, dolled up my girls in their cute outfits, and primped their hair.

I was elated as Jon drove our sweet family to Olan Mills Portrait Studios a few weeks before he was to be deployed on the aircraft carrier USS *Theodore Roosevelt*. This would be our first formal family portrait to include Taylor, who had been born six months earlier. While I dreaded the thought of Jon being at sea for the next six months and me having to hold down the fort alone, I was thankful we could capture an image of our growing family at this moment in time. As I posed for the picture, all I knew was that with Jon by my side, life was good, and the future was bright.

What I didn't know was that my picture-perfect life was about to be shattered into a million pieces as every wife's worst nightmare became my reality. The smiles would be replaced with gut-wrenching grief, the sparkling eyes would overflow with tears, and the innocence of my daughters' childhoods would be stolen by a harsh and tangible loss. My optimism, contentment, and happiness would be overcome by heartache, confusion, doubt, anger, uncertainty, and loneliness in ways I never could have imagined.

I also didn't know that out of the rubble of my shattered life, hope would return. That out of disaster, my life would reemerge, not destroyed but redeemed. That my daughters—who were too young to truly know their father—would grow into lovely young women filled with purpose and a reflection of their father's strong character. That Jon's firstborn would have a precocious, lively, radiant daughter of her own named Isabella, who would fill our lives with love and laughter. And that through Isabella, I would once again enjoy Jon's high-energy personality and famous sense of humor.

Twenty-five years have passed since that family portrait was taken, and I have decided the time is right to take the photo off the shelf and tell Isabella the story behind the picture. She knows the basics already: "Daddy Jon was kind, loving, and caring. He was a flight attendant in the navy and died in a plane crash." I guess that in the mind of a seven-year-old, a flight attendant and a naval flight officer is pretty much the same thing.

Jon would have grinned at her explanation. And he would have belly-laughed at her reaction to his college wrestling picture taken in the late 1970s. "Why did he have poufy hair and wear those weird clothes?" she asks, frowning. I show her other pictures of Daddy Jon in his flight suit and of his plane, the E-2C Hawkeye, along with some of his patches and his flight jacket.

She has more questions. Jon passed down not only his physical traits to his daughters and granddaughter but also his personality traits as well. One of those traits is an inquisitive mind. Isabella is full of questions!

"When and where was he born? How did he become a flight attendant? Why did he go into the navy?" Glancing through the pictures, she asks again, "And why was he a wrestler who wore funny clothes and had poufy hair?" (Her inherited sense of humor was on full display.) In addition to the questions she wants to ask Daddy Jon, she also has things she wants him to know.

Jon Rystrom's Nebraska Wesleyan wrestling picture

"I'd want to tell him that Mom is doing great—that she got straight As and passed the bar." (My oldest daughter, Jordyn, recently became a lawyer.) Isabella lowers her voice noticeably and adds, "I wish he was still alive. I don't like sad endings."

No one likes sad endings—or sad middles or sad beginnings. And yet life is filled with them. Some of us had childhoods loaded with burdens and traumas, whereas others had wonderful childhoods. Suddenly, like me, they found themselves blindsided by the unthinkable and are left reeling from the heartbreaking consequences. Whenever and however your "sad" comes, questions are certain to follow: Why? Why me? Why us? Could this have been prevented, and why wasn't it? How can I go on? How will I survive? Is it even possible to do so?

The questions go deeper as your world is rocked to its core: Where is God? Why didn't He stop it? Why didn't He fix it? How can a loving, powerful God let something like this happen? Does He understand my pain? Does He see me at all? Does He even care? Does He even exist? Is there one good reason why I should live another day?

These are questions I've asked myself, and while I struggled to find answers, I remembered promises Jon and I made to each other and promises God made to us—promises of hope and a future, of peace that passes understanding, of never forsaking us, and so much more. Even as I remembered them, I questioned them. And like a spinning compass whose needle eventually points to true north, I found myself returning to what I had always known to be true.

Isabella understands about promises and has already made several of her own: "No matter what happens, I will always keep my promises to God. I will never, ever, ever not keep my promises to the Lord, my family, and friends." That's easy to say when you're seven years old and playing with toys; it's much harder to say when you're several decades older and life has hit you hard in the gut. Suddenly, you find that keeping your promises is much harder and costlier than you ever imagined.

And what about God's promises to us? Isabella has ideas about that as well: "God never breaks His promise—*never*." And what about all the evil and pain and suffering in the world? "The devil made sin," she explains. "The devil is mean, cruel, and unfair. One day, the devil will be destroyed. Finally, he's gone forever!"

As simple as a second-grader's theology can be, it does raise some meaningful questions: Does God ever break His promises? Does He keep His promises safe? And when the storms of life overtake us, what do we hang on to and what do we let go of? Do we keep our own promises safe? I've made promises I intend to keep, as Isabella says, no matter what—promises to Jon, to myself, to my family, and to God. This book is born out of the resolve not only to keep my promises but also to provide promise to others—to provide promise to you—the promise of healing, redemption, and peace. By sharing my journey from grief to hope, I wish to offer you a rope you can hang on to during your storm and healing from the pains of your past. If God can mend a shattered heart like mine, He can certainly do the same for you.

With this book, I also want to leave a legacy for my daughters and to honor Jon's memory and sacrifice for our country. As a public speaker, I have shared my experience with thousands of people but never with this level of detail and never in writing. With the benefit of twenty-five years of perspective, now is the perfect time to present these precious—and sometimes painful— memories and the valuable, life-giving lessons I've learned.

So how do I answer Isabella's questions about Daddy Jon, both the ones she asks now and the ones she hasn't yet known to ask? And how do I do it while providing God's promises to anyone who reads this book? I do it using the power of story—Jon's story, which is told here as a narrative based on my first-person accounts and those of his family and friends, along with lengthy research into his service records, interviews with military personnel, personal letters, photographs, newspaper articles, and other documents and memorabilia. To honor his service in the navy, I describe Jon's career with accuracy. As fictionalized as the story may seem, it is true.

If this were the end of the story, what a sad story it would be. But it's only the beginning. Jon was the kind of man you meet only once in a lifetime—he truly was—and I'm not the only one who thought so. Jon's love for life, his unselfish nature, and his strong work ethic rubbed off on all who had the privilege of knowing him. He almost never complained, and he treated everyone around him fairly. He loved kids, dogs, and underdogs, and I'll be forever blessed that Jon loved me.

When people first hear about my loss, they always want to know: How did you survive? What was it like to lose your husband and the father of your children? How did you find hope?

But to comprehend what I lost that fateful March morning on Seagrass Reach, you need to grasp the depth of the extraordinary love Jon and I shared and the lasting impact of his character, affirmation, and affection on my life. Once you know what I lost, you'll more fully appreciate what I suffered and what I eventually gained.

Let me begin our story by introducing you to my beloved Jon. Isabella's first questions about her grandfather were about when and where was he born, so I think that is as good a place as any to start.

Jon's story touched many lives, but it is his and my story alone that I am telling. Ours is a story of love and loss, romance and remorse, heartbreak and healing. So, readers, as you journey with me to the highest highs and the lowest lows, we'll face some tough questions—and to be honest, I won't have all the answers. But my goal through it all is to Provide Promise to you—God's promises. Promise of Joy. Promise of Peace. Promise of Hope.

* * *

My dear Isabella, the old family portrait is off the shelf, and it's time now for Grandma to tell you the story—the whole story.

1

Growing Up

SPRINGTIME 1965
1400 CENTRAL TIME ZONE
STROMSBURG, NEBRASKA, USA
41°11′53″ N, 97°59′16″ W

Midwestern towns have their own unique charm, and Stromsburg was no exception. With streets laid out in perfect grids, quaint storefronts lining the old city square, and modest homes dating back to another time, "The Swedish Capital of Nebraska" created an island of trees, homes, shops, and churches in an ocean of prairie. Located in the East Central region of Nebraska, Stromsburg, with a population slightly north of a thousand, was the largest city for miles around.

Outside of town, the land opened to wide prairies and endless acres of cropland punctuated with the occasional farmhouse and barn and a windbreak of trees, all topped with a sky so big you could see a thunderstorm coming from miles away. The unhindered winds created waves of swaying green in the summer and massive snowdrifts in the winter. Under the gentle, flat-to-rolling land lay some of the richest and most productive soil on the planet. (There's a good reason Nebraska is known as the Cornhusker State.)

Along with their five children, Mervin and Josephine Rystrom lived in a humble, two-story, wooden-clad, white farmhouse that had seen its fair share of bitter winters and sweltering summers. Farm life was a wonderful way to raise their family. With acres of corn, milo, and wheat to raise and an aging house to care for, there was always plenty of work for Barb, Martin, Laurie, Pat, and Jon to do. But it wasn't all work and no play. The farm's outbuildings were a child's year-round playground where, in the dead of winter, snowdrifts could reach the roof of the barn, and the old, narrow grain crib created a makeshift indoor basketball court.

While the Rystroms' soil and love for each other was rich, their bank account was not. As part-time farmers, both Mervin and Josephine worked other manual-labor jobs to keep their family clothed and fed, but money was always tight. Doing without can make you either greedy or grateful. For the Rystrom children, the latter was true.

As the youngest of five children, Jon was the live wire of the bunch, and he was always joking with and playing tricks on his older siblings. Truthfully, the family relished Jon's outgoing personality, and he was his parents' pride and joy. Despite the harsh Nebraska winters and the challenges of living in a large family with minimal resources, there was always a wealth of fun and activity when Jon was around.

> *Promise:*
> *"For I know the plans I have for you," says the Lord, "they are plans for good and not for disaster, to give you a future and a hope."*
> *Jeremiah 29:11*

Even from an early age, Jon showed distinctive qualities that would follow him into adulthood: a tactical, strategic mind, combined with practical problem solving; a persistent, can-do attitude; an active, high-energy personality; a contagious sense of humor; and yes, a sweet tooth. As he grew into adolescence, his family and friends quickly learned this blond-haired, blue-eyed Swede could beat them handily at pitch or chess as easily as he could pin an opponent to the ground in wrestling. (As a high school wrestler, Jon came in second place in the state. Twice.)

But no one really minded losing to Jon. Jon was the kind of guy everyone loved being around. Due to his Midwest upbringing, he was rooted in a down-to-earth nature and genuine value of relationship that would mark him for life. While those closest to him realized the typical Nebraska farm life would never be able to satisfy his adventurous nature, no one could have guessed how far Jon's unique qualities would take him.

Jon's childhood home, the Rystrom farmhouse, Stromsburg, NE

Almost Heaven, West Virginia

My own childhood was quite different from Jon's. While Jon came from a large family and had to work for everything, my parents sacrificed so I wouldn't have to. My middle-class family consisted of my parents and only two children—my older brother and me. They raised us in the capital city of Charleston, the most populated city of West Virginia.

My parents, Chuck and Doris Windham, both worked, but they didn't have high-paying jobs. My dad was a civil engineer, and my mother was a cartographer, a unique job choice for a woman in the 1970s. Our family wasn't poor, but my parents had to be creative to provide what we needed and wanted. We always drove used cars, and vacations usually consisted of camping trips built around Southern Gospel sings in our region.

Growing up in Charleston was filled with fun and entertaining activities. My brother was involved in the local little league baseball and football programs, while I cheered beside the teams as a Kanawha City Colt cheerleader. On clear days, we rode our bikes to school surrounded by the beautifully landscaped homes in our suburban neighborhood. Summer days always included trips to the local pool with friends or boat rides down the Kanawha City river. It was an exciting day for our community when Pizza Hut opened its doors only a few blocks from our house. It turned into the local hangout for my friends and me as we ate pizza and learned to play Pac Man.

My parents were loving and caring, happily married, and never fought with each other. They were strong Christians and very involved in our local church. Though I did have a genuine conversion experience with God when I was nine years old, my own faith was more of a formality than a lifestyle. I was in church every time the doors were open, but I was more interested in being popular and having all the things I saw my wealthier classmates enjoying.

I was blessed to be part of such a kind family but realized that life could get tough even as a child. In fifth grade, I experienced for the first time rude and cruel remarks from my classmates. I was a skinny, awkward preteen, and my classmates bullied me without mercy, calling me "bush woman" because of my frizzy, curly hair and abnormal big eyes. One day in sixth grade, I had to give a report in front of our English class. When I walked up to the front of the room, several boys started howling like a dog. Some even pretended to gag and vomit as I read the report. After- school cry sessions became the norm in my bedroom on those days.

As I transitioned into middle school, I found extra-curricular activities could fill my pain and loneliness. I played the clarinet for the Horace Mann Junior High marching band but always dreamed of marching in front of our band with the popular majorettes. Determined to make the corp, I rode the city bus to downtown Charleston each week to take baton lessons at a local dance studio. Every day I practiced my twirling routines in the front yard of our modest home. Although the bullies' ugly remarks continued into middle school, I didn't let them keep me from trying out for the majorette corps. To my accusers' surprise, I made the corp, and my journey to coveted popularity and significance began.

Neither of my parents, who were both incredibly accepting of me, knew how driven I was to feel significant. My determination to overcome insults from my peers led me to work extra hard to earn straight A's in all my classes, but nothing healed the sting of their rejection, and their rude remarks would haunt me for years.

Krissy Windham as a majorette
Horace Mann Junior High marching band, Charleston, WV

2

The Next Steps

26 FEB 1978
1200 CENTRAL DAYLIGHT TIME UTC-5
MINDEN HIGH SCHOOL
MINDEN, NEBRASKA, USA
40°49'54" N, -98°57'20 W"

With his high school years behind him, Jon's farm-life work ethic took him to college at Nebraska Wesleyan University in Lincoln, Nebraska. Seeking a career in education, Jon dove into college with hard work and determination. Jon was not only part of Wesleyan's wrestling team but also worked full time at night to make ends meet. After graduation, he was offered a job as a teacher, guidance counselor, and football/wrestling coach at a small-town high school in Minden, Nebraska. It seemed to be the perfect fit.

Although Jon thought he was following his dreams, after a year of teaching, he felt discouraged with where his life was headed. The meager paycheck he earned was a joke; he'd expected better after graduating from college with a bachelor's in psychology. He couldn't even afford decent housing and had to live in one of the poorest sections of this Midwest farm town. That was not the kind of life he had dreamed of, and if he ever wanted a future with his college sweetheart, who he was still dating, he'd have to do much better.

When a navy recruiter visited the high school one cold winter day, Jon, as the guidance counselor, coordinated his visit with students. Before he left, the recruiter took a long look at Jon and asked, "How good are you at math?" Jon smiled. He was a math teacher after all. He had excelled in math during his college days and loved the challenge of problem solving. When the recruiter offered to fly him down to Florida to take the Aviation Selection Test Battery, Jon took the offer, wanting to see if he had what it took to be a naval aviator. Turns out, he did.

Then came a serious decision to make. Should he leave the high school classroom and become an officer in the navy? The timing seemed right. There was little to aim for where he was, and the navy offered adventure, financial security, and a career he could be proud of. Additionally, it offered a sense of significance, which was important to Jon and was one of the main reasons he was considering a career change. His college sweetheart was reluctant at first about this change in Jon's career and their future, but with some thought and coaxing, she eventually gave her blessing.

Jon wanted to fly, and, like the career of every aviation officer in the navy, that path always started in the same place: Aviation Officer Candidate School (AOCS) in Pensacola, Florida. No matter what their duties or where they served, all naval aviators forged a bond through the shared crucible of Pensacola, and Jon wanted to be part of this band of brothers.

When the school year was over, Jon, without hesitation, quit his teaching job, packed up his little green Triumph Spitfire convertible, and set off to sunny Florida.

Silver Dollar Salute

26 SEPT 1978
1200 CENTRAL DAYLIGHT TIME UTC-5
NAVAL AIR STATION PENSACOLA
PENSACOLA, FLORIDA, USA
30°35'57" N, 87°28'83 W"

Arriving in front of Building 626 with its iconic white columns, Jon and the other eager aviation cadets didn't know what to expect of their new training camp. And they certainly didn't know what to think of Staff Sergeant McAffee, a marine drill instructor. McAffee was known for his unmistakable gruff voice that would rapidly shoot out commands like hot lead through a machine gun. If commands were not followed exactly as Staff Sergeant McAffee demanded, they found themselves on the ground doing countless pushups. McAffee was like a dad to AOCS Class 15-78. He put them to bed at night and woke them up at "0-dark-30" each morning. He marched them off to class, yelled at them through endless hours of physical training, and made sure they ate their meals in less time than anyone thought humanly possible.

The cadets knew not to speak to the sergeant unless spoken to, and only in the position of attention. That meant heels together, feet at a forty-five-degree angle, thumbs on trouser seams, fingers curled, shoulders rolled back, and eyeballs looking straight to the front. Jon and his classmates understood quickly that they didn't do anything unless told to do it!

It turned out there were many things Jon and his classmates unexpectedly had to endure. When he left his high school teaching job to start his career as an aviation officer in the navy, he figured he would be spending his time studying aerodynamics and aviation physiology. He didn't count on learning how to properly stand in line or neatly make his bed or practice endlessly the detailed technique of polishing shoes.

The cadets learned that their assignments would be difficult but significant for the protection of the United States. The sobering realities became front and center when Jon and his classmates were confronted for the first time with an anti-personnel bomblet. This small, metal, baseball-sized object was designed to blast hundreds of high-velocity steel pellets in every direction with the intent to maim and kill human targets. Three hundred sixty of these pellets were packed together into one cluster bomb with the combined capability to take out an entire enemy position with one strike.

Am I ready to drop one of these and kill people? Do I know why I am here? Jon was faced with serious questions, and only he could answer them for himself. *I am here to become a flight officer in the United States Navy, to protect our country from enemies far and wide, and to carry out orders that will require me to drop bombs and fire missiles at the enemy with the intent to kill. If that's not what I'm here for, I need to leave—now.*

Over the next several weeks, Jon saw several of his fellow candidates do just that. They left. Due to the endless grueling hours of physical training and the high-pressure tactics of McAffee, several of Jon's classmates chose the "Drop on Request" option. Jon, on the other hand, had made a lifelong commitment and was not a quitter. He and his twenty-nine fellow candidates chose to stick it out. They pushed themselves and each other. Jon thought running through Nebraska snowdrifts was hard, but that was nothing compared to slugging through miles of Pensacola sand in sweltering heat and humidity.

Navy cadet Jon Rystrom, Aviation Officer Candidate School,
Pensacola, FL 1978

As the weeks went by, Jon noticed that he and his companions were becoming a real team, focusing on perseverance, attention to detail, and the discipline they would desperately need if they were to succeed in the navy environment. While each came into AOCS with a four-year college degree, they were all receiving a priceless education that would alter them forever. As AOCS wore on, the boot-camp atmosphere transformed. More responsibilities shifted to the officers-to-be, and classes began covering topics such as pre-flight training and aerodynamics.

All candidates, regardless of their path, received critical sea- and land-survival training. They practiced ditching out of a plane with an ejection seat and exiting an aircraft underwater. Sometimes they practiced "Dilbert Dunker," a cockpit that is ridden down a slide and then flipped over into a deep pool. Other times they practiced with its evil cousin, "Helo Dunker," where students were buckled inside a simulated fuselage, which was lowered into the water and turned upside down at random positions. Though the candidates hated this exercise, they knew they needed to be prepared. No one, including Jon, ever wanted to experience what the Navy called "panic in a drum" for real.

* * *

After thirteen weeks of school, the only thing left for Jon and his classmates to do was to put on their dress whites and line up for their graduation ceremony. Jon was pleased to see his parents and college sweetheart had made the long drive from Nebraska to watch him graduate and be commissioned as a navy officer.

After crossing the stage and shaking hands with his commanding officers, Jon faced Staff Sergeant McAffee one final time. McAffee carefully looked Jon over from head to toe. The young man he saw before him was quite different from the bearded dude with permed, curly hair that he'd met thirteen weeks earlier: shoulders straight, head held high, hair carefully trimmed, and every part of his uniform perfectly in place, down to the impeccably polished white shoes. McAffee had to smile to himself. Another job well done.

"Ensign Rystrom, good morning, sir," Staff Sergeant McAffee said as he saluted Jon, who crisply saluted in return.

"Congratulations," McAffee said, smiling as he reached out and firmly shook Jon's hand. Following navy tradition, Jon reached into his pocket and gave the sergeant a silver dollar to pay for the first salute he ever received.

Later that day, when the new ensigns stood under the Blue Angels jet for their final class picture, Jon felt a sense of pride and accomplishment. He had been searching for more—more purpose, more excitement, more challenge. He knew his navy training had only begun, and he could hardly wait to move on to the next step of naval flight officer instruction and to the future that his new career held.

Wake Bound

While Jon was embarking on his new journey in the navy, I was graduating from high school and ready to launch into a new life of my own. Even though I had been mercilessly bullied in middle school, I earned the senior superlative of most popular. However, my quest for popularity had a dark side. My need for significance was like a black hole, and no matter what awards I earned, what achievements I accomplished, or how many compliments I received on my appearance, it was never enough.

My quest for success granted me another hard-fought-for prize: acceptance at my number-one college choice, the prestigious Wake Forest University in Winston-Salem, North Carolina. While I wouldn't admit it to myself at the time, I chose this respected school more out of pride than anything. With a low acceptance rate, tough academic reputation, and a list of respected alumni, Wake Forest was a magnet for the offspring of well-moneyed Southerners looking to propel their children into successful lives. I desperately wanted to be in the inner circle to finally achieve a status that my middle-class parents could never give me. Thankfully, my academic achievements, as well as a long list of extracurricular leadership positions, granted me the coveted position of a Wake Forest University freshman.

Like most young adults, I wanted to spread my wings and get as far away from my hometown as possible. My hardworking parents didn't have the money to pay a Wake Forest tuition, but somehow, between government aid and their own sacrifice, they found a way. I was oblivious to what my college choice cost them, and I was so focused on my own success that I didn't care. My life was all about performance and checking the boxes. Great grades? Check. Good looks? Check. Thin waistline? Check. Head majorette? Check. Most popular? Check. My faith in God hardly made the list, except to check off the *Christian* box as a sort of insurance policy and a way to appear respectable.

I wanted to be seen as a good girl, yet I desired the money, good looks, and successful career that I considered the yardsticks of significance. I took God off the throne of my heart and put myself there instead. I was learning how to get the affirmation I desired through my own efforts and inner drive, and I didn't need faith for that.

As I was making plans in my final months as a high school senior, Jon was continuing the next phase of his naval training and making choices that would have life-changing consequences for both of us.

Flying High

14 MAR 1979
0800 CENTRAL TIME ZONE
VT-10, TRARON TEN
NAVAL AIR STATION PENSACOLA
PENSACOLA, FLORIDA, USA
30°35'04" N, 87°31'00" W

The T-34 scurried down the runway under sunny skies and calm winds. Pulling back on the stick, the flight instructor coaxed the single-prop plane into the air, leaving the tarmac at Saufley Field far behind. Directly behind the experienced pilot sat Ensign Jon Rystrom, a naval flight officer (NFO) in training. Jon loved getting out of the classroom and into the air. The T-34's bubble canopy provided excellent views of the Florida Panhandle coastline below.

Before arriving for AOCS, each recruit had received a thorough physical and screening to see if they met the exacting requirements for flight operations. While Jon was highly intelligent and physically fit, his eyesight wasn't good enough to qualify him as a pilot, so he was assigned to be an NFO. This classification meant that Jon would not fly an aircraft but operate the missions in the back of the aircraft. Jon was thrilled to be part of the aviation world regardless of what his assignment entailed.

Even though Jon was training as an NFO and not a pilot, he was learning important lessons in basic flight characteristics and navigation. Straight out of AOCS, Jon and the other fresh ensigns continued their training in various squadrons, depending on their designations. All air squadrons for fixed-wing aircraft start with a "V," and as a student NFO, Jon was sent for six months to Training Squadron (VT) 10, which, like AOCS, was located at Naval Air Station, Pensacola. VT-10 was known as the Wildcats, and their stated mission was to "provide world class Primary & Intermediate student Naval Flight Officer training and prepare aircrew to fly with courage, fight with honor, and lead with commitment."

The young ensigns, all feeling confident, were convinced they were prepared to do exactly that. They were eager to move beyond AOCS and proceed with the next phase of their training. However, they quickly discovered that they had much to learn before they could earn their ultimate prize—the Wings of Gold from the United States Navy—and take to the skies.

Hours of classroom instruction in weather, flight rules, and, of course, the T-34 flight manual, along with extended time in various computer simulators contributed to their extensive training. The ensigns didn't require Marine DIs to keep them in top physical condition; the sense of pride these aviators-in-training had in being naval officers was the only motivation they needed.

While Jon knew he wanted to be an NFO, he didn't know on which aircraft he would serve. During his time at VT-10, Jon was presented with several options, based on his performance during his training. After carefully considering which path to take, Jon chose the E-2C Hawkeye, a five-seater, twin-engine, turboprop plane with a large, round rotodome on top–used as an early warning radar detection and mission coordination aerial platform.

Jon had yet to earn his NFO wings, but after completing his six-month training with VT-10, he was one step closer. He was beginning to find the "more" he had been looking for, and the camaraderie he experienced fit in well with his gregarious personality. However, at age twenty-four, Jon was ready to invest himself in something that mattered. He missed his girlfriend back home. Maybe when this initial training was over, he would finally marry his college sweetheart and they could begin their lives together wherever the Navy planted them.

However, there was still some serious work ahead before Jon could truly launch his navy career. He had to stay focused on the task at hand and perform at his best if he ever wanted to escape the poverty and dead-end life he'd left behind in Nebraska.

Navy cadet Jon Rystrom next to the T-34
Training at Aviation Officer Candidate School, Pensacola, FL

3

The Hawkeye

I was excited when I drove through the perfectly
landscaped entrance of Wake Forest University at the start of my
freshman year. But as the semester began, that thrill was soon
replaced with sheer panic, and I had only myself to blame. Full
of confidence when I registered for my first semester, I chose the
most challenging courses, but once classes started, it didn't take
long to figure out that I was in way over my head. I even turned
to my faith in desperation and put Bible verses on my walls, looking for divine intervention!

It became painfully clear that my high school strategy of
working harder than anyone else wouldn't cut it at this highly
ranked university. After only one semester, I was in danger of
flunking out of my number-one college pick. In truth, I really
didn't belong there. I was surrounded by brilliant students who
were better prepared than I was for this demanding environment. I loved being at Wake—the picturesque campus, the upper-class students, the Greek life, and the exciting football
games. I didn't want to leave, and I definitely didn't want to get
kicked out of my dream college and go back to my hometown in
shame, but that fear was quickly becoming a real possibility.

Attending those exciting football games was one of the few
reprieves from my pressure-filled study sessions. Joining the
34,000 cheering fans at Groves Stadium to watch our Demon
Deacons take on their Atlantic Coast Conference rivals filled me
with a sense of pride to be part of such a distinctive community.

Krissy Windham, cheering at a Wake Forest University football game,
Winston-Salem, NC 1981

At the center of all the excitement was the Wake Forest cheerleading team dressed proudly in Wake's traditional black and gold colors. As I watched the team's routines, I envisioned myself performing those cheers and stunts. Although I wasn't a trained gymnast—only a dancer at heart—I was willing to work out and train hard to learn their special skills. Finding significance academically wasn't working out, but maybe I could earn a spot on the cheerleading squad.

That idea kept rolling around in my head as I managed to eke out passing grades in all my classes and avoid the disaster of a one-way trip home. I was relieved when I could register for the spring semester, and this time I had the wisdom to sign up for easier courses.

Spring tryouts for the cheerleading squad weren't far away. I ignored the voices in my head that kept saying, *If you can't make the grades, what makes you think you can be a varsity cheerleader?* Apportioning the same work ethic I had applied to the rest of my life, I went to tryouts fully prepared. When the cheerleading squad was announced, I was ecstatic to find that I had made the varsity team. My win proved to me that with hard work and determination, there was nothing I couldn't achieve. Finally, as a varsity cheerleader at an NCAA Division 1 school, the status and popularity I desperately wanted was within my grasp.

Eye in the Sky

11 FEB 1980
1200 EASTERN TIME ZONE
RVAW-120, CARAEWTRARON ONE TWO ZERO
NAS NORFOLK
NORFOLK, VIRGINIA, USA
36°94'25" N, 76°29'05" W

Sitting in the dark interior at the back of the E-2C Hawkeye, one of the most unique-looking aircraft in the navy, and surrounded by some of the most advanced electronic surveillance technology on the planet, Jon felt like a kid in a candy store. The sixty million dollars that this aircraft was worth could certainly buy a lot of candy, and Jon was enjoying learning how to operate the E-2C's highly advanced systems.

Two months earlier, he had finally earned the coveted wings of gold, and he proudly wore the title of naval flight officer. But the training never stopped. His assignment with Carrier Airborne Early Warning Training Squadron 120 (RVAW-120) had been challenging from the beginning. For starters, students had to know the E-2C NATOPS manual backward and forward, all 750+ pages of it. But that was only the beginning of Jon's education.

Multiple hours logged in weapon system simulators, classroom instruction, and missions flown in the E-2C to gain experience in high-stress situations prepared Jon and his classmates to join squadrons operating around the world. This extensive preparation was crucial because the real mission of the E-2C was what happened in the back of the plane, where the three NFOs did their jobs. But before those critical tasks can be understood, an introduction to this unique aircraft is needed.

Nicknamed the Hummer, an E-2C Hawkeye was often heard before it was seen due to the distinctive sound of its twin turboprop engines. The Hawkeye was not a sexy aircraft like its fighter-jet counterparts. In fact, to the non-aviator, the E-2C's sixty-million-dollar price tag might have seemed like a mistake. Thanks to the large, gray, pancake-looking rotodome on top of its fuselage, the E-2C had the most unique silhouette of any U.S. Navy aircraft. Inside, in the two-person cockpit, conditions were cramped, visibility was limited, and the instruments appeared rudimentary.

The E-2C's main function was to know where the enemy was and what they were doing. Gaining this information from a great distance increased the time for sea, land, and air forces to successfully respond to enemy threats. The E-2C's sophisticated capabilities allowed it to see everything happening for three hundred nautical miles in all directions, or three million cubic miles of airspace, rightly earning it the Hawkeye, or Eye in the Sky. There was almost no operation of a carrier strike group that didn't involve the Hawkeye. In peacetime, the E-2C also assisted in humanitarian crises, search, and rescue (SAR) operations, drug interdiction, and air traffic control.

> Promise:
> "The Lord keeps watch over you as you come and go, both now and forever."
> Psalm 121:8

While it was true that any aviation squadron had to work as a team to be effective, teamwork was essential in a VAW squadron. To execute these missions and capabilities, each of the three NFOs had different responsibilities. Jon's responsibilities were that of the Combat Information Center Officer (CICO). Much like the quarterback on a football team, the CICO oversaw the coordination of his crew and the execution of the mission, all while listening to six or more radios, maintaining situational awareness, maximizing the performance of his weapon system, and keeping all the warfare commanders in the loop. The work was tedious and exacting, requiring great mental focus, which was made even more difficult by the mighty roar of engines. NFOs would be both mentally and physically exhausted when their mission was complete.

Learning the Hummer from tip to tail was critical because the mission of all the other aircraft in the air wing depended on the E-2C functioning properly. An E-2C NFO could never stop learning and could never know enough. Life and death, success and failure, could depend on the crew's collective knowledge and skill.

As Jon's time with RVAW-120 was coming to an end, he prepared to receive his orders. But he also was preparing for something else: marriage. He hoped to tie the knot with his long-time Nebraska college girlfriend and start their life together. His first tour would be sea duty, but he would train several months with his new squadron before deploying on an aircraft carrier. Hopefully, that would give him and his bride time to enjoy being newlyweds before he went off to sea. He had joined the navy, in part, to see the world. But what part of the world would he see first?

The E-2C Hawkeye

4

Freedom's Flagship

I thought I was prepared for what lay ahead when joining the Wake Forest cheerleading squad and continuing my sophomore year. On the outside, it looked as if I had it all together: I was getting noticed around campus, enjoying sorority life, and loving all the fraternity parties. Cheerleading before thousands of people at Deacs' football and basketball games was a total rush. I was checking off the boxes of "perfection" in my life with popularity and significance once again.

I loved being a part of the Wake Forest academia life, and I decided that the communications department had a lot to offer me in a major. I now had found a path forward in finding the perfect match for me professionally. Television broadcasting and interpersonal communications were exactly what I wanted to pursue for my future career. Once I took classes in my areas of interest, my grades climbed to the A/B scale. Getting a 4.0 was way out of my reach due to my horrible freshman year, but I could now see that in only two years, I would accomplish the coveted prize of becoming a WFU graduate. But there was another grading scale I was fighting to control—the scale of my weight.

Sometimes I would take a break from my hectic schedule and clear my head by taking late-night runs through the historic, tree-filled university campus. My evening runs had a darker purpose, however. For years, I was driven to control my image, success, popularity, and future. Once I joined the cheerleading squad, controlling my weight was added to the list.

I remembered having been careful about my weight the summer before entering college, keeping an eye on my plate and my scales. But once I became a varsity cheerleader, I set a personal goal of staying under 112 pounds, and I was determined to achieve it. I decided to limit myself to five hundred calories a day. This became increasingly difficult to maintain, especially on a college campus where pizza, ice cream, and soft drinks were the norm. I started a calorie journal to track not only my caloric intake but also my caloric burn. At the end of each day, I would tally the numbers, and if I

> Promise:
> "You made all the delicate, inner parts of my body and knit me together in my mother's womb. Thank you for making me so wonderfully complex! Your workmanship is marvelous—how well I know it."
> Psalm 139: 13-14

was over, I'd make up the difference by going for a run or doing aerobics in my room. If I didn't have time for exercise, I would make myself throw up instead. I dropped some weight, but I was never thin enough—at least not in my eyes. Because my body image was distorted, each time I met a weight goal I would think, *You know, I could be five pounds less,* and I would double my efforts. Before long, my weight got so low I even stopped menstruating. I found myself thinking, *Do I starve myself today or tomorrow?* I cheered for the Demon Deacons while the demon of anorexia took over my life.

Little did I know that while my life was spiraling out of control, my future husband's was just taking off.

Gonzo Station

27 JAN 1981
1400 GULF TIME ZONE, UTC+4
GONZO STATION
USS INDEPENDENCE (CV-62) WITH CVW-6, VAW-122
24°71'42" N, 58°72'47" E

Winds upward of thirty knots (thirty-five miles per hour) swept over the flight deck as the five-man crew of 602 proceeded to their E-2C parked between elevators 1 and 2 on the ship's starboard side. Dressed in olive-green flight suits, flight boots, survival vests, life jackets, and helmets, they walked slowly around the plane, reviewing their crucial pre-flight checklist: rivets popped, prop surfaces smooth, no fluid leaks, etc.

Jon was the first to enter the plane since his seat was the farthest back. He, along with the other two NFOs, proceeded down the narrow corridor, being careful not to catch their gear on any of the equipment as they scooted past. Once in their seats, they strapped themselves in and entered that mission's pre-flight data into the system. On word from the pilots that they were ready to taxi to the catapults, the NFOs turned and locked their seats forward and reported that they were prepared to taxi.

In the cockpit, the pilots finished their preflight procedures and steered the plane to follow the yellow-shirt handler as they started their taxi to the catapult. Even though the flight deck resembled a three-ringed circus with multiple planes and personnel in constant motion, the pilot kept his eyes on one person alone: his handler, who used a variety of hand signals to instruct and guide the Hawkeye to the launching point. Jon could feel the lock-in and the stretching of the plane as the launch gear was connected to the powerful steam catapult system. The pilots responded to the yellow shirt's signal to ramp up the twin turboprop engines to full military power.

As a final check, the NFOs made sure their seats were facing forward and locked and their helmet visors were down. The CICO reported to the pilot that the NFOs were ready. The pilot silently signaled readiness to launch to the yellow shirt with a salute, and the catapult officer returned a salute. The aircraft sped down the flight deck accelerating from zero to 150 miles per hour in 2.5 seconds. As the E2-C catapulted itself into the air, the force of the acceleration slammed Jon and the other crewmen back into their seats.

Disappearing rapidly behind them was USS Independence, an aircraft carrier serving in the Gulf of Oman Naval Zone of Operations, otherwise known as Gonzo Station. The Gulf of Oman, located between the Arabian Peninsula and Iran, could be a hotbed of activity. However, as a lowly nugget (an aviator on his first sea tour) with the Steeljaws of VAW-122, Jon's days rarely had a high level of excitement. There was one important job, though, that Jon and all the other nuggets in the air wing shared: adjusting to life in their new home away from home, the aircraft carrier.

Many kinds of ships, boats, and planes make up the greatest naval force in the world, but everything in the navy centers around one class of ship: the aircraft carrier. The aircraft carrier is as long as the Empire State Building is tall. Nearly six thousand people are required to run this floating city on the sea. In Jon's day, that was six thousand men, as only men could then serve on carriers. With a world-class airport, kitchens that crank out thousands of meals a day, a fully-functional hospital, a post office, laundry services, a daily newspaper, stores, a chapel, a library, and even a jail, it's easy to see how a sailor could serve on a carrier for more than a year and still not see the entire ship.

One thing Jon had to get used to while living on a carrier was the noise. With jet engines being tested, catapults launching, and planes landing, it was an everything-humming-24/7-kind-of-noisy. Sleeping was a major challenge with planes launching and landing at all hours, but after about two weeks onboard, he was so tired he learned to sleep through anything.

The long deployments made each day at sea seem much like the day before. The ship-based crew that worked below the upper decks could go weeks at a time without seeing the light of day. The only way to communicate with folks back home was through snail mail, with emphasis on *snail*. The monotony of carrier life was broken up by a few ports of call, Saturday pizza nights, or the occasional steel beach party where the flight deck turned into a mega barbecue picnic. But these distractions were few and far between.

Still, Jon had no regrets about switching careers and joining the navy and could see himself rising in the ranks and achieving the success he'd always wanted. However, his marriage was suffering. He'd been married for less than six months when the Indy started her Indian Ocean cruise. Letters from his new bride had been terse and critical, and the separation was causing serious strains in their fragile relationship. His wife had to handle unexpected storm damage to their roof and manage to make ends meet on Jon's meager ensign salary while far from family and all alone. Hopefully, when he returned, he could make up for his six months at sea and get his marriage on track.

But USS *Independence* still had a few weeks of sailing left before the air wing departed the carrier en masse for the traditional fly-in and welcome home. After his first deployment, he had no idea what would be waiting for him at home.

5

Single and Searching

As I finished my sophomore year at Wake Forest,
I decided the thrill of cheering was fading. After some serious
falls and injuries, I decided to hang up my pom-poms and find
something else that was just as fulfilling but a bit safer to fill my
"box-checking" college life. After taking a class in the dance department, I found myself wanting more. I was thrilled to be accepted into the Wake Forest Dance Company. Along with
holding leadership positions in my sorority and joining other
campus clubs, I found myself flourishing in my junior and senior
years. My perfect life was going just how I planned, but there
was another harsh reality that I had to face—my eating disorder
still had a grip on me.

Because I had starved myself for so long, my metabolism
slowed down to the point that I needed less and less to keep going. With my body in starvation mode, when I ate normal
amounts, I gained weight and gained it quickly, becoming
chunky and, at least in my eyes, unattractive. I turned to my cal-
orie-counting ways, but with my body screaming for food, it
didn't last long. Since I was still not menstruating, my mood
swings could take me to extreme highs and lows.

I so desperately wanted to be "normal" like my classmates.
My friends seemed to be happy and excited about planning dinners out or pizza runs. They were oblivious to my food and
weight obsessions. My mind was constantly plagued with the
heaviness of making food decisions. "Am I going to enjoy food
with my friends knowing that it will make me get fat?" or "Do I

make up some excuse not to join them because I am in a starvation stage that day?"

Sometimes I tried to break free from the madness and eat whatever I wanted in a bingeing craze, but depression and disgust came crashing in, and once again, the anorexic/bulimic cycle consumed me. As I wrestled daily with my eating disorder, ugly voices told me I was a waste and could never find love or acceptance. I wasn't resting in God's unconditional love for me but instead chose to make my own path of doubt that would haunt me for years.

Despite my struggles, I had loved my years at Wake Forest, but it was time to turn the page on my crazy college days and step into the future a more mature woman. I only hoped as I left the Demon Deacons behind that my own personal demons wouldn't follow me.

My job prospects after college didn't look promising. My Wake Forest education was top-notch, but to be more marketable in my chosen major, mass communications, I needed additional experience and skill. A master's program seemed like a logical solution, but where?

This brought up another question in my search for a master's program—where could I study that had a pool of eligible men to date? I hoped to find a man of faith to love me—someone like my own father—a godly man who would be devoted to me in the same way that my dad was devoted to my mom. But I needed to find a place that had more men of the marrying type who shared my Christian faith. I was being drawn to my relationship with God again, which had been put on a back burner as I pursued my version of happiness. I was ready to return to my spiritual roots and try to find the peace that had eluded me for so long.

Krissy Windham, single and searching, Virginia Beach, VA

As I looked for master's programs in mass communications, one choice seemed to check all these boxes: CBN University, associated with the Christian Broadcasting Network, in beautiful Virginia Beach, Virginia. Their program looked extremely promising, and the student body would be packed with eligible Christian men. And surely my failing faith would flourish in the university's spiritual atmosphere.

Put to the Test

06 JUNE 1983
0900 EASTERN TIME ZONE
COMOPTEVFOR
NAS NORFOLK
NORFOLK, VIRGINIA, USA
36°92'59" N, 76°29'22" W

After his stint with USS *Independence* and the Steeljaws of VAW-122, Jon left his three-year sea duty behind and started his next shore tour at the navy's Commander Operational Test and Evaluation Force (COMOPTEVFOR) in Norfolk, Virginia. Working down the road from where he had started his E-2C training years before with RVAW-120, Jon remembered how excited he had been to get his hands on the Hawkeye's advanced technology as an NFO-in-training. Here at COMOPTEVFOR, Jon had a similar feeling, but even more so.

COMOPTEVFOR performed a critical job for the navy and the Department of Defense. Its mission was to test and evaluate ships, systems, weapons, and other essential items under real-life conditions and judge their effectiveness, durability, and affordability. Everything the navy needed to carry out its mission was tested, from the latest destroyer ship to ordinary life vests. COMOPTEVFOR's green light was like the Good Housekeeping Seal of Approval. Without it, nothing could be rolled out or receive funding. Testers of any rank had the power to say whether something passed or failed. Jon's role as an E-2C NFO was as an operational test director of the E-2C Airborne Early Warning Projects, and his work was considered classified.

Jon had left the Steeljaws highly confident, for he had earned his CICO designation and rose in rank from a lowly O-1 ensign all the way to an O-3 lieutenant and ranked number one out of fourteen lieutenants in the squadron. But when he arrived at the testing center, a major operational test was already underway, and he had to jump in and get up to speed much faster than was usually expected of junior Air Warfare Division officers.

Jon buckled down. He leaned heavily on his Nebraskan-farmer work ethic and problem-solving skills to become a valued participant in the test, earning the respect of his commanding officer as well as other military support and civilian personnel. In this demanding environment, Jon's natural tactical skills were unleashed, but instead of playing chess with a king, bishops, and knights, he was using advanced radar and other technologies to maximize the E-2C's unique capabilities in an active wartime environment. He relished the opportunity to benefit the entire VAW community and cherished the fact that his opinions were sought out and respected, giving him affirmation that he was a valued asset to the testing team.

If only Jon were as successful in his personal life. After his first sea duty, he had hoped he could patch up things with his wife before he went to sea again a year down the road. But as his second cruise on USS *Independ-*  *ence* drew near, his optimism faded. The strain between his wife and him increased. The navy life wasn't easy, and his wife was struggling with Jon's long absences.

This time, the *Indy* was headed to the Mediterranean Sea, with several ports of call planned along the way, and Jon and his wife arranged for her to meet him at one of them. Perhaps being able to spend some time together in the middle of his deployment would make the six-month separation easier to handle. Those ports of call were suddenly put into jeopardy, however, when Israel invaded Lebanon, forcing the navy to change the *Indy*'s mission.

By the time the crew of USS *Independence* finally could enjoy its ports of call, Jon was anxiously anticipating a much-needed reunion with his wife. But instead of welcoming him with open arms, she greeted him with divorce papers in hand. The weeks that Jon was away on workups and the long months at sea were too much for her to handle. The stresses of navy life had taken a toll, and their young marriage lasted slightly over two years. Jon was crushed. He knew their relationship was in trouble, but he certainly hadn't expected this. When the cruise was over, Jon returned home with a heavy heart and tried to convince his wife to change her mind, but his efforts were in vain. She had already moved on with her life and had no interest in being married to a man who was rarely home. Jon was the first person in his family to get a divorce, and he found no pride in this distinction. Months went by before he even told his family the sad news.

Perhaps that was why the respect and affirmation Jon received during his tour of duty at the navy's testing center meant

> *Promise:*
> *"He heals the*
> *brokenhearted*
> *and bandages*
> *their wounds."*
> *Psalm 147:3*

so much to him. Jon felt like a failure, and the success he had working on the various important projects for the E-2C was salve on an open wound. At age twenty-eight, this unattached sailor was lonely, but he didn't want to rush into another long-term relationship. Jon realized that not every woman was suited for the stress of navy life, but he hoped that somewhere out there was a woman who could earn his seal of approval and, in turn, he could earn hers.

Plans Gone Wrong

With my own dreams of finding a soul mate, I headed to CBN University, convinced that surrounding myself with Christian professionals would give me a better chance of finding a husband and getting my chaotic life on track. Although I was still struggling with my weight and self-confidence, I was hoping to meet people who had a heart for God who would overlook my imperfections. But things didn't work out exactly as planned. At twenty-one, I was the youngest student enrolled in their master's program. Most of my classmates were considerably older, and many were married with kids—not exactly the best husband-hunting environment.

I also hadn't counted on feeling so uncomfortable in this Christian-saturated culture. Some students would participate in late-night Bible studies and lengthy prayer sessions; I wanted to focus on my studies, earn good grades, and make enough money at odd jobs to cover my expenses. These super-Christians were much more serious about their faith than I was, and I couldn't relate. However, one positive change I experienced was the inspirational power of contemporary Christian music. It was a new world to me, and I surrounded myself with the songs of Amy Grant, Russ Taff, DeGarmo and Key, and the Sweet Comfort Band. My eating disorder followed me to Virginia Beach, but the music of these artists, along with many others, planted seeds of comfort to my searching soul.

I finished my master's degree in communications in a record eighteen months. The only thing left to do was to complete my dissertation, but there was no rush to do so. I needed to focus on finding a job—a real one, not the dead-end side jobs I'd worked to pay my way through grad school. Finding a decent-paying job in the mass communications sector proved difficult, though. I searched earnestly for jobs in Charlotte, North Carolina, where many of my Wake Forest friends had relocated, but my attempts proved futile.

Then a job opened in Virginia Beach at a weekly fashion and entertainment publication serving Hampton Roads called *Portfolio*, which featured local political issues; sections for arts, entertainment, and travel; restaurant and movie reviews; personal and classified ads, and the like. They were looking for an advertising account executive, and working on commission for a magazine that was only two years old was attractive to me. As Charlotte was clearly a closed door, I applied for the *Portfolio* job in the spring of 1985. When they offered it to me, I took it.

Finally, years of classes, studying, and test taking were behind me, and I could focus on one full-time job. Surely with the pressures of school and job hunting behind me, my long-term eating disorder would become a distant memory, but my inner despair only worsened. While many of my college friends were sending me wedding invitations, I was giving up on ever finding true love. Disgusted with my distorted body image and growing weary of my eating disorder, I briefly despaired of life itself. I was the lowest I had ever been, and my internal demons had replaced my fun-loving personality with brokenness and distress. Life was not turning out as I had planned.

My job at *Portfolio*, while not the high-profile one I'd dreamed of when I was younger, was a bright spot in my otherwise drab life. Finally making real money, I started a savings program to give myself a more secure financial future. I enjoyed the office atmosphere. Many of my fellow workers were young, single women like me. We'd laugh and joke around with one another, and after working there a few months, we became good friends. I had no idea these friends would do me the biggest favor of my life.

Dating Going Nowhere

25 MAY 1985
2315 EASTERN TIME ZONE
HAMPTON ROADS, VIRGINIA, USA
36°88'68" N, 76°23'40" W

Jon was ready for his personal life to match his professional one. At work, he felt confident, competent, and valuable, and he was growing in his skills and responsibilities. He was scheduled to receive training as a casualty assistance calls officer (CACO). CACOs were officers who personally notified the next of kin whenever a service member was injured or had died in the line of duty. A CACO walked alongside the affected families, helping with funeral arrangements and guiding them through the necessary paperwork to receive the benefits they were due. It was a solemn responsibility that Jon hoped he never had to carry out.

As Jon reflected on his accelerating military resume with the added experience at COMOPTEVOR, he found himself growing restless with his personal life. He knew there had to be a better way to find meaningful female companionship than blind dates and the bar scene. How could a highly trained NFO like himself know how to detect all types of aircraft from three hundred miles away and not be able to find one compatible woman in a metro area of nearly a million people?

Perhaps he'd been going about this dating thing all wrong, Jon realized. It was time for him to put his extensive training and problem-solving skills to work once again. How could he decrease the false hits of incompatible dates and increase the probability of successful ones? As an alternative idea, Jon had picked up the latest edition of Hampton Road's local fashion and entertainment magazine called *Portfolio*. As he thumbed through the pages, he flipped to the personal ads in the back.

Long before there were Internet matchmaking sites and dating apps, people looking for love turned to the trusty personal ads found in the classified sections of nearly every newspaper. These short and simple notices used a special code to quickly communicate essential information: "S" stood for single, "D" for divorced, "W" for white, "B" for black, "F" for female, "M" for male, and so on. A DWM was a divorced, white male who might be looking for an SWF. Here was a concise list of nearby available females, along with their descriptions, occupations, likes and dislikes, and specifics on what they were looking for in a man.

Jon wasn't sure about the accuracy of the descriptions provided in the personal ads, but it might be worth a try, and surely, he couldn't do worse than his latest blind date. Sorting through those entertaining personal ads seemed promising. All Jon had to do was send a letter and a photo of himself to the paper, reference that ad's box number, and wait to see if he received a response.

Jon realized his job couldn't give him the internal satisfaction he desired, and at age thirty, he was ready to share his life with someone special. Almost two years had passed since his painful divorce, and the bachelor's life was growing old. He took another glance at the *Portfolio* personal ads and decided to act.

6

Green-Eyed Lady

Summertime came to Virginia Beach, and my coworkers and I were looking for a little fun to liven up the atmosphere around the *Portfolio* office. It all began when one of our coworkers confessed that she had been thinking of running a personal ad in our paper. We were all a bit surprised, as this woman seemed to have no trouble finding dates. I was even more surprised when she suggested that all of us should run personal ads at the same time!

Most of my coworkers were enthusiastic about the idea, but I wasn't one of them. I thought those ads were ridiculous. Only losers resorted to such tactics, and I told them so. Their stories of happy couples who had met that way didn't change my mind. But when one of the copywriters offered to write my ad, after I gave the excuse that I wouldn't know what to say, I finally gave in.

Before the day was over, the others had their ads ready to submit. My copywriter friend proudly handed over a draft ad for me. I scanned it quickly, making sure she had the facts straight, but it wasn't quite what I expected. She had used a word to describe me that I didn't think men would understand, so I asked her to remove it. She explained that it would make me sound exotic and mysterious. I reluctantly agreed since I was not putting much confidence in the whole experiment anyway. What could possibly come from a tiny personal ad other than a handful of sorry letters from a few desperate men?

Tawny

17 JULY 1985
1845 EASTERN TIME ZONE
HAMPTON ROADS, VIRGINIA, USA
36°88'68" N, 76°23'40" W

Jon had been working extra hours at COMOPTEVFOR on the E-2C Update Program, an assignment that required his detailed focus. The work left him exhausted. One evening after work, Jon picked up that week's edition of *Portfolio* and took another look at the personal ads.

He passed over several ads posted by women who seemed either desperate or uninteresting. Then he saw one that piqued his interest. He read it once, and then he read it again:

> GREEN-EYED LADY. SWF, 23, advertising account executive, tawny, athletic, energetic, and fun. Looking for SWM, 26-35, who has "IT," that elusive quality that can only be recognized, never defined. He should also be educated, artistic, funny, and attractive. No machos, no wimps need apply. Box #6575.

Tawny? What the heck does that even mean? He read the ad a third time. This woman was the right age, and she had a job. She was tawny—whatever that meant—and it sounded like she would be a good match for his own high-energy personality. He was in the age range she specified. He didn't know if he had "IT" or not, but he was college educated and well-known by his friends for having a great sense of humor. No one had ever accused Jon of being a wimp. As an avid cyclist, he often rode his bike twenty-five miles one way to work, but he doubted biking, or his one-armed pushups, would qualify him as macho. He wasn't sure about the artistic or attractive requirement, but maybe she'd be so overwhelmed with his "IT" factor that she wouldn't notice.

Tawny. That word intrigued him. He still wasn't sure what it meant, but he'd like to find out. Fighting his doubts about writing a letter to a mysterious woman on the other end of a personal ad, he decided to give it a try.

Jackpot

A week went by, and then one morning, I walked into an atmosphere of excitement at the *Portfolio* office. My coworkers were all laughs and chatter. When I got to my desk, I found out why. There, stacked in a pile, was a massive mound of letters—more than sixty of them. I had hit the jackpot! I wasn't the only one with a stack of responses, but my ad brought in the most. My copywriter friend was all smiles.

I had dismissed the personal ad completely, for I had recently adopted a new puppy from the shelter and had been preoccupied with house training her. My new puppy was a black terrier mix that I named Sophie. I adored my little puppy, who gave me love and affection, and now, looking at the stack of letters, I allowed myself to hope that I might meet someone to share my furry companion with.

After sorting meticulously through each letter, my first promising candidate was a graduate from West Point, an army officer. Since I was hoping for an established professional type, I thought this was an obvious option. On my girlfriends' advice, I suggested that we first meet at a public place, and he agreed.

The guy was nice but not really my type. Although I was impressed with his West Point education and career possibilities, he seemed a bit dull and uninteresting. He did not have "IT." There was absolutely no chemistry between us. I marked him off my list. My second choice was another army officer and West Point grad, but all he wanted to talk about that evening was politics—not my favorite subject. And to top it all off, it turned out that he was good friends with date number one. Another matchmaking blunder.

I wasn't a quitter, so I was willing to give it another try. Living in a military community, I had quite a few servicemen who responded to my ad. I decided to choose a different branch of service. I found a letter from a navy officer, an aviator named Jon. He had included a photo of a group—three guys looking impressive in their navy dress whites, along with a girl in a fabulous dress. Obviously, they were attending some formal function. The attached note said, "I'm the good-looking one." I smiled. Ah-ha, he had a sense of humor as well. Of the three guys pictured, none of them were bad looking. I might as well give him a chance.

When I dialed his number, he wasn't home. Not quite ready to give out my name, I left a message that the "green-eyed lady" had called, and I gave my phone number. It wasn't long before "the good-looking one" gave me a call. After my lackluster experiences with the army officers, I wasn't as eager to go on a date, so we talked on the phone several times, taking time to get to know a little bit about each other.

It turned out that Jon loved dogs, and with his recent experience as a Norwegian elkhound dog breeder, he gave me helpful advice for my new puppy. A few weeks later, when he asked to meet in person, I agreed. Again, I asked to meet somewhere in public, which also provided an opportunity to duck out early if I decided this was another dating disaster. We chose the next Monday evening to meet at Darryl's, a casual restaurant in Virginia Beach. I was hopeful yet, at the same time, wary.

When I arrived at the restaurant, I caught my reflection in the glass of the entrance door. I had dressed nicely for the evening, but I was still a little heavyset from my eating disorder. Hopefully, Jon wouldn't notice. To this point, I still hadn't seen Jon in person, so I wondered how I would find him. But when I walked inside, there was a man sitting at the table nearest the door. One look at me and he stood up, walked over, and held out his hand.

"Kris?" he smiled.

"Yeah. Jon?" I asked.

He nodded as we shook hands.

As he led me to our table, my first impressions of him were somewhat promising. To be honest, the "good-looking one" wasn't that attractive, but his athletic build was noticeably appealing. He had dressed nicely for our meeting, and I was flattered by his effort. His clothing choices of a short-sleeved, baby-blue striped dress shirt with white summer cotton pants were a flattering look. I tried to look past his distinctively sharp nose and military, bowl-cut, blond hair to perhaps make a new friend. Our lengthy conversations on the phone over the past few weeks had stirred my curiosity, and I wasn't going to dismiss him this early in the evening just because he didn't look like a GQ model.

What happened next, however, took me by surprise. As we sat down, he looked at me, turned his head slightly to the side, and said, "You know, you remind me of someone," he paused, thinking of the name: "Brenda Vaccaro."

"Who?"

"You know, the actress with the husky voice."

Jon could tell by the confused expression on my face that I had absolutely no idea who he was talking about, and if he meant it as a compliment, he was failing miserably. I knew he was seven years older than me and figured the age gap must be why I wasn't familiar with that actress. It was an awkward moment for both of us. Jon realized his social blunder and after a few painful seconds simply said, "Hold it."

He stood up and calmly walked out of the restaurant. I was so taken aback that I didn't know what to do, but as I turned around, I saw him walk straight back in, cool-headed and unflappable, with a smile on his face. He approached me and held out his hand. "Let's try this again. Kris?" I had to laugh as we shook hands for the second time, and Jon took his seat. Not only did he have a sense of humor but also a sense of confidence. The ice finally broken, we started talking, introducing ourselves to each other. And we kept on talking. We even closed Darryl's and moved on to a beach restaurant that stayed open later.

I learned a lot about Jon that night: how his parents were humble farmers in Nebraska, which probably explained his pickup truck; how he'd been a state runner-up in wrestling twice in a state where wrestling is everything; his year of teaching high school math and how he'd made the decision to join the navy; even his failed marriage with a college sweetheart who couldn't adapt to the navy life. The most important things I learned weren't about Jon's background but about who he was. From the moment we met, his humor and confidence were obvious. And as the evening went on, I was able to look past the bad haircut to see a genuinely kind, personable, intelligent, and wise man. By his appearance and his vehicle choice, Jon was clearly a down-to-earth guy. As we got to know each other on that late-summer night, I couldn't help but wonder if I had met the man who had "IT," that elusive quality that can only be recognized and never defined. I did know that for the first time in my life, I had met a man who cared more about others than himself.

I liked him, but I didn't really see him as the successful, handsome, professional man of my dreams. At the time, I had no idea what it took to become a naval flight officer, and I certainly had no clue about Jon's specialized skills. He was a true professional in every sense of the word, but I was looking for a man in a suit and tie who ran a successful business or had a C-suite title.

After many years of searching for my preconceived idea of Mr. Right, I had trouble seeing Jon as my Prince Charming. But then, how did Jon view me? Could he see a chunky, somewhat dysfunctional twenty-three-year-old as his dream come true? I wondered what had caused him to respond to my ad in the first place, so I asked him.

"It was that word you used—tawny," he replied with a grin. "I found it intriguing."

I confessed that my copywriter friend at the office had come up with the word, and it was fitting, as my summer skin had taken on a golden tan from the weekend beach days—a golden tan that Jon seemed to like.

Even though I had reservations, I didn't resist when he kissed me goodbye. The evening was far better than any I'd had in some time, but this was not love at first sight. As I drove home through the nearly empty streets of Virginia Beach, I decided that if he asked me out again, I'd probably say yes, but

> *Promise:*
> *"So let's not get tired of doing what is good. At just the right time we will reap a harvest of blessing if we don't give up."*
> *Galatians 6:9*

I wondered how far this relationship realistically could go.

Best Day of My Life

20 AUG 1985
0912 Eastern Time Zone
COMOPTEVFOR
NAS Norfolk
Norfolk, VIRGINIA, USA
36°92'59" N, 76°29'22" W

At last, after months—no, no, years—of relentless searching, he'd found a woman who touched his heart. August 19, 1985 would forever remain one of the best days of his life. He couldn't explain it, but from the moment he'd looked into her big, green eyes, Jon knew that Kris was special. And by the time the evening ended, he knew that Green-Eyed Lady was "the one" he'd been looking for. He'd also found out what *tawny* meant and decided he liked it. He liked it a lot.

He's a Keeper

Due to the late night, I was a little tired at work the next day, but all my friends wanted to hear about my date with Jon. They all cringed when I told them about the Brenda Vaccaro comment but smiled when I told them how he'd handled it and how we'd talked until the wee hours of the morning. I told them that he was genuinely a nice guy but really wasn't my type, and I didn't think we could be much more than friends. I had to rethink those words later when a gorgeous vase with a dozen, long-stemmed, red roses was delivered to my desk. His attached card read, "Thanks for the special evening. Jon." As my coworkers admired the lovely bouquet, I realized that Jon had been wise to send the roses to my office instead of my home, knowing that my fellow office workers would be impressed at his romantic gesture and sing his praises. But it would take more than a dozen roses to win my heart.

Jon wasted no time in asking me out again, and before long, we were spending more and more time together. Sophie became a part of our relationship, and through our common love of dogs, I could see more of Jon's tender, loving nature. I was beginning to warm up to this lively, funny, pick-up-driving Nebraskan, but I still had reservations.

Nevertheless, Jon's influence on my life was having effects on me that others noticed. A coworker pulled me aside one day and asked me if I had been losing weight. When I got home, I hopped on the scales and saw that I'd lost ten pounds without even trying! I was amazed. My anorexic/bulimic cycle had been fading away as my relationship with Jon grew deeper.

Soon after we began dating, I confessed to Jon my struggle with a distorted body image. "Don't you think I'm fat?" I fearfully asked him.

"No," he replied, shaking his head with a smile. "You're sturdy."

His matter-of-fact response made me realize that Jon didn't have an issue with my weight, and in time I began to see myself the same way.

Jon's approach to food was freeing as well. He was an excellent cook, and sometimes instead of eating out, he'd fix delicious meals for the two of us. Before long, I was eating three regular meals a day and joining Jon for bike rides and walks with Sophie. However, even with all that, it was his unconditional love and acceptance that made all the difference. Now that I was feeling valued and no longer focusing on achieving and performing, the weight came off. The grip of my six-year eating disorder was finally being loosened by the gentle love of one special man.

In the same way that Jon helped me with my eating disorder, I helped him get in touch with his faith. I invited him to join me at First Baptist Norfolk on Sundays, and I could see how his heart was being awakened by God's love. Growing up as a weekly church attender, I knew much more about the Bible and spiritual truth than he did, and yet so little of that truth had penetrated my heart. As we experienced God together, both of us were finding new meaning in our spiritual lives.

Even with all the good that was happening between us, I still wasn't sure Jon was the man for me. Giving up my long-held image of Mr. Right was proving hard to do. I needed clarity and an objective opinion on our relationship. We'd been dating for a few months, and Thanksgiving was approaching. Perhaps it was time to take Jon and Sophie to Charleston, West Virginia, to meet my parents. Maybe they would see Jon in ways that I couldn't. Jon, a relational guy, was enthusiastic about meeting my parents and looked forward to having Thanksgiving with my family. My dad had been an enlisted sailor in the navy in his younger days, so I knew the two of them would have plenty in common.

My parents met Jon and Sophie with open arms, and right away, Jon and my dad hit it off. Mom and I came up with a nickname for them: the friends. For the rest of the weekend, the friends spent hours playing chess and cribbage and reliving Dad's old navy days. They couldn't have gotten along any better.

As the weekend wound down and Mom and I were alone in the kitchen, I asked her what she thought of Jon. She got a misty look in her eyes and smiled. "Krissy, the first time I saw him hold your puppy, I knew he was a keeper." Mom had an innate sense of people that I cherished, and her words helped me see Jon through her eyes.

I also knew that my dad wasn't pretending to bond with Jon just for my benefit. Their connection was genuine and warm, and the way he honored my father and enjoyed his company spoke volumes about Jon's character.

I couldn't deny that since Jon had come into my life, I'd experienced peace and contentment as never before. That Thanksgiving trip to Charleston provided the clarity I needed: Jon was a keeper. On the way home, I could finally tell this blue-eyed, down-to-earth Swede, "I think I'm falling in love with you."

7

Welcome to the Navy, Mrs. Rystrom!

07 DEC 1985
1500 EASTERN TIME ZONE
HAMPTON ROADS, VIRGINIA, USA
36°88'68" N, 76°23'40" W

With Christmas fast approaching, Jon had a lot on his mind and needed to sort through a jumble of thoughts and emotions. His tour at COMOPTEVFOR was successful but coming to an end. He'd been a major force in the development of the E-2C Updated Development Program and the testing of APS-138, 139, and 145 radars. His high-performing unit had been awarded the Naval Unit Commendation a few months earlier.

Now it was time to look to the future. With Jon's shore duty soon ending, he had received his new orders. The navy needed him to transfer to San Diego, California, where he would begin with a Replacement Air Group (RAG) refresher training at Miramar Naval Air Station and then move on to sea duty with VAW-114 Hormel Hawgs and the carrier USS *Carl Vinson*. This was no surprise to Jon. Navy careers alternated between three years of sea duty and two or three years of shore duty, but the timing and type of assignment weren't the best for Jon's personal life.

He'd met Kris less than four months ago, and he'd much prefer to allow their budding relationship to grow gently over time. If his sea duty had been based out of Norfolk, little would need to change in their relationship, but having to move thousands of miles away meant he had to consider some significant decisions much sooner than expected. Would Kris be willing to relocate to join Jon's life in California? Was Jon ready for that step? He knew that not only would Kris have to choose to join his life, but he would have to choose to join hers.

From the beginning of their relationship, Jon understood that faith was clearly a priority for Kris, but was Jon willing to make faith a priority as well? Over the weeks and months that they had known each other, Jon had felt a rekindling of faith in his own heart. He remembered going to a church camp when he was a teen and responding to a tug inside of him pulling him toward God and His grace. While that was a genuine experience for Jon, years of neglect and outward focus had diminished that flame to a dim flicker. However, that little spark had been rekindled after being with Kris, attending church services with her, and once again hearing of God's amazing love and mercy. While Jon still had many questions about spiritual matters, he could not deny the growing desire in his spirit to grow closer to Christ. Could a relationship with God be part of the "more" he had been looking for all along?

With a tour change to San Diego in less than six months, Jon knew it was decision time for him and Kris. The path forward wasn't completely clear, but he couldn't deny the growing love in his heart.

Forty or Fifty Years

As we rang in the 1986 New Year together, Jon and I had a lot on our minds. With his upcoming move to California, I had some serious conversations with myself. My love for Jon continued to flourish, but was I ready to change my entire life for a man I had only known for five months? There was much uncertainty about our future together, especially when the world of the military is involved, but no one could avoid uncertainty.

A special holiday was fast approaching. Being a new couple, I was anxious to see what Jon had planned for our first Valentine's Day together. Jon and I had made lunch plans, and I anxiously waited for him to pick me up at the *Portfolio* office. Jon arrived, handsomely dressed in his navy khakis and holding a big heart-shaped box of chocolates. My heart skipped a beat and couldn't wait to see what other surprises he had waiting for me. As he stood in the middle of the office, he casually opened the box of chocolates and playfully said, "Would you like a chocolate?" As I gazed at the assortment of truffles and caramels, my eyes went to the center section where one chocolate confection had been replaced by a gorgeous diamond ring.

To the delight of all my coworkers, Jon promptly got on one knee, held my hand, and said, "Krissy, will you marry me?"

His twinkling, blue eyes met mine in an eager gaze, and my heart skipped a beat as my own eyes began to fill with tears.

"Yes! Yes, of course, I will!" I fervently replied.

He gently took the chocolates from my hand and lovingly placed the beautiful marquise diamond ring on my finger. The office staff applauded as we sealed the sacred moment with a passionate kiss.

What a surreal moment it was. In six months, I had gone from debating whether I should place an ad in our magazine to committing to spend the rest of my life with my personal-ad love. (And to think that some people say advertising doesn't work. I beg to differ.) For years, I'd been trying to put a square peg in a round hole, looking for popular, successful, upper-class guys to fill the void in my life. What I'd needed all along was a man of character and substance. I'd been envious of all my friends tying the knot right out of college and despaired of ever finding a soul mate of my own, but I'd found true love at last, and I couldn't have been happier.

Now that I'd said yes, a whirlwind of activity quickly ensued. Jon had to report to his new squadron in California by mid-June, so we picked May 3 as our wedding date. That would give us time for a honeymoon and a cross-country move, but we had less than three months to prepare. To keep things simple, we chose a full-military wedding at Dam Neck Naval Base, which had a beautiful gazebo right on the beach for the wedding ceremony and the nearby officers' club for the reception. My mother and friends helped me pull all the details together in record time, and I felt as if I were living a dream.

After all the years of my personal struggles to find significance and value, I was experiencing for the first time the promise of security and unconditional love from a man who would soon be my husband. Everything was happening quickly—getting married and leaving behind my job, the East Coast, my parents, and my old life. Jon and I knew that our whole lives were going to be different, but we were eager to begin our new adventure together.

After our whirlwind engagement, our wedding day arrived. The cool, spring breeze coming in from the ocean was so strong that the musicians had to hold their music in place with clothespins. Jon's navy groomsmen, all dignified in their dress whites and sabers, looked comical as they tried in vain to lay down the flimsy bridal aisle runner on the wooden deck leading up to the gazebo.

As I took my father's arm and walked slowly down the aisle, I could sense his pride and excitement. I was gaining a husband, and my father was gaining a son. I hoped that my hat wouldn't blow off in a sudden gust, but once I locked eyes with Jon— standing confidently on the gazebo stage and looking handsome in his navy dress whites—I forgot all about the wind and the hectic weeks leading up to this special day. This was a moment I knew I would cherish forever. As my father took my hand and placed it in Jon's, the robed minister reminded us of the solemn oaths we were about to take and then continued to address the audience, "A vow and covenant once made should not be broken."

Lt. Jon Rystrom and Krissy Windham's wedding day
May 3, 1986, Dam Neck Naval Base, Virginia Beach, VA

"Jon, will you have Krista to be your wedded wife, to live together after God's ordinance in the holy estate of matrimony? Will you love her, comfort her, honor and obey her, and keep her in sickness and in health and, forsaking all others, cleave only unto her so long as you both shall live?"

"I will," Jon promised.

I promised the same.

The minister was right. There should be a "profound sense of seriousness" in the vows we take. As a dewy-eyed bride, I had little idea of the true weight of the promises Jon and I were making to each other.

After the exchanging of rings, the minister pronounced us husband and wife and gave the final prayer. "And now, Father, give them the strength to keep the vows they have made to be loyal and faithful to each other and to support each other throughout their lives. May they bear each other's burdens and share each other's joy. Help them to be honest and patient with each other and to be loving and wise parents one day. In their future together, may they enjoy each other's lives and grow through each other's love. Keep them faithful to You, and at the end of this life on earth, receive them and us all into Your Heavenly Kingdom. Amen."

The minister then turned to Jon and spoke the words we'd all been waiting for: "You may kiss the bride!"

Jon wasn't one to question orders, and he willingly complied. I was happy to be Mrs. Krista Rystrom and relieved that my hat hadn't blown off during the final prayer. With military precision, Jon's fellow officers marched down the aisle before us and created the Arch of the Swords –a saber tunnel for us to walk through. As we were about to pass the last two officers in the line, I could feel Jon slowing down, and I was surprised when they lowered their sabers and wouldn't let us pass.

Arch of swords at the Rystrom Wedding – May 3, 1986
Dam Neck Naval Base, Virginia Beach, VA

"Welcome to the navy, Mrs. Rystrom," one groomsman called out, and I felt a sharp little slap on my bottom as one of them gently swatted me with a saber. Jon laughed, delighted that I was completely surprised by this traditional introduction to the navy. I laughed along with him and knew it would be the first of many revelations to come. I had not only married Jon but also the navy.

Our reception was filled with congratulatory toasts and joyous smiles. There were also tears as we said goodbye to dear friends before we moved across the country. After we used a saber to cut our wedding cake, Jon shared his thoughts on this special day with our guests.

"One thing I can tell you," he said with a smile, "is that eight months ago, I wasn't thinking about getting married. And it wasn't until I met this wonderful lady that I began to look forward to having a great time with her for the next forty or fifty years." I felt the same way as we stepped into our getaway car and headed out on our weeks-long honeymoon, staying at several bed-and-breakfasts as we trekked across America. We were certain that we had the next forty to fifty years to love each other.

The Rystrom Wedding, front cover feature in Portfolio
Hampton Roads, VA, May 1986

8

Highway to the Danger Zone

The earth-shaking rumble of jet engines jolted me from sleep. In frustration, I glanced at the alarm clock beside the bed: 2:36 a.m. Beside me, Jon was sleeping like a baby. How did he do it? I put a pillow over my head in a failed attempt to shut out the noise as another jet passed overhead. I hated that sound—the sound of F-14 fighter jets going through their paces in the desert air over our new home, a small apartment at Miramar Naval Air Station.

Thankfully, we only had to live here a brief time before we could move off base and into a duplex we had purchased. But until then, I had to endure the constant cacophony of aircraft as they carried out their training day and night at this massive military airport. As I tossed and turned, I couldn't help but reflect on our wedding day when I got the traditional saber slap from one of Jon's groomsmen stating with pride, "Welcome to the navy, Mrs. Rystrom." Experiencing for the first time the world of a military wife, this midnight wake-up call from jet blasts was not the welcome I had expected.

Jon was assigned to Miramar for what he called RAG, or refresher training, required for all aviators before they could reenter active flight. In four months, he was scheduled to join the Hormel Hawgs of VAW-114, who served on the aircraft carrier USS *Carl Vinson*. Not having much time to enjoy being married before he went to sea was frustrating, and living on base caused sleep deprivation and even more irritation for me. Jon knew I needed an evening out, so he suggested the movie *Top Gun*. This popular action flick about navy fighter pilots had been released while we were on our honeymoon, and Jon was eager to see it. Much of it had been filmed at Miramar, also known as Fightertown USA. In real life, Top Gun—the United States Navy Fighter Weapons School—trained naval aviators in fighter and strike tactics. Every day as I drove from work to our apartment on base, I would pass the hangar where the real Top Gun was operating.

I wasn't nearly as excited as Jon was to see the movie. I'd had my fill of jets, thank you very much. But I didn't want to disappoint him, so I agreed to go. Surprisingly, I was hooked from the first scene, which was set on a bustling carrier flight deck. As the high-energy music of Kenny Loggins' "Danger Zone" filled the theater, I was seeing Jon's world for the first time. This was his life.

The danger and drama of the missions, the Soviet MIG intercepts, the intense training, the bravado of the men, and of course the romantic love story totally transformed the annoying rumble of late-night flyovers into an intoxicating aphrodisiac for this new bride. Of course, Jon flew in the E-2C Hawkeye, not the F-14 fighter jet, but when he was dressed up in his flight suit, he was just as handsome as Tom Cruise.

After the movie, I asked Jon about the death of Goose, who played Tom Cruise's radar intercept officer (RIO) in the movie, and the dangers of flying. He tried to reassure me.

"Don't worry, Krissy, I fly the safest plane in the navy." Jon fibbed a little on that one, because it wasn't true, but it was the safest plane on an aircraft carrier. Goose was an NFO like Jon, but he told me he couldn't eject in the E-2C as Goose had in the F-14. I was oblivious to the fact that the E-2C was commonly referred to as "the flying coffin" in some military circles because if there was a need to escape, there was no ejection available. Instead, they had parachutes and other survival gear attached to their seats in case of an emergency.

The Rystroms at Miramar Naval Air Show, San Diego, California

That helped alleviate my fears a little, but his joke about CA-COs certainly didn't: "If you see a white car parked on the street and naval officers in their dress blues coming to the door, you'll know I didn't make it."

He said it with a laugh, but I didn't see the humor. I tried to get the image of naval officers coming to my door out of my mind, especially as Jon's RAG training ended and the time came for him to go to sea.

While he was packing his bags for his Indian Ocean tour, I was unpacking boxes from our cross-country move. I found it comforting to know that while Jon was away, I wouldn't be all alone. I had made friends with the squadron wives from the

Hormel Hawgs and with co-workers at my new job selling newspaper advertising in San Diego. Also, Jon and I had joined the College Avenue Baptist Church and choir, and we were forming new relationships there as well.

The carrier was already out to sea, and Jon would be joining USS *Carl Vinson* (or as he called it, the "Chuckie V") mid-tour, meaning he'd be gone only four months instead of six. *Only* wasn't the right word, though, because I couldn't imagine going one day without him. I was dreading the separation tremendously, especially since we'd be missing many firsts as a married couple, such as my birthday, Thanksgiving, and worst of all, Christmas.

I could tell, mainly by the smell of chocolate cake, that Jon was getting stressed too. In our few short months of wedded bliss, I'd discovered that even optimistic, upbeat Jon had a bad day occasionally. And on those rare occasions, he often would bake a chocolate cake to unwind. While my cooking was improving, it was Jon's efforts in the kitchen that kept me eating three square meals a day, which held my eating disorder tendencies at bay. I would miss Jon's cooking, along with his smile, his voice, and his kisses—but most of all, his pres-

> *Promise:*
> *"I will not fail you or abandon you. Be strong and courageous."*
> *Joshua 1:5-6*

ence. Being around him made me feel safe and secure and loved. I knew his first marriage hadn't survived because of the stress of long deployments, and I couldn't help but wonder how it would affect us.

Because Jon had to meet up with the carrier sailing somewhere in the Indian Ocean, we said goodbye at San Diego International Airport. I drove away in a puddle of tears, barely able to function, and ended up taking the afternoon off from work. Opening the door and entering that quiet, empty house—all alone except for my little dog, Sophie—was too much. I was only hours into the first deployment of my navy-wife life, and I wasn't sure I could make it.

Dear Jon

Before I could check off the first day of Jon's 1986-87 *Chuckie V* cruise, I needed to write him a letter. Before the days of cell phones, email, texting, video calls, and the internet, the only way to regularly communicate with a sailor at sea was by mailing letters. (And if you think snail mail is slow, imagine trying to get letters back and forth to a ship out in the middle of the ocean!)

The time lag between when a letter was sent and when it was received could be as little as a few days or as long as a month, with the average being around ten days. Sending and receiving mail was affected by the weather, the ship's location, the mission of the carrier strike group, and even postal bags falling overboard. Letters could stack up for days, both on the ship and at shore, before a plane, called a COD (Carrier On-Board Delivery), could land on the carrier to transport them. As a result, letters never came in the order they were written or mailed. Numbering letters was critical; otherwise, you'd never be able to read them in order or know which ones were still to come.

With two prior cruises under his belt, Jon knew all about writing letters, but this was a new experience for me. Before he left, we made a solemn promise to write one letter to each other every day of his deployment. We were determined that our marriage would be even stronger when he returned, and this daily investment of time and love was a token of our commitment to each other.

As I got out pen and paper, I thought about what to say. I didn't want Jon to worry about me, so should I put on a brave front and act as if my first day was a breeze? Or did I risk making him feel guilty by letting him know how much I'd cried and how awful our first day apart had been? I decided on the latter. I knew Jon wanted me to be completely honest and open with him, and there was no way we'd grow closer if I tried to hide my feelings and deepest struggles. Knowing my words would travel around the world to my husband's heart, I sat on the couch, turned on the television to relax, and began to write:

Oct. 6, 1986

Hi sweetie!

Well, here goes my first letter of many to my dear, sweet, wonderful, strong, sexy navy husband. It is 10 p.m. Monday night, and Sophie is digging in the trash can and scratching her fleas. I'm sitting in the den watching Cagney & Lacey. It's been a rough day...

Four pages later, I signed my letter and put it in an envelope, making sure to add a circled number "1" on the back, like Jon had shown me. I went a step further and started a letter log of my own to track the dates of letters and packages that I sent to him during his cruise. This wouldn't bring him home any sooner, but it helped to give me a sense of accountability and a way to count down the days.

When I got home from work on Tuesday and checked my mailbox, I nearly jumped for joy when I found my first letter from Jon. The postmark said Los Angeles, and with the next post-mark coming from overseas, I knew it would be several days before I could expect another. I ran inside the house and flopped down on the den couch. Sophie cuddled next to me as I ripped open the envelope and read my first letter from Jon, written in his unmistakable scribble.

6 Oct. 86, 1335

Of course, Jon would use the military form for dates and time. I needed to subtract twelve to remember that *1335* was 1:35 p.m.

Hi Krissy,

Here is letter #1, and I hope you can read my writing. First off, **I love you**!

This part was written in larger letters and underlined three times. His words were like a warm hug.

Now that I have that off my chest, I am sitting in LAX (Los Angeles International Airport); it is 1135 a.m., and I had to wait over one hour to get my ticket. I am not stopping in Korea. I am stopping in Tokyo, then to the Philippines.

It still hasn't really hit me that I won't be seeing you for a while. I don't think I will mention actual numbers, as it will depress me.

That's how I felt. I couldn't bring myself to look at the calendar; February seemed so far away.

I just hope and pray that nothing major happens soon and that you can develop a routine.

How sweet of him, though I wasn't sure how I'd ever get used to this navy life.

Well, sweetie, time to close so that I can mail it before I leave. I will write every day of my fears, joys, expectations, friends I meet, and my favorite topic, my girl (I should say woman), Krissy.

I miss you.
Love, Jon

I savored his heartfelt words. Having Sophie next to me helped ease the loneliness of our first night apart. Receiving this letter had been a blessing but knowing this was how Jon and I would be relating to each other for the next four months was a sobering thought. I was glad we wouldn't just be sharing facts with each other but also our deepest feelings. Perhaps that would be one silver lining to this dark deployment cloud. I scanned the letter again and realized that he should be meeting up with USS *Carl Vinson* any day now. I wondered where on the other side of the world my sweet husband was and what was he doing.

DIEGO GARCIA

10 OCT 1986
16:42 IOT, UTC+6
USS CARL VINSON
00°05'57" S, 65°32'28" E

Jon glanced out the porthole to see the blue waters of the equatorial Indian Ocean as 601 made its final approach to the flight deck of USS *Carl Vinson*. The E-2C Hawkeye was the last aircraft to land, and Jon was glad to have his first flight of the cruise under his belt.

The pilots dropped their hook and began their counter-clockwise holding pattern over the carrier. They lowered the throttle, let down their landing gear, and began their approach. Jon could finally spot the white, frothy waters of the carrier's wake, which was his cue that in a few moments, he'd be aboard Mother, the naval aviators' traditional nickname for the carrier that was their home away from home. He was glad to be back on the water.

The rush of landing on a carrier and being in his beloved Hawkeye gave Jon a pleasure that was hard to explain. Pilots' heart rates were often highest within seconds of landing on a carrier. Arresting wires (long, thick, steel ropes stretched about fifty feet apart across the landing area), as well as a larger system of cables and hydraulic cylinders located under the flight deck, could bring a jet plane going one hundred fifty miles per hour to a complete stop in about two seconds.

After a nearly four-year hiatus from carrier life, Jon found that, for the most part, little had changed.

After hitting the rack early, Jon was wide awake at 3:30 a.m. The stresses of travel and getting readjusted to carrier life was enough to make anyone's sleeping schedule out of sorts. Jon figured since he couldn't sleep, he might as well write Kris her daily letter. He was anxiously awaiting his first letters from her, but he knew they were on the way. In the meantime, he couldn't wait to wish her a happy birthday.

Krista,

I want to wish you the happiest birthday you could ever have. I know I am not there with you, but I love you and care for you more than I ever thought I could love any one person.

Jon glanced over longingly at a framed wedding picture he had on his desk and sighed.

I never want to lose you.

If only he could be there to celebrate with her.

Lt. Jon Rystrom, VAW-114 Hormel Hawg's E2C

9

Love Letters Across the Sea

Missing special days together was one of many adjustments I had to make to the navy-wife life, but the letter-writing ritual was one of the greatest gifts I received from this season of my life. These daily letters began to deepen and solidify my love for Jon. I certainly loved him before, but even in our short dating time, and even shorter engagement, I wasn't filled with a deep love for my Cornhusker Swede. The security he gave me is what drew me to him. But the man I discovered as we endured this forced time apart went well beyond that basic need and touched a deeper part of my soul that I never knew I had.

After my birthday, letters from Jon began arriving in my mailbox and sometimes at work. But it took a few weeks before we could tell we were receiving each other's letters. I found it funny that Jon received my first letter on my birthday, eight days after I'd written it on October 6.

> To my wonderful birthday bride,
>
> What a great day—my honey turned 25, I am feeling better, and I, Jon Rystrom, got my first letter from you, I love it. I didn't realize how one person can make me feel all gooshy inside. I swear I have read your letter 10 times already. Oh, I truly love you.

As you told me in your letter how your first day went, my heart wept when you did. I could feel the same emotions that you were feeling. I bet you were really out those four hours that you took for sick leave too.

Both of us struggled with the irregularity of letters, and Jon understood my frustration.

I promise you, hon, that I have written every day and that I will continue to write one letter (minimum) a day to my favorite person in the world.

I am so glad you are finally getting my mail. As you can see, I have been writing every day. Now that you have had several days of no contact with me until the letters came, you may be able to understand what I was talking about when I said how important mail is on the ship. It is a two-way street—mail is just as important to you. Oh, how I love you.

My heart would explode with joy whenever my mailbox was full.

As a young newlywed, I eagerly shared my warm feelings, reaching out across the miles to let Jon know what his love meant to me.

Before you go to sleep tonight, I want you to read this letter again and think of me. Know in your heart that you have a woman who cherishes you, Jonathan, adores you, worships you, and will always be there—waiting for you, loving you, giving you a happy home, having your children, supporting you and your career and living beside you, taking every step with you as you live your life. Remember that as you close your eyes, my love, for your wife sends you these truths across the miles to your pillow.

* * *

I'm in love with this man. He is out on an aircraft carrier right now, protecting our country. He is the "coach" up in the air. He has strong legs, beautiful eyes that sing with fun and happiness when he smiles, and a loving and kind heart that no other man in the world has. His name is Jon and I am his wife forever ... I love you, Jonathan, more than you could ever, ever know. I think about you constantly. I give you the best I could ever give. No conditions, no demands, no expectations ... Just me, with all my faults and flaws, the entire package ... And it is all yours forever.

Jon was not a poet, but he had his own unique way with words, especially when they came straight from his heart.

I think about you more than I should, cuz when I do, I realize how long I must wait before I have you in my arms. But to bring me back up in spirits, I think in relative terms—what is four months out of 40-50 years—and knowing how we feel about each other makes me feel GREAT! Now I can face anything.

* * *

I have gained so much knowledge and wisdom about you through your letters. Sometimes I can feel your pain, your hurt, your joy, your intense desire to please me in your letters. When I read your letters, I read between the lines and marvel at what an incredible woman I have married. Kris, I knew from the first day I met you that you were a special person in my life, and you have not disappointed me in the least. I have grown to love and care for you more and more every day. I love it!!!

* * *

I guess you realize that my two favorite things in the whole world are loving you and college football. And in that order!!!

Missing Jon was one of my regular letter topics, but writing him helped me process my feelings of loneliness.

It seems so strange without you. I've really been doing well keeping myself busy but at night when I lock up the house, turn on the alarm, and tuck Sophie in, I look beside me at this empty space and I long for you … It's only been six days, but it seems like forever.

* * *

It seems like you've been gone forever. It is almost like I'm married to a man, live in his house, sleep in his bed, watch his TV, and drive his car, but there is no man around. I know it sounds weird, but everything around me seems like you are here, but the laundry I do is mine, the messes I clean are mine, and the conversations I have are with me too.

Now, don't worry, I'm not freaking out. I'm explaining my feelings as I am going through this the first time. Sometimes I call home to hear your voice on the answering machine ... What a laugh! I missed you more today because I didn't get a letter ... But you know I'm so patient these days, thanks to the Lord putting us through our frustrations and wait. He was really preparing me for what was ahead. Pretty neat, don't you think?

* * *

You seem so far away now. It is amazing that out of the billions of people in the world, there is one little boy on one side of the world loving one little girl on the other side and vice versa, and all because of one little 2" x 1" ad that ran in August 1985. Amazing, isn't it? I love you, sweetheart, more and more each day.

* * *

I was thinking about you so much yesterday evening that I got in your closet, smelled your clothes, and even put on one of your flannel shirts so that I could smell you all evening!

Anytime someone we love is far away, we worry about their safety. But imagine how much you'd worry if your husband was flying off a busy aircraft carrier thousands of miles across the ocean. My anxiety even showed up in my dreams.

Hi, hon. It is Friday morning (7:30 a.m.) and I'm at work. I woke up this morning at 5:00 a.m. because I was having a terrible dream about you. That you were killed in an accident. It really shook me up, so I started praying for your safety. I love you! I love you! I love you! You ARE my happiness and life. Krissy

Maybe it was because Jon had a degree in psychology, or maybe it was his optimistic personality, but he seemed unflappable and cool-headed in every situation. He didn't stress out the way I did, and he could handle my wide range of emotions.

I just today got your little note written on the 17th and, honey, I hope you do not have any more nightmares, cuz I am fine, honest, and I won't let anything happen to me, OK?

Even when Jon was far away, he still tried to care for me, especially after I wrote about my poor meal choices and weight loss.

GO TO THE STORE! I knew you would eat bad while I was away. When I was by myself, I would eat cereal or SpaghettiOs. But please try to eat a balanced meal. Buy a lot of balanced frozen dinners. I don't have an answer but try to eat more balanced meals and get some vitamins. Enuf said.

* * *

Kris, one serious note – you are not becoming anorexic, are you? If you are eating but still losing,

OK, but I love you and I want you healthy. I worry about you, OK? Let me know.

* * *

Remember that I fell in love with you over a year ago, when you were sturdy.

From across the ocean, Jon knew how to love me and motivate me. I heeded his words and started eating regular meals. My weight stabilized without my anorexia rearing its ugly head.

During this first cruise, we learned the importance of consistently encouraging each other in our letters. When the days were hard, we'd read those words of hope and affirmation time and time again.

I finished watching "An Officer and a Gentleman." Boy, did that ever give me goosebumps. I am so proud of you every time I think about what you've had to go through and what you are going through now. I am so lucky to have found someone so dedicated, hard-working, loyal, and loving as you. I will love you till the day I die, and even then, I'll still love you because we will be together in heaven.

* * *

I love you more and more every day, Jon, and there are a lot of people praying for your safety. Keep up the good work and remember that you have a happy, safe, and loving home to come home to. Loving and missing you but coping fine. Your wife, Krissy.

Jon's warm words helped carry me through times of doubt and frustration, especially when appliances broke, my car needed repairs, or the lawnmower had issues. I would ask myself: *What would Jon do? How would Jon handle this?* As the weeks and months went by, I found myself taking on more household repairs and growing in confidence. His natural optimism began to rub off on me and gave me a healthier perspective on life.

If you didn't have a terrible day occasionally, you wouldn't be able to feel so great when a great day happened. I hope this makes sense cuz I am trying to be upbeat about life in general. I also feel and know that when I am feeling low, I think of you and the love you have for me, and I immediately feel better and know I can face anything with that type of love and caring.

Kris, I have never wanted to be loved by somebody so badly in my entire life as I do with you. I think of past times of us together, plus the excitement of the future, and it gives me a rush like you wouldn't believe. Knowing that I have most of the next 50 years with the woman I love, I can't have a bad day knowing that.

* * *

I always had the utmost confidence in you, Kris. I knew what a gem you were the moment I met you. I don't remember ever doubting that you were the one for me. I just knew. Love is grand, isn't it!! You realize, the more you like yourself and believe in yourself, the more of you that you can give me.

* * *

You can do it, Kris. I have faith in you!

Jon was great at giving advice, but there were times when he was forced to follow it himself. Even unflappable Jon had a bad day occasionally. And this time, his bad day affected both of us.

Good News, Bad News

04 DEC 1986
23:32 IOT, UTC+6
DIEGO GARCIA
USS CARL VINSON
7°18'11" S, 72°24'38" E

Cruise life was typically mundane and boring, but this day stood out as one to remember. Jon was approached about being on the Anti-Aircraft Warfare Board, where he would help plan how best to defend the carrier strike group in a war scenario. On top of that, he'd officially qualified as a CICO with the Hawgs and could finally get his own crew. Jon was walking with confidence and was a valued member of the team.

As he sat at his desk to write his daily letter to Kris, he smiled in satisfaction at his situation.

> *Everything is falling into place. My beautiful wife and marriage, and work is good for me. God takes care of everyone who wants to let Him into their lives. I am so glad that we found each other. I have never been happier or more content in my entire life.*

The small, framed wedding picture Jon kept on his desk caught his eye.

Thank you, Kris, for saying yes. I am bushed, so it is time to close. I love you, I do, I do, I do.

The next morning, as Jon started his morning routine, he didn't anticipate the aching in his right foot. In a few minutes, he found the pain so intense that he couldn't stand much less walk. Jon realized that this was a serious problem and needed to get a medical evaluation fast. Once in the medical ward, the flight surgeon informed Jon that the same slipped disk that had plagued him during his high school wrestling days–pinching his sciatic nerve–had flared up again, and the treatment was the same: bed rest for at least one week. Life had seemed so perfect the night before. How quickly circumstances can change. Jon was humbled by the suddenness of it, but he didn't panic. If his last bout with back pain was any indication, he'd be in severe pain for three days and return to normal in fewer than ten. Until then, he knew he would have to let Kris know but also didn't want her to worry.

> *Promise*
> *"So be strong and courageous! Do not be afraid and do not panic before them. For the Lord your God will personally go ahead of you. He will neither fail you nor abandon you."*
> *Deuteronomy 31:6*

Hi, Krista Kaye.

How is my No. 1 lover and friend? I have some good and bad news. The good news is I love you more and more every day. In fact, I can't get you off my mind. It's great. The bad news is that I am flat on my back in the hospital ward with my back acting up again. Now don't worry. At first, I wasn't going to tell you until I was flying again, but I knew

I should be honest with you. It is no worse than before, and the flight surgeon said the same thing: one week of bed rest, and then we will go from there, so let's keep our fingers crossed. ...

The next few days brought little improvement to Jon's condition. There had been little to distract him from his discomfort besides a quick bedside visit from famous country music singer Loretta Lynn, who was making a celebrity stop at the ship that day to encourage the troops. He even had his picture taken with her!

Now Kris, don't get too worried over this. I am not going to die. It is not life threatening; it is like what happened in January, and I have seven doctors looking out for me, so I am in good hands.

But Jon showed a chink in his armor:

I wonder if I will have this for the rest of my life, not like a broken leg that heals, but this won't totally go away, so include me in your prayers as I will pray for you.

After eleven days of care, the flight surgeon ordered Jon to be flown to Clark Air Force base hospital in the Philippines for further testing and possible surgery.

This was not the Christmas Jon had anticipated.

Miserable Christmas

Our first Christmas as newlyweds wasn't what either one of us had expected. Jon was stuck in a military hospital in the Philippines with no real improvement while I was alone and worried on the other side of the ocean. What a miserable Christmas it would be. The day before Christmas Eve, I wrote him this heart-felt letter:

Dear Jonathan,

It is Tuesday night, and I talked to you today. Oh, how I needed to hear your voice, to reassure me that you were OK. I cried for an hour after we hung up, out of hurt for your pain, your loneliness, your frustration, your boredom, for you. I went straight to bed and fell asleep out of exhaustion from my emotions.

I guess it all hit me today, the fear, the worry, the frustration, and wanting to be beside you to comfort you, to make you laugh and smile. To know that you will be spending Christmas alone, in a hospital bed, tears me apart. If only I had the money, I would fly right to your side to hold you and tell you how much I love you. But I can only do that in my thoughts, prayers, letters, and dreams.

There must be a reason for all this. What is it? Only the Lord knows. We can always second-guess it. Maybe we've gotten too secure and cocky with the navy and your success. Maybe this is directed at me for taking your career for granted. I don't understand how we could have so many problems in our first eight months of marriage. Why? What have we done? Is this to make us stronger? Secure our love for each other? Prepare us for major hardships in the future that normally could be devastating—only not for us, since we have survived so much? Is this to make our faith in Christ stronger?

No one really knows, only that the sun comes up every day and there are three sure things going for us: (1) There is always tomorrow; (2) God loves us so much; (3) We love each other more than any husband and wife ever could. With these things, Jon, we can do anything! Believe me, I'm telling myself this more than you because, after today, I need it! I love you, honey, and I'll keep living one day at a time looking for the day when our lips can meet again....

Loving you,
Kris

The next day, on Christmas Eve, I called Jon on the phone in his hospital room. How I wished I could travel through the phone line and be there with him. When he wrote me his letter that night, it was clear that he felt the same way.

When you called today, I wanted you to whisk through the phone so that I could hold you in my arms and cuddle and pamper you. Kris, I want to bawl. I wanted to be near you so much. Your voice and your love mean so much to me. Words will never be able to express how totally in love with you I am, but I try. I want to take you in my arms so that you never have to worry again. I realize that is impossible, but please don't worry as much cuz God is looking out for me.

* * *

I'll never forget that January day when Jon came home. He didn't arrive to a hero's welcome at the squadron's celebratory fly-in. Instead, he was rolled in a wheelchair from a small military plane to our car. While we were thrilled to be reunited, with Jon lying flat on our den floor, the homecoming was bittersweet. But as the days went by, we were blessed; Jon's back made a full recovery. And when the Hormel Hawgs squadron returned home in February, he resumed full duties with them.

The cruise was not at all what I had expected, but I was thankful for the experience. Had we changed—Jon and me? Absolutely. Our goal of strengthening our relationship had been met with flying colors. Our love for and understanding of each other was even deeper than before. I had gained tremendous confidence and independence. As Jon once said, "You never know what you can do until you have to do it." And as it turned out, this navy wife could do quite a lot!

10

Back at Sea

Jon and I grinned at each other as we put on our
snorkel gear and slipped over the side of the boat and into the
magical world below us. The crystal-clear waters along the San
Diego coast and the bright, afternoon sun combined to deliver a
showcase of vividly colored tropical fish dancing among the variety of corals as if on parade. The breathtaking beauty of this
underwater paradise was so inspiring that when we got back
into the boat, we decided to become certified scuba divers. And
why not? With the scare of his back injury in our rearview mirror, Jon and I plunged straight ahead, making up for lost time
and enjoying life to the fullest.

We were still newly-
weds after all, and with
the stress of the cross-
country move and Jon's
first deployment behind
us, we finally had the luxury to simply enjoy each
other. After working dur-
ing the week, we'd travel
all over on the weekends,

often finding ourselves somewhere near the beach or on the water. We also added a new member to the family: Max Deacon, an
adorable Norwegian elkhound puppy. Sophie and Max often
joined us on our beach adventures.

Now that Jon was home, he rejoined me in the church choir, and we attended an in-depth Bible study together. Jon had never been discipled in his faith, and this season of solid Bible study and meaningful relationships with fellow Christians grounded him in his beliefs.

Both Jon and I had a deep-seated need for significance and security, and we struggled to turn this over to God and let Him handle it. From our beautifully decorated home to my top-quality business suits, it was obvious I still had desires to surround myself with the trappings of success. But at the heart of it all, we both knew we had no real control over our lives, and the only way to move forward was to find significance in our relationship with Christ.

On the professional front, Jon's navy career was moving forward according to schedule, and we looked forward to his planned promotion to lieutenant commander. Jon and the rest of the Hawgs would start workups in the fall in preparation for USS *Carl Vinson*'s 1988 cruise. Jon was well acquainted with his squadron, and the stress of being the new guy was over. He was nearing an important milestone as an NFO: two thousand flight hours logged in the E-2C Hawkeye — quite an accomplishment!

As Jon's 1988 cruise approached, we finalized our plans for his six-month deployment. We were excited about meeting each other five months later in Hong Kong, where the ship had a port of call. To stay connected and growing in our faith, Jon and I would be reading through the same marriage devotional while he was away.

For the first time, I experienced a proper sendoff of the squadron, gathering with other families at the Miramar VAW-114 hangar of the Hormel Hawgs to watch our guys fly away to meet USS *Carl Vinson* at sea. I was much better prepared for another goodbye but knew the "navy wife hat" would need to be once again in place.

As USS *Carl Vinson* began her six-month voyage, life on the carrier resumed normal activities and duties. The beginning of this deployment looked different for Jon in that he was being considered for his long-anticipated promotion to lieutenant commander. The promotion board was in the review process, and he would learn of his future with the navy soon. His outlook for the next six months would be determined by one thing—the frocking of the coveted lieutenant commander stripes. The stripes sewn on officers' uniforms were significant, and as a naval officer's wife, these stripes would eventually become a haunting vision for the rest of my life. If only Jon could see his future, but for now, he would have to trust in God that his future was held in His hands.

> Promise:
> *"For I hold you by your right hand—I, the Lord your God. And I say to you, 'Don't be afraid, I am here to help you.'"*
> Isaiah 41:13

Cloud Nine

The Fourth of July arrived a few weeks after Jon left. Even though I attended a huge party, I felt alone and missed Jon terribly, especially on such a patriotic day. The meaning of the day was still on my mind when I wrote Jon my daily letter that evening:

Happy Fourth of July!!!

I love you and am so proud of you. I thought of you all day today—knowing that because of you, we can celebrate freedom every day and especially today. Thank you for allowing me to have freedom, sweetie. You are a special and honorable man to give so much for your country ...

One of our friends was telling people how wonderful you are. She said that you are so special, the kind of guy you meet once every 20 years. I agree with her all the way! You radiate with warmth. That is why I married you and, most of all, why I love you—because to me you are the kind of guy you meet once in a lifetime. I love you. Thank you for choosing me to live your life with you.

After I finished my letter, I went to bed, only to be awakened a few hours later by the phone ringing. I was still half asleep when I answered it. "Jon? Is that you?"

"Call me Lieutenant Commander Rystrom!" he exclaimed excitedly, and even the static from the overseas phone call couldn't diminish the joy in his voice. We were thrilled that he'd been promoted, but that wasn't the end of the good news. He'd also been involved in the first Soviet MIG jet fighter interception of the cruise, and—best of all—Jon was nominated for the Hawkeye of the Year award, a high honor in the VAW community. Jon was on cloud nine, and I was proud of him and happy for us. Now we could relax and look forward to our Hong Kong reunion.

However, he had another matter to consider and a major decision to make. Jon's tour with the Hormel Hawgs would end a few months after this cruise was over. Where he served next was important because his goal was to command a VAW squadron someday, which required following a specific career path. He carefully weighed his options in the months that followed.

Day by Day

While Jon was flying over the ocean, I was literally diving into it. One of my strategies to get through Jon's cruises was to keep myself busy with activities. On Jon's second cruise, I took a class to earn my advanced scuba certification. One of my favorite dives was off Catalina Island. We were 110 feet underwater. The water was cold and clear, but there wasn't much to see that far down — no fish, no sharks, no corals, no wrecks like we'd seen on other dives. Nothing of interest except that our blue wet suits turned a deep purple at that depth. I enjoyed earning my advanced scuba certification and was surprised at how comfortable I had become in the water. I couldn't wait for Jon and me to dive together when he returned home.

Another thing I couldn't wait for were letters. Having experienced typical letter delays during the first cruise, I thought I would be fine when Jon's letters were slow in coming the second time around, but that wasn't the case. Sometimes I could get downright mean about it; at other times, the lack of letters made me depressed.

Another day without a letter, but today I was more prepared ... Think of submarine families that go without mail for months ... You seem so far away, almost like you must be a man in my dreams. I'm finding that in order to deal with this horrible emptiness, since I haven't had any contact with you, I put my deep feelings way back in my mind so that I can get through day by day.

When I'm alone, I think a lot about our future, our next year, and the next few months before I see you again. I really, really miss you ... Why are we putting ourselves through this? Does it all really make sense? Boy, not getting letters from you must be the toughest thing yet. The thought of losing you, your love for me, or even your desire for me would literally break my heart.

Of course, the letters came eventually, and over time, I learned to have faith that even if I wasn't hearing from Jon the way I desired, he still loved and cared for me. This navy wife was learning to trust. Little did I know how much I was going to need this more than ever in the days ahead.

Sophie and Max Deacon Rystrom

11

Hong Kong Homecoming

As I saw my mailbox being filled with letters once again, I realized that Jon was right. I kept my head up and my attitude positive, and the letters came. But some of what Jon wrote was downright disturbing and brought fearful images to mind that were hard to shake.

> What a day! VF-111 lost an F-14 jet tonight. In fact, three hours ago, and my crew was involved in the rescue. From start to finish it only took 55 minutes. The F-14 had gone down in the water about 45 miles from the Carl Vinson. The RIO had back injuries—we don't know how serious—and went into shock aboard the helo, but he's stable now. The pilot was in good shape. The cause of the crash? No one is talking. I'm sure we will hear more in the next day or two. Well, that's the big news and, no, we weren't heroes—just doing our job.

Regardless of what Jon said, I considered him and the men he served with to be heroes, but I feared for his safety all the same.

Another image appeared to me in this same time period— one that would haunt me for years. It wasn't in a letter from Jon but on the cover of a local newspaper. Living in a military community, I was accustomed to seeing articles on planes and service people all the time, but something about this image grabbed me by the throat and wouldn't let go.

It was a picture of a young widow of a navy aviator holding a folded flag that had been presented to her at her husband's funeral. His F-14 fighter jet had been on a training run when it developed mechanical trouble. Both the pilot and the RIO ejected, but the RIO got tangled in some power lines and broke his neck. He died of his injuries the next day. The plane itself crashed into a local airport, causing several injuries on the ground.

As I looked at that mournful image and the grieving face of the navy widow, this thought went through my mind: *One day that will be me.* Why would I think such a thing? Her husband flew one of the most dangerous fighter jets in the navy. *Jon is in the safest plane in the navy.* I shuddered at the thought and tried to erase it from my mind, but the memory of that front-page photo seared into my subconscious and would resurface in the most unexpected moments.

Once in a Lifetime

I pushed these dark premonitions aside and focused my energies on something much more delightful: our upcoming reunion in Hong Kong. I couldn't wait to be safe and secure in Jon's arms again. The long-anticipated November day came, and while experiencing the exotic wonder of this bustling city gave me a rush, it could not compare to the thrill of being reunited with my beloved Jon. With the luxurious Kowloon Hotel as our home base, Jon and I spent nearly a week together touring the harbor, shopping for pearls, purchasing custom-tailored silk suits, and experiencing Hong Kong's unique cuisine. We shared many activities with other couples from the squadron but still had plenty of alone time to reconnect and rekindle our love.

Jon seemed as excited about discovering and buying Hong Kong treasures for me as I was to receive them. He didn't have a selfish bone in his body—at least not where I was concerned. He went to great lengths to make sure I had plenty of meaningful mementos from this once-in-a-lifetime adventure. During that week, we also had Jon's official frocking ceremony, where I was proud to place Jon's new lieu-tenant commander stripes on the shoulders of his dress whites.

> Promise:
> "Take delight in the Lord, and he will give you your heart's desires."
> Psalm 37:4

At the end of our visit, all the wives rode the liberty boat out to USS *Carl Vinson*, where our husbands gave us a guided tour of the carrier, including their personal staterooms. How surreal it was to be sitting in the same O-4 bunk room where my Jon wrote me every night while we were apart.

Saying goodbye to Jon for the second time during this cruise wasn't any easier than the first, but we knew we had less than one month to go before he and the rest of his shipmates would return in time for Christmas, a real Christmas homecoming. Around the middle of December that year, I joined the other VAW-114 squadron families at the Hawgs' home base in prepar-ing a special homecoming for our aviators.

As the ship neared its San Diego port, the air wing prepared for the fly-in, where all the planes left the carrier and returned to their home bases across America. With our San Diego home so close to Miramar Naval Air Station, I had grown accustomed to the engine blasts of F-14 jets and the thrilling flyovers of Blue Angels in tight formation. But nothing stirred my heart like the unmistakable sight and sound of Hummers in the sky. As Jon and his squadmates walked across the tarmac dressed in their flight jackets, this was the homecoming I'd always hoped for. As Jon and I embraced, our kisses mixed with tears of joy and relief.

Kris visiting Jon's stateroom on the USS Carl Vinson
during their Hong Kong reunion

You Make Me Complete

As I thought about our first full six-month cruise, I was happy knowing we had not only maintained but also grown our close relationship. Outside of our fairytale trip to Hong Kong, what I remember most is how we expressed our love for each other through daily letters.

To Jon Alvin Rystrom:

Three years ago tonight, I met a man that would change my life. This man would teach me about the navy, about finances, about buying a house, about using a drill, about Nebraska football, about Norwegian elkhounds, about moving cross country, about operating two VCRs, a stereo, and a TV at the same time, about patience, about listening, about giving, about accepting, about lovemaking, about snuggling, about responsibilities, about security, about waiting, about flexibility and positive attitudes, about marriage, about ... love.

I will cherish the wonderful memory of our meeting for as long as I live. Oh, to think that it has been three years and look at how much we have been through and what lies ahead. What a thrilling thought. I love you with all my heart. Thank you for being the man I prayed for all my life and, most of all, for giving love a try again in your life. Because this time, babe ... it worked!

You changed my life and taught me how to live it. Thank you, Jon Alvin. I will love you for eternity.

Your "Green-Eyed Lady"

* * *

I am so lucky to have you as my better half. I absolutely adore you. I love it when guys complain about me getting so many letters, but they don't realize it is a two-way street. If I didn't write as often as I do, you would find it tougher to write to me so much. I am glad we agreed to try to write every day, and I think that overall, we have done well.

I'm not sure I handle the pain of things correctly. But because of you in my life and opening my eyes again to God, I can accept the little things that go wrong—as long as God is on my side and I have my faith and our love for each other.

I love you.

Jon and Kris at Balboa Park, San Diego, CA

12

Go Big Red

With the New Year came the need to make our final decision on Jon's new orders. A Joint Service tour, where Jon would serve alongside service members from other branches of the military, would be the best move for Jon's career and would likely increase the chances of his future promotion to commander. That narrowed our options, but one of the choices was, of all places, Nebraska. The National Emergency Airborne Command Post (NEACP), or the Flying White House plane, was based at Offutt Air Force Base south of Omaha. Jon would need special clearances to qualify for the position, but he had been told that NEACP was the best-kept secret for duty tours because of the time you were able to spend at home.

When I thought of Nebraska, all I could see was shoveling through chest-high snowdrifts surrounded by endless acres of corn and being awakened by tornado sirens. Nebraska had one thing going for it, and it was a big one—family. Jon's navy career meant that visits with his family were few and far between. The possibility of being based so close to his parents, most of his siblings, and their families made Nebraska a hard option to dismiss.

Relationship was important to Jon and me, and with NEACP on the table, we prayed long and hard about the direction we should take and asked God to give us clear guidance. To be honest, Nebraska was not my first choice, but I was prepared to go if that was God's will for us. After much prayer and many late-night conversations, we both had peace about God's guidance and our decision. My cornhusker husband was going home.

Bellevue Baby

Before moving to Jon's new post in May, we spent the last few months in San Diego tying up loose ends and saying goodbye to our home and backyard, with its citrus trees and rosebushes that Jon planted for me. Pulling up roots of the life we had established in San Diego was another harsh reality of the navy life I had chosen.

However, that reality became much sweeter when I discovered something else right after we accepted the NEACP tour—I was pregnant! The next chapter of our lives would include Baby Rystrom. God's guidance to leave the beaches of Southern California for the cornfields of Nebraska now made complete sense.

We decided to rent out our duplex instead of selling it, keeping it as an investment in the rising real estate market. As boxes were being packed, my own personal checkboxes were changing.

Great house? Leaving it.

Great job for me? Leaving that too. We decided that until Baby Rystrom arrived, I would be a stay-at-home wife. I could go back to my career afterward.

Great marriage? Yes, that one box was still checked.

Faith? We loved our church home in San Diego, and I was comfortable with my relationship with God. Finding a new church home would be a priority.

Great family? My growing tummy was a constant reminder that life was about to change for us forever. Whatever adventures lay ahead, Jon and I would face them together.

Moving into our new home in Bellevue, Nebraska—a suburb surrounded by cornfields and situated about thirty miles from Omaha—was nothing like the fast-paced, beach-centered lifestyle to which we were accustomed. Several military families lived in our neighborhood, and I was thankful that they quickly accepted me into their circle. As the birth of Baby Rystrom approached, we found it easier to slow down and embrace a simpler, calmer lifestyle. We traded in our Jeep for a minivan, our vacations for trips to see Jon's family, and late nights out for cookouts and barbecues with Jon's new squadmates.

In September, four months after moving to Nebraska, we experienced one of the best days of our lives—the arrival of our firstborn, a baby girl named Jordyn Deay Rystrom. Her middle name came from the maiden name of Jon's mother, and sharing her birth with Jon's family made this milestone even more precious. As I held my newborn daughter in my arms, my entire life was transformed.

In the same way that Jon's unconditional love had brought healing to my eating disorder, becoming a mother and experiencing the affectionate bond I shared with Jordyn brought healing to my need for significance. My intention had been to return to work soon after delivery, but once Jordyn was born, my heart was full, and my desire to gain affirmation by climbing a career ladder diminished.

Jon was shocked that his once highly competitive businesswoman-wife was now content to stay home with our baby girl and hang out with other moms and their children. If someone had told me in San Diego that I'd be embracing the mom life, I wouldn't have believed it.

Jon and I found a meaningful church home at Christ Community, a Missionary Alliance church in Omaha. There, at Jordyn's baby dedication, Jon and I promised before God, the congregation, and each other to raise our daughter in the faith and in a home that honored Christ, to surround her with God's people, and to teach her the truths found in God's Word.

The President's Nightwatch

The NEACAP fleet was made up of four Boeing 747s known as the Doomsday plane, or Nightwatch. Disguised to look like Air Force One, the military version performed a critical role in the

United States defense strategy. In case of a nuclear attack or other national emergency, the president and the Secretary of Defense, along with the Joint Chiefs of Staff, could carry out their duties safely from the air for days at a time, if necessary, without having to land to refuel. To accomplish this mission, the massive jet was packed with the latest top-secret technology and operated by a team of highly skilled crew. NEACP crews rotated watches so that one plane was ready to go 24/7. Jon was proud of his assignment with NEACP, working primarily as a strategic operations officer. To say Jon's job was classified was an understatement.

For a navy wife who had spent nearly half of her marriage apart from her husband, Jon's new work schedule was total bliss. He served on one of three NEACP crews that rotated responsibilities on a weekly basis securing the air space within two hundred miles of President George H. W. Bush. He was used to working all hours of the day and night, so helping with baby Jordyn's care in the wee hours of the morning was a pleasure for him. And his rotation schedule allowed us to travel and have fun if we didn't drive too far away from the base when he was on call. We agreed that the NEACP tour was indeed the best-kept secret in the navy.

The President's "Nightwatch,"
Offutt Air Force Base, Bellevue, NE

Nebraska Family

Because the NEACP tour was a Joint Services tour, Jon had the honor of serving alongside service members from other branches of the military: the army, air force, and marines. The camaraderie built among the members of the crew was deep and would last a lifetime. Many said the best relationships they developed in their military career were those forged at NEACP. The long hours spent together being on call far from home; the stresses of the overwhelming responsibility; and the cooperation, trust, and professionalism required to accomplish the mission forged a special bond among these crewmates. And that bond translated to their families as well.

I was the youngest officer's wife with a baby. I loved spending time with these more experienced military moms and grew close to them. We shared dinners and cookouts together, including special gatherings at a double-wide trailer near the base that was placed there specifically so we could spend time with our husbands when they were on call. This was especially meaningful if Jon was on call on Christmas or other special days; we wouldn't have to spend so many holidays apart. Of course, if a thunderstorm or other emergency interrupted our meal with a klaxon call, the guys would jump up, run out the door, and hightail it through the gate.

As meaningful as spending time with the NEACP families was, what really made our tour in Nebraska special was the time we were able to spend with Jon's family. Jon's hometown was only a ninety-minute drive away, and we'd often travel through miles of prairie and cornfields to his parents' humble, two-bedroom home in Stromsburg for birthdays and anniversaries or simple visits. Whenever we visited my

> *Promise:*
> *"Deep in your hearts you know that every promise of the Lord your God has come true."*
> *Joshua 23:14*

in-laws, within minutes of arriving, I'd be in the kitchen with Jon's mom while "Jonny" and his father would be outside working on some project.

How rare it was for a navy officer to be stationed in Nebraska, near his hometown and his family and with an assignment that gave him precious time with the people he loved. And even though Jon's responsibilities were considerable, the country was not at war, so life was easy. We were still newlyweds in many ways, and the lack of stress allowed us a unique season of enjoying each other and our family. Jon excelled at his job and won his highest-ranking medal to date, the Joint Services Commendation Medal. As for me, once Jordyn was a toddler, I found a way to work part time as an adjunct professor at the University of Nebraska Omaha, where I taught advertising classes.

But this tour couldn't go on forever, and as 1990 ended, the time came for Jon to receive his new orders. Once again, we had options. But whatever he chose, we knew his next tour would be sea duty. If Jon ever wanted a chance to move forward in his career as a senior officer and one day command his own squadron, his next billet needed to be a VAW department head. We could have returned to San Diego, but now that we had a daughter, we wanted to avoid the high cost of living and hectic lifestyle of California, and we also wanted to be closer to my parents in West Virginia.

In the end, we chose to return to Norfolk, where Jon and I had roots. I was going home. In August 1991, we packed up our belongings, said tearful goodbyes to our family and new friends, and headed east for our next adventure, where Jon would join the Bear Aces of VAW-124 and later deploy on the carrier USS *Theodore Roosevelt* for a 1993 Mediterranean cruise to start in March and end in September.

13

Seagrass Reach

When we returned to Norfolk, I was by far a dif-
ferent woman than the one who had left five years earlier. I still
had my competitive nature, but I loved mom life, and I was much
more relaxed and experienced in my navy-wife role.

Our decision to keep and rent out our duplex in San Diego
while we lived in Nebraska had turned out to be a wise one.
Thanks to California's booming real estate market, we had a nice
chunk of equity when it came time to sell. Compared to California, land prices were much cheaper in Chesapeake, a growing
area south of Norfolk where many military families found af-
fordable housing. That meant we could build the home of our
dreams without the cost forcing me to work. We chose a lot lined
with tall pine trees in a developing neighborhood called River-
walk on the Elizabeth. Even the name of our street sounded like
a fairytale forest: Seagrass Reach.

We planned all the details of our custom home together. We
chose a gorgeous, two-story, Georgian-style facade in a tasteful,
light brick, with curved brick steps leading up to beautiful, glass-
front double doors. The peach-tiled, vaulted entry displayed a
grand, white-spindled staircase that led to the upper-floor bed-
rooms, including a playroom over the double garage. The downstairs living area included a lovely formal dining room off the
generous kitchen. Some couples say they want to divorce after
enduring the stress of a house-building project, but not us. We
had no fights or arguments; our goal was to make each other
happy. The way we handled this massive task reflected the trust,

honor, and space we willingly gave each other. Jon visited the construction site every day to make sure everything was done according to his high standards. He would personally do some of the outside jobs, like the fencing, sprinkler system installation, and landscaping.

Jon and Kris' Seagrass Reach home under construction

As we prepared to move into our dream home in December 1991, we had another reason to be thankful: I was expecting again! Somehow, getting pregnant and moving seemed to go hand in hand for us. We couldn't have been more excited, and our new home would be perfect for our growing family.

Checking Off Boxes

Once again, I found myself unpacking boxes. It seemed the navy life was all about boxes—constantly packing boxes to move out and unpacking boxes to move in. As I mentally checked off my own "boxes," life could not have been more perfect.

Perfect home? Yes, and more than I could have imagined.

Perfect marriage? Oh yes, and only getting better with time.

Perfect family? Of course, especially with our second child due in August and us now living closer to my parents in West Virginia.

Perfect church? Having lived across the country, Jon and I were thrilled to return to our roots. We chose First Baptist Norfolk as our home church. We were excited to sit under the biblical teachings of our new pastor and get involved with this new family of believers. Jon and I immediately joined the choir and a couples' Sunday School class. We began teaching youngsters in Mission Friends and enrolled Jordyn in the church preschool.

Perfect friends? Reuniting with our old friends as well as meeting new ones from Jon's squadron, neighborhood, and church family provided numerous opportunities for relationship. Everywhere we had lived, Jon and I dove head-first into community, and our Norfolk move was no different. Besides our church activities, we cooked out with Jon's squadron and got to know our neighbors. One special friend was Jennifer, who was often alone because her husband, a navy officer, served on a submarine. She lived down the street, and she and Jon enjoyed talking about yard work.

Perfect finances? We had a solid foundation, though I always seemed to be stressed about it. Perfect job? Jon was secure in his navy career, and with our return to the Norfolk area, I was ready to prepare myself for the future. Regent University, formerly CBN University, graciously allowed me to rejoin their master's program and complete my thesis. Jon finished his training and joined the Bear Aces in January. I knew he would be following his new squadron to Panama in the spring of 1992 for drug-interdiction missions, but I figured I could effectively manage being the pregnant mom of a preschooler, completing my master's thesis, plus getting settled into a new home all by myself. I was still a bit of an overachiever.

The one downer in our lives was that my dear old friend—my beloved Sophie—passed away right after we moved into our new home. We were devastated to lose our sweet companion of more than six years, but at least faithful Max—our Norwegian Elkhound fluff ball—was still by our side.

Hellos and Goodbyes

The next few months were a blur. I juggled all my responsibilities mostly alone. With Jon away in Panama, we were able to phone each other occasionally, but our daily letter writing resumed. I shared with Jon how Jordyn was dealing with experiencing his long-term absence for the first time:

> *Hi, Babe,*
>
> *Well, this is the beginning of another letter-writing relationship between Kris and Jon. I'm sure this tour will fill up lots of shoeboxes ... On the way home from church, Jordyn asked where you were. When I said at work on the plane, she started crying. So I said you were hunting bad guys and then she was OK!*
>
> *Jordyn has been such a good girl—she keeps me laughing with all her antics. She started crying, wanting Daddy today. Occasionally, she'll surprise me with wanting you, just out of the blue.*

Even though we were writing letters to each other again, our topics were different from the lovey-dovey letters of our newlywed days. Many of them centered on parenthood. I tried to keep Jon up to date on the details of Jordyn's life that he had to miss:

her growing love of the ocean, fun times she had with other kids, and, of course, her health.

> *I realized Jordyn felt really HOT, so I took her temp and it was 102°!! Poor thing had a fever! So in the five weeks you've been gone, she has had a stomach virus, a sinus infection, and now 102° fever. I hate to see what it is going to be like with two kids while you are at sea for six months!*
>
> *I'm really concerned about the cruise. Hopefully, the baby will make it go faster and by then I'll be back to choir, Bible study, maybe working out again. Anyway, I've been staying busy, but there is still a void, a loneliness, and I get so tired ... but again, that could also be the pregnancy and still the weight of getting this thesis out of the way. Ugh.*

As I read Jon's letters, I began to learn about some of his squadron mates. I was looking forward to getting to know their wives. I knew from experience that a strong sisterhood formed with other wives during deployments. This cruise would be different from Jon's previous ones, though, since I was now a mom of two small children. I was going to rely on the Bear Ace wives for parental support this time.

His Panama duty ended in mid-May 1992, but by mid-June, workups on USS *Theodore Roosevelt* began, with Jon rotating between sea and land time. Another hello-goodbye period had begun, but we also hoped it would be one of our last. Jon had a good chance of being promoted to the rank of commander when the next promotion board met soon after the start of Jon's 1993 cruise. I could tell by his workup letters that his priorities were shifting.

Hi, My Love,

Well, another period of being apart, but at the same time, I realize that you are kept so busy with Jordyn that the loneliness is not as strong, except at certain times...

Kris, going to sea is not what it once was. I miss you and Jordyn too much and love you like crazy. I pray that this tour gives us what we want for my career. I know that if it is in my power—I really mean God's power—after this tour, no more sea duty for us. I love you and miss you. Jordyn, give mommy a hug! Love, Jon

Unexpected Phone Call

One evening while Jon was home from workups, the phone rang. Jon answered, and although I couldn't hear the conversation on the other end, the look on Jon's face told me something was wrong. After asking a few questions, Jon hung up with a look of despair.

"Jon, what's wrong?" I asked, with my stomach in knots.

He sighed, trying to find the words. "There's been an accident with an E-2C—not from our squadron." He paused. "All five men were killed."

My heart froze. Killed? Dead? All five of them? Jon gave me the rest of the details. An E-2C from VAW-126, the Sea Hawks, was coming back from a routine training flight off the aircraft carrier USS *John F. Kennedy*. They were minutes from landing when a fire broke out in the cockpit, filling the plane with thick smoke. They sent out a distress call, but only four miles from the ship, the plane tumbled out of the sky and into the water. One body was recovered, but the remains of the other four men were never found, and they were declared lost at sea.

The VAW community was a tight-knit one, and even though these men weren't in Jon's squadron, they were considered his. The crash of the Sea Hawk's 602 sent a jolt through the entire VAW community. And it sent a jolt through me too. Jon had told me that E-2Cs never crash. Obviously, that was not the case. I could only imagine what the wives and children of those men were going through. Immediately, the memory of the front-page picture of a navy widow holding her husband's folded flag—the one I'd seen in San Diego years before—flooded my mind.

Our Chesapeake Baby

As Jon started preparing for his upcoming six-month deployment with the Bear Aces, we were able to have picnics and dinners with the aviators from the squadron and their families.

I loved finally getting to match the wives with the guys in the squadron after I had heard about so many of them through Jon's letters when he had first joined the squadron in Panama. He had told me about Shelly Messier's husband, John—also known as Frenchy—whom Jon thought was the best stick (pilot) in the squadron. I'd already taken a meal over to Paola Dyer, the wife of another pilot, Billy Ray, after the birth of their baby son.

I finally got to meet Jon's best chess buddy, unattached Patrick Ardaiz—Aardvark. Then there was Katy Forwalder's husband, Bob, who was training to be a CICO like Jon. They were expecting their first child in the spring during the deployment. We were all disappointed that Bob couldn't stay home for the birth of his son and then meet up with the carrier. The military unfortunately had the final say in that decision.

Kris, Jon, and Jordyn at a Bear Ace picnic, Norfolk, VA 1992

Although we were all preparing for our husbands' upcoming deployment, the wives enjoyed getting to know each other at our monthly meetings together. Aviator's wives have a unique bond, and I was thankful to be part of this tight-knit community. Jon's deployment was going to be easier to get through with so many fun ladies in our group.

Summer came, and I cherished the days that Jon and I could be together working on projects around our dream home. Jon worked unusually hard to complete his tasks, knowing he wouldn't be home for almost half of the upcoming year. The house was coming along, but our favorite part was working on the nursery. By now, we knew we were having another girl, and my due date was only weeks away. Life was turning out just as we had planned.

We celebrated in late August the birth of our second daughter, Taylor Windham Rystrom. Thankfully, my biggest fan and best birth coach, Jon, was there beside me and not training at sea. Even at birth, it was obvious that beautiful, fair-skinned Taylor looked like her father, which made her daddy extremely proud.

Jon returned to USS *Theodore Roosevelt* for workups, and I added caring for a newborn to my list of duties. When Taylor was about six weeks old, she became sick with a 103° fever. I instantly took her to the doctors. They couldn't determine the cause of her fever and admitted her to the hospital. I tried to stay calm, but as more tests were run and the doctors couldn't give me any answers, I became hysterical.

I was able to contact Jon where they were operating near Puerto Rico. But as much as he wanted to come home, he wasn't allowed to leave. I was devastated. This was my first true crisis without Jon there to calm and reassure me and to balance my intense emotions with his cool-headed manner. Our church rallied around me and our girls, and I stayed by Taylor's side, feeling helpless and afraid. As I lay next to her in that hospital room seeing all the tubes in her, the fear of parenting alone was overwhelming. This experience took the stresses of the navy-wife life to a completely new level. Thankfully, Taylor fully recovered.

Significant Events

Summer turned to fall. Bill Clinton defeated George H. W. Bush in the November presidential elections, and though I wasn't into politics or world affairs, the military certainly was. The navy had already experienced budget cuts, but one benefit allowed Jon to double the amount of his Servicemembers' Group Life Insurance policy. Because of the dangers of their jobs, navy aviators—unlike civilians—found it difficult to buy traditional life insurance, so this benefit was sorely needed.

"If I die, you'll be well taken care of," he joked with me one day.

I was not amused. "Don't talk like that, Jon! Stop!"

Maybe it was all the stress of this workup period getting to me, but at times, I would look at Jon's hands, his face, his skin, memorizing his scars in case I needed to identify his body one day. That old dreadful feeling was returning—the same one I'd felt years ago when I saw the widow's picture in the newspaper in San Diego. And Jon talking about life insurance policies certainly didn't help.

This navy wife was weary—weary from her husband's comings and goings. I found myself wondering if our lives would ever be normal.

> *Jon,*
>
> *I really hate being alone so much. I know there is nothing you can do, and you've built this beautiful house for me, but it is so hard going day and night, knowing it is still days and weeks before you are home and, basically, only for a visit. It doesn't even feel like I'm married sometimes, and when you are home, all your time is devoted to Jordyn, getting stuff done around the house, and work, again. Sounds like a lonely housewife having a pity party...*
>
> *I'll just say, after this tour—you will get a shore tour with no separation. We've never had any length of time when you aren't gone for long periods of time for over six years. It is time that you start being a full-time husband. OK?*

Jon missed Thanksgiving with us, but he was home for Christmas. In keeping with tradition, we decorated our Christmas tree together, with Jordyn's help, who was now three years old. Five days before Christmas, we had Taylor's baby dedication service at First Baptist Norfolk. Like we had done with

Jordyn, Jon and I promised before God, our church family, and each other that we would raise Taylor in a Christian home connected to the body of Christ, with a respect and love for God's Word, and would encourage her to have a personal relationship with God.

With our year-old home decked out in holiday cheer, our growing family getting to celebrate the season together, and our meaningful connection to our church family and other friends, that Christmas was a special one. With the New Year, we began our final push to prepare for Jon's cruise set to begin in March. We'd met another navy family in the neighborhood, the Purcells. Mike was deploying on USS *Theodore Roosevelt* too, though he wasn't a part of the air wing. He and Jon hit it off right away, and they made plans to share some hobbies together when they got back home.

> *Promise:*
> *"Don't be afraid, for I am with you. Don't be discouraged, for I am your God. I will strengthen you and help you. I will hold you up with my victorious right hand."*
> *Isaiah 41:10*

Jon and I talked a lot about his career after this cruise, and he had been investigating possible tours. One option included moving to London, but we weren't sure we wanted to uproot our family, sell the dream home we'd lovingly built together, and move overseas. But what if that was the only way to continue his naval career? He'd hoped to retire from the navy and become a financial advisor, and with the O-5 promotion board set to meet in March, Jon would get a good idea of where he stood with the navy.

Jon's parents celebrated their fiftieth wedding anniversary in February, and we took time out of our hectic schedule to travel to Stromsburg with our girls to celebrate this milestone event with Jon's family. Before we left, we went to Olan Mills Portrait Studio to have a formal family portrait made—the first since

Taylor was born—to display alongside photos from everyone in Jon's extended family. After our NEACP years, Nebraska held even more fond memories for me, and we were happy to introduce everyone to our newest member of the Rystrom family.

Once we were home from our trip, my world became small. All I could focus on was my own family and Jon's upcoming deployment. My navy-wife hat was about to be worn full time, and, to be honest, I was ready for this cruise to get started so we could be done with it.

Little did I know that on the other side of the world, there was a hopeless mother clinging to her starving children in fear .... waiting ... waiting for relief in her war-torn country, while here I was, a privileged housewife and mother clinging to her husband who had a mission. A mission called *Operation Provide Promise*. Neither she nor I knew that Provide Promise would save her life and destroy mine.

14

Iron Grip

02 MAR 1993
2143 CENTRAL EUROPEAN TIME, UTC+1
CERSKA, HERZEGOVINA
44°15'18" N, 19°01'34" E

The thin, plastic sheeting stretched over the bro-ken window glass did little to keep out the icy chill that penetrated the remote mountain enclave. In the dark interior of the shell-damaged cottage, a despairing Bosniak Muslim mother and her three young children huddled together in a vain attempt to keep warm. Her husband, most likely shot or captured by the attacking Serbs, had disappeared weeks ago while foraging for whatever food could be scavenged from the surrounding snow-covered forests. Random gunfire punctuated the gloomy night as the few remaining village defenders, with their feeble light weapons, endeavored to hold back the far-superior Serb forces who had encircled the village with an iron grip.

> Promise:
> *"The Lord is a shelter for the oppressed, a refuge in times of trouble."*
> Psalm 9:9

Life hadn't always been like this in the rugged, scenic region of Eastern Bosnia, where the Muslim majority had once lived in relative harmony beside their Serb neighbors. All that changed when the collapse of the former Eastern Bloc and the splitting of Yugoslavia fanned regional and ethnic divisions and aspirations into full flame. The Serbs, the second-largest ethnic group in the area, wanted Bosnia-Herzegovina to be a part of a greater Serbia, but the more numerous Bosniak Muslims stood in their way.

Backed by the Yugoslav army, Serb forces began a strategy of ethnic cleansing by surrounding and shelling Muslim communities, slowly starving them, and eventually forcing them out of homes that had been in their families for generations. Men and boys who weren't executed and left in mass graves and women and girls who weren't rounded up and raped went on foot by the thousands as refugees in search of safe areas many miles away. To be fair, no ethnic group was innocent of wrongdoing during this convoluted conflict, but the complicated nature of the Bosnian War was irrelevant to a besieged mother in Cerska trying to help her forsaken children live to see another day.

A small number of United Nations convoys had reached her village early in the conflict, but the few medicines, food supplies, and plastic to cover broken windows that they provided was like putting a band-aid on a severed limb. The villagers knew it was only a matter of time before the Serbs moved in and their fate was sealed.

The UN had proven incapable of ending the conflict, and the humanitarian airlift called Operation Provide Promise, which began in July 1992, couldn't erase the effects of the hostilities. Cerska's only hope was a report from a shortwave radio operator nearby who heard that the president of the United States had authorized airdrops of food rations to their area. While the multinational coalition forces running Operation Provide Promise had been airlifting food and medical supplies into Sarajevo for months, this would be the first time that food rations would be delivered to the beleaguered and isolated Muslim areas of Eastern Bosnia.

Large C-130 transport planes flying out of air bases in Europe would drop their loads from high altitudes to avoid being hit by enemy fire. This also meant the accuracy of airdrops would be inconsistent, but the Pentagon felt that even if some shipments missed their mark, the rations that made it through would be worth the effort.

Perhaps with the Americans getting involved, Bosniak Muslims hoped they could hold out long enough for a diplomatic solution to end the fighting. And while they were waiting, maybe they could at least receive some rations to ease the gnawing in their stomachs.

The thin night air was interrupted by an unfamiliar sound: the low drones of United States Naval C-130 transport planes. The mother gasped, and her children clasped their hands in hope. Perhaps they would live to see another day after all.

15

Rosebushes and Goodbyes

March arrived, and we had eleven days until Jon would be deployed to the Mediterranean. Jon was excited to learn that he could participate in three-year-old Jordyn's preschool class's career day before he had to leave.

Jon, dressed in his flight suit, took his gear and a model of the E-2C plane to Jordyn's class at First Baptist Norfolk. I was proud and thankful that Jon placed a high value on spending meaningful time with our children.

Jordyn looked proud holding her daddy's hand as they entered the classroom. Several parents had come to share, and after several presentations, it was Jon's turn. Some of the kids already knew "Mr. Jon" from the Mission Friends class he taught at church, but they'd never seen him in his flight suit.

"Good morning, boys and girls!" Jon began his presentation, as he sat down in a little preschool chair with a wide grin on his face. Jon's natural connection with children and his enthusiasm for his job were obvious as he clearly explained his role in the navy in ways only a three-year-old could understand. "I fly planes in the navy to keep America safe—in a plane that looks like it has a big pancake on top." Jon illustrated by pointing to his model. "That pancake lets me look at the other planes in the sky, and then I can see the bad guys coming and tell the good guys where to go."

The children were fascinated with his explanations and were hanging on his every word.

"Let me show you my flight suit and my survival gear," Jon continued. "My dark-green flight suit covers my whole body, and it's made of fabric that can't burn. And my shoes," Jon demonstrated as he hit the end of them with his hand, "are steel-toed so that my feet can't get hurt. I also wear these gloves and this helmet with a visor that I lock down to keep my head and face safe."

"What's that part wrapped around your legs?" asked one little boy.

"That's a good question," Jon replied. "I have this special webbing that I step into, and it's not only around my legs but also around my waist, my shoulders, and chest too. See?" Jon stood up and slowly turned completely around so that the children could get a better look. "And I must make sure it's snug and tight because if something happens, this webbing is what holds me to my parachute. And it can really hurt if the webbing is loose when the parachute comes out."

"What's all that stuff stuck on it?" another little girl asked.

"Well, it's all part of my survival gear. Let me show you. Around my neck and waist, I have things I can inflate with air—like one of your pool floaties. That helps keep my head above the water if I must leave my plane over the ocean. Here's my flashlight, and I've got lots of pockets. I have things I can use if I'm out on my own for a while, like fishing line and hooks, a signal flare, and something that makes smoke and a mirror so that I can let other planes know where I am. I always like to carry a Swiss army knife with me, and I keep it in this pocket. And all of us on the plane have one of these."

Jon took out a small canister that had what looked like a scuba diver's breathing device on one end. "This is a bottle of oxygen—a bottle of air—and that way if our plane goes down in the water, I can pull this out and breathe in here," Jon explained as he put the device up to his face. "That will give me time to find my way out of the plane."

As the eager children asked more questions, Jon patiently answered them all. The kids were clearly entranced by Jon's captivating presentation. When he finished and sat down next to Jordyn, the smile on her face was priceless. I knew the basics of Jon's job, but I didn't know the details about his survival gear. Getting out of the tight confines of the E-2C in an emergency would be difficult, and knowing he had a bottle of oxygen with him brought me some comfort. Not that I ever wanted him to have to use it.

Promise Me

Our last Sunday before the cruise, we followed our usual routine and attended church as a family. Jon and I usually went to our Sunday School class together, where he was always so sweet to bring me a cup of coffee. The friendships Jon and I had made in that weekly class were meaningful to us. Several military people went to our church, and everyone there understood the demands that deployment put on military families. I was thankful for that group of people who would help support me during Jon's cruise.

However, that Sunday, I took my turn helping in the church nursery. When class was over, several of my girlfriends from class were anxious to tell me about Jon's sweet request. How they described the scene took me by surprise but warmed my heart as they told me word for word what he asked.

Jon had presented briefs, projects, and lectures countless times over the years in front of powerful civilian contractors, Pentagon brass, and all ranks of the military, but based on my friends' description, it seemed that what he shared in our Sunday school class that day made all those times seem insignificant.

As he stood in front of our class with his hands behind his back, he began his remarks. "As most of you know, I'm going on a cruise to the Mediterranean for six months starting this Thursday. I want you to promise me something: I want you to promise that you will take care of Kris and the girls."

"Oh, Jon, of course," one lady said, laughing softly, familiar with Jon's antics and jokes in class.

"No, I'm serious," Jon said firmly, with a solemn look and tone that instantly changed the room's casual mood to a grave one. He paused slightly before continuing. "I want you to promise me that you will take care of my family when I'm gone."

No one had ever addressed the class like that before. Walking alongside military families when a father was deployed wasn't a new idea to the class. Another member named Dave was currently deployed on USS *John F. Kennedy*. Many people in our class had been looking after Dave's wife and kids and including them in family activities. What surprised our friends was not his request but the soberness in which he delivered it.

"I promise, Jon," answered one husband on the front row. "I'll help Kris and the girls in any way I can."

"We both will," his wife joined in.

"Me too, Jon. You can count on me."

And in a moment, everyone in the class had given Jon the promise he'd asked for. Jon thanked the class and took his seat, satisfied that we had the support of our classmates. This wasn't Jon's first cruise by any means, but it was his first with children, and that made all the difference. He would do everything in his power to provide for us and leave the rest in God's hands.

Storm of the Century

The final days before Jon's Thursday departure were a whirlwind of activity. Jon put on his Nebraska overalls and completed every household task that he could, including planting rosebushes along the side of the house.

The *TR* itself was preparing not only for the cruise but also for a special visitor. The newly elected President Bill Clinton had planned to deliver his first speech as commander in chief onboard USS *Theodore Roosevelt* on Friday, the *TR*'s first full day at sea. He would be accompanied by other high-ranking officials and members of the national media, making this a significant and widely covered event.

As powerful as the president was, even he couldn't control the weather. I didn't usually keep an eye on the forecast, but I couldn't help but hear about a crazy weather system heading our way later that week. Being hailed as "the storm of the century," meteorologists described it as a hurricane with snow and potentially lots of it. It would impact most of the Eastern United States, but exactly how it would affect us in the Norfolk area was unclear.

Wednesday came—the final full day before the cruise. That evening at church, Jordyn enjoyed one more fun evening with her daddy teaching his last Mission Friends class for a while. When we got home, Jon put on his overalls and completed the finishing touches on our new rosebushes and made sure that our house was buckled down for the approaching storm due to hit that weekend.

Changing Priorities

When Jon finished his work, I joined him on the front steps and we talked about our future. In a few weeks, we'd know whether he'd be promoted to O-5 commander. His detailer told him that he might not be able to find a shore duty in the Norfolk area and possibly would have to move to London after all. As we sat together on our front porch steps, I wondered if we would have to sell our custom-built home before we had a chance to raise our family in it.

Jon suddenly became solemn, which wasn't like him. "Do I still want to do this?" Jon asked, thinking of his fifteen years of service in the navy. We talked about whether we wanted to spend the next five years having to uproot our lives and move away so he could retire after twenty years and receive his pension. Now that we had children, our priorities were changing. Jon adored his girls and wanted to be there for them.

As we put the girls to bed and the house grew quiet on our final evening together, we both took comfort in knowing that this should be one of Jon's last cruises. If we could make it through the next six months, we should have a long break before Jon had another extended deployment. At least that was our hope.

When we woke up on Thursday, we discovered that the time for Jon's departure had been moved up unexpectedly, and we were rushed to get to the base. There was no time for emotions or sentimentalities. We pulled into the parking lot at the hangar, and Jon grabbed his bags. A quick hug and kiss for me and the girls, and he was off.

As I watched him run across the parking lot and into the hangar, I felt relief. The girls and I would begin the countdown for Daddy's return home. Workups had been stressful, and, like Jon, I had my orders. The time had come for me to assume my duties and power through one of the last cruises of Jon's navy career. Jon had prepared me well. With my navy-wife hat firmly in place, I drove home and jumped into being a single mother and handling all the other details of our lives.

> Promise:
> *"Look at the lilies and how they grow. If God cares so wonderfully for flowers, he will certainly care for you."*
> *Luke 12:27-2*

The first task at hand was to make Daddy's countdown chart. I decided it would be more fun for the girls if we made a paper chain instead. Jordyn and I diligently crafted a paper chain out of colorful construction paper. Jordyn picked out special stickers to put on each holiday, birthday, and other special occasions while I wrote the numbers to help us all count the days until Daddy came home. I planned for us to remove one link together each night as we prayed for Jon's safe return. Cutting the last of the 183 links couldn't come soon enough.

16

Paper-Chain Prayers

12 MAR 1993
1100 EASTERN STANDARD TIME, UTC-4
USS THEODORE ROOSEVELT
EAST COAST WATERS, USA
36°57'50" N, 74°20'50" W

The unmistakable sound of a Sikorsky Sea King filled the air as *Marine One* prepared to land on the flight deck of aircraft carrier USS *Theodore Roosevelt*. The sunny skies and calm seas gave no hint of the massive storms to come as the *TR* welcomed its commander in chief.

President Bill Clinton, donning a green flight jacket, accompanied by his secretary of defense, exited the helicopter. He returned the salutes of the multi-colored flight deck as he strolled across the tarmac to meet the assembled navy brass. Warm handshakes, eager smiles, and polite banter ensued as the tour continued. The president went below deck and through the enlisted mess line to share a meal with the sailors. Secret Service officers blended discreetly in the background as a few sailors with cameras took snapshots of the smiling president, who posed for picture after picture.

After viewing various aircraft and chatting with the aviators who flew them, the president and other dignitaries gathered on a platform in front of the thousands of sailors and aviators packed into the massive hangar bay to hear the president's speech. Wearing his new USS *Theodore Roosevelt* dark blue ball cap, he stepped up to the podium, adorned with the presidential seal, and addressed the crowd.

I am honored to be here. As many of you know, it is a great blessing and a great honor to be elected president of the United States. But there is no greater honor in the office than being the commander in chief of the finest armed forces in the world today and the finest that America has ever known.

Our armed forces are more than the backbone of our security. You are the shining model of our American values: dedication, responsibility, a willingness to sacrifice for the common good and for the interests and the very existence of this country.

This carrier can extend our reach. These planes can deliver our might. They are truly extraordinary tools, but only because they are in the hands of you. It is your skill, your professionalism, your courage, and your dedication to our country and to service that gives the muscle, sinew, and the soul of our strength. And today, I'm proud to be here to salute you.

This world remains a dangerous place. Saddam Hussein confirmed that. The tragic violence in Bosnia today reminds us of that every day ... today, there are different security challenges into which we must march. And at times, you who serve our nation in uniform may be called upon to answer not only the sound of guns but also a call of distress, a summons to keep the peace, even a cry of starving children.

I know this has been a difficult day for many of you. It can't be easy to leave family and friends for six months at sea, especially when the challenges before us seem unclear and when you wonder whether world events may or may not place you in harm's way. But I hope you understand that your work is vitally important to the United States and to the commander in chief.

This is a new and hopeful world but one full of danger. I am convinced that your country, through you, has a historic role in trying to make sure that there is, after all, a new world order, rooted in peace, dedicated to prosperity and opportunity.

The American people have placed their faith in you, and you have placed your life at the service of your country. The faith is well placed, and I thank you.

As the crowd politely applauded and the president shook hands with the dignitaries on the stage, the rest of the ships in Battle Group 8 were already steaming east to escape the hurricane-force winds to come with the predicted "storm of the century."

Life as Usual

The weather reports kept calling for severe weather that weekend, but you would never have guessed it in the days before. The weather was so nice on Thursday that I even tried to pick up where Jon had left off and planted a few shrubs around the yard. Jordyn enjoyed being outside playing in the dirt, and we both relished the fresh air. The weather turned colder on Friday, with the major brunt of the storm due to come late Saturday afternoon.

On Friday, the first full day of Jon's cruise, I resumed my letter-writing ritual. After dinner and some play time, I got the

girls ready for bed, and we prayed for Daddy as we cut off a link in our paper chain. I hoped that Jon liked my idea of helping the girls count down the days. Jordyn loved having the long, multicolored chain in her playroom, and it became a fun waiting-for-Daddy game. Once they were tucked into bed, I sat down to write my letter. Some nights I knew I would want to call a friend first, but tonight, I couldn't wait to get started on my letter.

As I wrote my first letter, I thought about one thing I hadn't done since Jon left — cry. What a contrast to the buckets of tears I had shed when I dropped Jon off at the San Diego Airport for our first mini-cruise. And I didn't plan on self-destructing whenever letters from Jon were delayed, which was inevitable. To help this cruise fly by, I already had a list of projects I hoped to complete and outings to attend with friends.

As I got ready for bed that night, I kept wondering how bad this anticipated storm would be and how it might affect Jon and the ships at sea.

Rocking and Rolling

13 MAR 1993
2308 EASTERN STANDARD TIME, UTC-4
USS THEODORE ROOSEVELT
OFF EASTERN SEABOARD OF USA
37°21'25" N 69°21'46" W

Jon felt the mighty USS *Theodore Roosevelt* rock and roll in the massive waves. As huge, seventeen-foot swells crashed into the *TR*'s steel hull, waves rose more than eighty feet, repeatedly covering the 4.5-acre flight deck, and the multiple planes chained to it, with a frigid saltwater spray.

The wind and waves were so severe that no one was allowed onto the flight deck for five days. But when the storm finally subsided and the damage surveyed, they discovered that every plane on the flight deck was encased in a quarter-inch layer of salt. Corrosion control teams would have their work cut out for them. The storm back home was on everyone's mind as the TR spent another night being rocked by rough seas.

Keep Daddy Safe

Back in the United States, much of the East had suffered significantly from the storm, all the way from the deep South to the Canadian border. Dubbed a "snowicane," the historic weather system caused everything from tornadoes, thundersnow, flooding, storm surges, damaging winds, and snowfalls measuring in feet instead of inches.

Here at home, the wind started howling like crazy on Saturday afternoon and continued well into the night, rattling window screens, bending trees, and causing poor Max to be distraught. But when I woke up Sunday morning, I was encouraged to find the storm had passed without any major damage. Other than the pilot light going out in the gas fireplace and a few branches down in the yard, all was well. Almost all. The girls were both starting to show signs of a cold, which had nothing to do with the storm. I decided to stay home from church and have a rest day instead.

Over the next few days, as the girls' colds ran their course, Jordyn wasn't sleeping well and kept coming to my room at night for comfort. To keep my focus off Jon's absence, I started some sewing and kitchen projects. In the evenings, the girls and I would cut off links from the paper chain and pray our nightly prayer: "Dear Jesus, please keep Daddy safe in his airplane. Amen."

No-Fly Days

18 MAR 1993 THURSDAY
1014 AZOT (AZORES TIME) UTC-1
USS THEODORE ROOSEVELT
NEAR AZORES
38°47'06" N, 36°34'19" W

"Sir, if you have a moment, I need your signature on something," said the chief yeoman as Jon walked into the Bear Aces' ready room.

"What is it?" Jon replied.

"It's about your life insurance policy, sir."

"I thought I took care of that back in December," Jon responded with a quizzical look on his face.

"That's right, sir, you increased it to the new maximum, but somehow your signature was missed. If you could verify this form is correct and sign at the bottom, please."

Jon looked it over, made sure his information was correct, and double-checked the beneficiary–his beautiful bride, Kris. Jon smiled politely as he handed the form back to the chief yeoman and took his seat with the other Bear Aces. Although they couldn't fly, they were training in other ways, including briefings. But the no-fly days needed to end and soon.

Hopes for leaving the bad weather behind as the ship headed east were futile, as one storm after another slowed their plan of intended movement. The days of no-fly conditions, combined with the ship's need to hightail to the Med, meant that pilots and crews were behind on completing the number of day and night landings (called traps) required to clear them for flight operations. Jon and others like him who were responsible for keeping crews qualified were feeling the pressure.

> Promise:
> "The Lord is close to the brokenhearted; he rescues those whose spirits are crushed."
> Psalm 34:18

On Saturday, the news came that an F-14 jet had gone down after a routine training flight near the North Carolina coast. The RIO on board, Lieutenant Commander Fred Dillingham, had been a former member of VF-84, the F-14 squadron currently deployed on USS *Theodore Roosevelt*. A memorial service for Dillingham was planned for the next day in the ship's forecastle, where the massive anchor chains were located. This spacious room at the bow, under the flight deck, was a convenient place to hold large gatherings such as weekly religious services and, less often, memorial services. The fact that Lieutenant Commander Dillingham was a husband and father of two children hit a little too close to home, and Jon was suddenly thankful that the chief yeoman had caught his missing signature.

That evening, Jon sat down at his desk and thought about what to tell Kris. His eyes rested on a framed picture of her and the girls that he kept on his desk. He couldn't help but smile as he gazed at their precious faces, and a little lump formed in his throat. Oh, how he missed them. He felt blessed to have such a beautiful wife, inside and out, and two amazing daughters. He wanted to make sure Kris knew how much she and the girls meant to him.

The next day, Sunday, Jon attended the lieutenant commander's memorial service. The somber affair had a great turnout, even from those who never knew the man personally. Naval aviators were a tight-knit bunch.

Finally, the weather was clearing, and that meant CODs carrying mail could fly in. Everyone on board was anxious to get news from home. As night fell, wishes came true as the first COD delivering mail arrived. It felt like Christmas morning when Jon ran to the Bear Ace ready room and found three letters from Kris waiting for him, along with some other mail. He knew any letters he'd written were either still on the ship or would fly out with the COD that had just landed. It would be several days until Kris would hear from him, but he couldn't wait to hear from her. He tore open the letters and savored every word. The letter drought had ended!

By now, it was after midnight, but he promptly found paper and pen and wrote to Kris before flying a nighttime mission. That night, there was an extra spring in his step as he crossed the flight deck and climbed aboard his E-2C.

LCDR Jon Rystrom in his flight suit, VAW-124 Bear Ace

17

Operation Provide Promise

22 MAR 1993
MONDAY
2200 WESTERN EUROPEAN TIME, UTC+0
USS THEODORE ROOSEVELT
APPROACHING ROCK OF GIBRALTAR
35°30'42" N, 9°56'42" W

Jon had everything ready to make a recording for
Kris: his list (so he wouldn't forget anything), a microcassette
recorder with fresh batteries, and a quiet room. He made sure
the tape was rewound all the way and then hit the record button. He sounded drowsy, as if he were at home and it was time
for bed.

"Well, honey, I love you very much, and it's 2200, or ten
o'clock, on a Monday night, the 22nd of March. It's been a quiet
day. I wrote ya–I think letter No. 9–yesterday, so this will be 10.
And the big thing is that I love you."

Jon's tone changed noticeably then, as if in those few
words the pain of being oceans apart from his soulmate became apparent. He quickly recovered though, glanced at his
notes, and went on to his next point. Jordyn, Daddy misses you
very much, and he's going to come back. As you whittle down
your chain–one for every day that I'm gone–you can see that
it's going to get closer and closer. It's going to be kind of hard
to do, but I'm going to get there."

Jon told Kris about his upcoming mission. "It's called Operation Provide Promise. I don't know if it makes the paper or
not. We're dropping MREs (meals ready to eat) to Muslims who
are being attacked by the Serbs."

Jon went on in his recording. "I got a letter from the Sunday School class. It's very nice; I really appreciated it. Lots of people wrote comments on it. Nobody knows how to spell my name or your name." Jon grinned. "But the intent is there." "We're going to go through the Rock of Gibraltar tomorrow, the 23rd, and enter the Med. On the 25th, we're going to do the turnover with *JFK*, so maybe I'll see our friend Dave from Sunday School and say hi to him." (Some officers, including Jon, would be heading over by helicopter to USS *John F. Kennedy*, where she—the *JFK*—would officially pass the baton to the *Theodore Roosevelt*.)

> *Promise:*
> *"Then Abraham looked up and saw a ram caught by its horns in a thicket. So he took the ram and sacrificed it as a burnt offering in place of his son. Abraham named the place Yahweh-Yireh (which means "the LORD will provide"). To this day, people still use that name as a proverb: "On the mountain of the LORD it will be provided."*
> *Genesis 22:13-14*

"Hope you find all this interesting, in the same way that I could listen to you talk all day about Jordyn and Taylor. I'm missing you so much. I'm lookin' at your letter No. 2. I'm glad you stayed home from church and took naps. And how long was your nap? Is Taylor sitting up? Does she grab things? Take those pictures; I'm ready! It's one-thirty in the morning on Tuesday the 23rd; I'll finish up the rest of this tape later."

Long-Distance Dad

The next evening Jon had time to finish his recording. Now that the details of his upcoming mission were more certain, he shared them with her.

"After we turn over with the *Kennedy* on the 25th, we actually start taking over the missions for Provide Promise that evening. Wish us luck here. Pray for us that everything goes okay. And Jordyn, if you're listening, I am definitely coming back as soon as we do our job over here. I must fly airplanes for a while, but I should be back around the time of your birthday, or when your chain gets done. Flip the tape over for a story! I love you, Kris. You take care. I hope everything is fine. I pray for you and love you very much, honey. Give my wonderful little children hugs. I love you. Bye-bye." Jon pushed the stop button and sighed. He knew how much hearing his voice meant to Kris, but he sure liked writing letters better.

Now for Jordyn's story. He wished he'd brought some simple bedtime storybooks to read to Jordyn on tape, but he hadn't. He'd have to make up a story, and he'd been thinking about one all day, remembering the names of Jordyn's little friends and all her favorite things. Hopefully, he wouldn't make a mess of it. He flipped the microcassette over and took a deep breath before hitting the record button.

"Hi, Jordyn. This is Daddy," he said in the gentle, lilting voice he used with his daughter. "I want to first tell you that I love you. Are you getting ready for bed? Have you brushed your teeth? Are you being a big girl for Mommy? Well, I know you are, and Daddy is very, very proud of you. I think you and Taylor are the best things that ever happened to me, and I love you very much. I really wish I could be with you, but I can't right now because of having to be on a big boat and fly. But I'm thinking of you all the time, and I know Mommy is taking care of you. Now, you sit with Mommy and you can listen to this story I'm going to tell you, okay?"

As Jon paused, the bang of a catapult launching a plane could be heard in the background. He began telling his story about Princess Jordyn and all her best friends who were playing in the forest and making up songs until the skies turned dark and cloudy and one friend disappeared.

Jon finished his story and said goodnight. "Daddy loves you very much. I'll tell you another story on the next tape, Okay? I love you. Bye-bye."

Jon realized that this was harder to do than he expected. In his next letter, he would ask Kris to send him some books that he could read to Jordyn. Making up stories was hard but not nearly as hard as being a long-distance dad.

News Travels

During a cruise, especially when there were mail delays, the Executive Officer (XO) would contact his wife and give her updates on the men. In turn, she would get the information to the phone tree so we wives could get the latest news. I knew that everyone was doing fine, that they'd made it through the storm okay, and that they'd arrived in the Med. I also knew they'd had their first mail drop. So hopefully, letters would start coming soon.

I continued to fill our days with activities that kept the girls and me busy. The highlight of our week was always Wednesday evenings at church. Although it meant late nights for us, it was worth it. My friends at First Baptist Norfolk were like a second family to me. Wednesday nights included a shared evening meal then teaching the two-year-old Mission Friends class, followed by rehearsal with our large choir. Although our girls were normally tired and ready for bed after our busy evening, we still managed to pray for Daddy and cut another link from his chain before I settled down to write my letter to Jon.

Hi,

Of course, it is late tonight because of choir (11:20 p.m.), so I won't make this letter long, but I always feel that my day isn't complete without talking to my honey. I had a flash tonight when I was in choir—what would happen if one night on Wednesday when I'm in choir, you come walking in to surprise me (obviously this is after you get ranked #1 or you get picked up for O-5 and they send you home early). What an awesome thought! Wishful thinking—I know I'm not even thinking such positive thoughts but, you know, it could be possible ...

The chaplain's wife from the TR that goes to our church said she got her first letter on Monday, so it is starting! I love you and can't wait for my 1ˢᵗ letter. Love, Kris & girls

Cool Guy

24 MAR 1993
WEDNESDAY
1910 CENTRAL EUROPEAN TIME UTC+1
USS THEODORE ROOSEVELT
MEDITERRANEAN SEA
38°21'39" N, 10°56'54" E

Jon looked over the *TR* patch freshly sewn onto his friend's flight jacket; it looked good. Mike was Jon's neighbor from Chesapeake, and though they didn't cross paths in their regular duties, the two had managed to meet up a couple of times on ship. Mike had shared some helpful information with Jon from his experience in combat, but he always believed he received more from Jon than he gave in the relationship. Jon's enthusiasm washed off onto everyone he encountered. He was one of those cool guys you wanted to be around. When Mike told Jon he'd been on the *TR* for months but didn't have anybody to sew a *TR* patch onto his flight jacket, Jon said he'd have his people take care of it.

Mike looked forward to returning the favor—maybe with a special dinner out when they got home. He and Jon had already been talking about new restaurants to visit together with their wives when the cruise was over. Until then, pizza night on the ship would have to suffice.

Ready to Launch

25 MAR 1993
THURSDAY
0700 CENTRAL EUROPEAN TIME UTC+1
USS THEODORE ROOSEVELT
IONIAN SEA, NEAR THE BOOT OF ITALY
38°31'45" N, 17°36'55" E

Jon rolled over in his rack and turned off his alarm. He'd been up super late the evening before getting a brief together for that night's first Provide Promise mission. Now he had to get ready to take a helicopter (helo) over to the *JFK* for the turnover. On his first cruise, when he was a younger man, getting by on fewer than four hours of sleep was a piece of cake, but not anymore.

A shave and shower helped him wake up before he headed to the officer's mess for a quick breakfast. The table talk was about the latest O-5 promotion board that had just ended. Jon wasn't the only lieutenant commander waiting to see if he'd been promoted to commander, but it would be at least a month, maybe two, before the official list was released. The waiting was always the hardest part.

Jon had even more waiting to do, as he found out that the helo he was slated to ride wouldn't launch for another hour. If only he could have had that extra hour to sleep. Until the turnover was completed, there was little else to do, so he returned to his stateroom. He looked at his messy rack and decided to make his bed for a change—something his roommate would probably appreciate. With housekeeping done, he sat down at his desk and found himself staring at the pictures of Kris and the girls. He usually wrote his letters at night after the day's work was done, but he might as well go ahead and write Kris now.

Jon had a lot on his mind, like the O-5 board. The significance of being promoted was different than when he was promoted to 0-4 when he was with the Hawgs. He wasn't the same Jon Rystrom as he was then. He had changed. Of course, he wanted the promotion, but through the uncertainty, God had given him a peace that he couldn't quite explain. He gazed again at his family's pictures and smiled. He knew what was truly important, and the rank of commander had nothing to do with that.

He thought about that night's Provide Promise mission. He would have sat out on it except the XO was away on assignment for a few days. As the next senior CICO, the commanding officer (CO) had assigned Jon to fly in the secondary E-2C, 603, while the CO himself would be CICO in the primary plane, 602. Jon's plane would be piloted by Frenchy Messier, with Billy Ray Dyer as copilot, and sitting ACO and RO next to Jon would be Aardvark Ardaiz and Bob Forwalder. Jon was pleased with his crew. Due to the difficulty of the mission (night flying, hazy conditions, the first time flying in the Adriatic, and the high-visibility nature of the mission), the higher-ups decided this was a varsity operation and wanted only their best aviators in the air.

After staying up until 0300 putting the brief together, Jon knew the details by heart—they would brief the crews at 1730, launch at 2100, and land at 0100 on Friday, the 26th. The aircraft from the *TR* would direct traffic and provide an escort for the large C-130 cargo planes that would drop much-needed food into Eastern Bosnia and the besieged capital of Sarajevo. USS *John F. Kennedy* had flown these missions for the past few weeks, but after the turnover, *TR* would take her place.

Jon looked at his clock. It was 0830. If he was going to write Kris a letter before he left on the helo for the *JFK*, he'd better get to it. He found her last two letters and made sure to answer any of her questions and ask his own in return. Three pages later, he was finished. As he sealed the envelope and left his stateroom, he really hoped he could find his good friend Dave on the *JFK*. Too bad they couldn't trade places and Jon could be the one heading home. Jon had enough time to get his letter in the mail before his helo was ready to launch.

USS Theodore Roosevelt

18

No Horizon

---

25 MAR 1993
THURSDAY
1700 CENTRAL EUROPEAN TIME UTC+1
USS THEODORE ROOSEVELT
IONIAN SEA, NEAR THE BOOT OF ITALY
38°50'72" N, 17°60'58" E

The aircrews of both 602 and 603 gathered in the
Bear Aces' ready room for their pre-brief. Crew assignments
were confirmed, and the mission parameters defined. At 1730,
the entire mission was briefed to all the participating air wing
crews via the onboard closed-circuit televisions found in each
squadron's ready room.

The nearly moonless night made it a challenge to pick out
the ship from the water. This meant that aircrews would most
likely be flying all night by instruments (called IFR conditions).
Below the fifteen-hundred-foot ceiling, the complete and total
darkness meant no horizon would be visible during the approach phase of the carrier landing. Not the greatest conditions, but certainly well within everyone's limits. The E-2C crews
concluded with an additional briefing of their own and
grabbed some dinner before their launch.

1800 Central European Time, Noon, Eastern Standard Time

As the girls and I went about our day as usual, I couldn't help
but think we were anything but "usual." Waiting and looking
out the window for the mail carrier to drive by was a constant

and nagging reminder that Jon was at sea. Maybe today would be the day I finally got a letter from Jon.

I heard a familiar sound from outside and smiled. It was a Hummer, an E-2C, probably flying off for a routine exercise. Living so near Norfolk Naval Air Base, aircraft of all kinds often flew overhead, but the daily sound of the Hummer always put a smile on my face. It reminded me of my Jon and how proud I was of him and the important job he does. One day, quite a few paper-chain links from now, I'd hear Jon's Hummer coming home at the September fly-in. What a sweet sound that would be!

2114 Central European Time, 3:14 p.m. Eastern Time

Flight ops for Operation Provide Promise began. The flight deck of USS *Theodore Roosevelt* was buzzing with activity as the various aircraft prepared to launch. As was customary, the "Plane Guard" helo launched first to provide an airborne safety net should any planes experience difficulties around the ship. The Bear Ace E-2Cs launched next, with 602 taking the lead, followed by Jon's 603. One by one, the jets launched in quick succession, their bright blue afterburners piercing the pitch-black night. All told, nine fixed-wing aircraft left the flight deck of the *TR*, including pairs of F-14 Tomcats, FA-18 Hornets, A6-E Intruders, and one EA-6B Prowler. This was a small and straightforward mission, but an important one.

One thing every pilot noticed, as they sped away from the ship and climbed through the fifteen-hundred-foot ceiling, was that the hazy conditions didn't let up.

Soon after launch, it was time for the NFOs in Bear Ace 603 to turn and burn, rotating their seats and switching their radar from standby to operate, but there was a problem: the radar wasn't working. Over a secure radio, 603 notified the primary E-2C of the issue. "Uh, 602, our radar is not working. IFF is functional. Do we RTB (return to base)?"

The Bear Ace CO and CICO in 602 thought a moment. He didn't want 603 to RTB if their IFF antennae that identified friend or foe were still functioning. "Negative, 603. Go to tanker duty, and we'll cover Control."

"Affirmative, 602. Moving to tanker duty."

Unfortunately, keeping the complicated equipment in top-working order was a challenge, especially with the budget cuts the navy was experiencing. Nothing on the sixty-million-dollar E-2C was cheap to fix, and maintenance crews worked hard to keep all the systems operating. This wouldn't be an exciting hop for 603, as guiding the various jets to a tanker plane to get more fuel was a basic job, but it was an essential one. There weren't many aircraft to control, so 602 would be able to handle that job just fine. As the C-130s approached their drop zones, hopefully their loads of relief supplies would land accurately.

> *Promise:*
> *"He will cover you with his feathers. He will shelter you with his wings. His faithful promises are your armor and protection."*
> *Psalm 91:4*

2200 Central European Time, 4:00 p.m. Eastern Standard Time

Finally, the mail carrier came. I rushed out to the mailbox, pulled open the door, and there it was: Jon's first letter! I was thrilled. It had been so long since I'd had contact with Jon, and I was desperate to find out how he was doing.

"Look, girls, a letter from Daddy!" I exclaimed as I ran into the house, waving his letter in the air.

"Yay!" yelled Jordyn, as we sat down and I ripped the envelope open. The back had the number "5" on it, so that meant there were four letters before this one. I read aloud the first words I'd heard from Jon in two weeks.

Midnight, 18ᵗʰ

Dear Kris,

An uneventful day today, still no flying because of …x and being behind PIM.

I frowned slightly as I couldn't make out his scribble in front of the "x," and I had no idea what "PIM" meant.

Well, we are now up to dinner. I had dinner with the flight surgeon and the chaplain from our church choir. Had a good conversation. It's nice being able to talk to somebody different than Bear Aces. I know quite a few other O-4s of other squadrons. I am glad—it is a nice change of pace.

Jon was such a social guy, and I was glad to know he was enjoying making the rounds.

Well, good looking, how was that for a day? Then the squadron watched a movie called Sneakers. I'd never heard of it. Excellent movie, not real serious about computer hackers. Very enjoyable. Still no mail, so I hope everything is OK. I love you and miss the girls.

Love, Jon.

"Mommy, where's my name?" Jordyn asked when I finished, with a puzzled look on her sweet face.

"What do you mean?" I asked, looking again at the letter. "Oh, I see. Daddy said he misses the girls, and that would be you and Taylor, wouldn't it?" Her face told me she was hoping for something more than that.

I read through the letter again and again. Holding it made me feel closer to him, knowing his hands had touched it. I smiled as I put the letter away, and I was already thinking about what I would write to him that evening. I'd start by asking him the meaning of some of the abbreviations he used.

2228 Central European Time, 4:28 p.m. Eastern Time

"Wave-off, low approach," radioed an LSO from USS *Theodore Roosevelt* as some of the first planes from Operation Provide Promise began to return to mother. That's not what 512 wanted to hear, as the A6-E Prowler ascended past the ship to make a second pass. The pilot had the sensation that he had over-rotated. A quick glance at the instruments in his cockpit told another story. He hadn't rotated enough. Such was the phenomenon called *vertigo*, the bane of every pilot.

Flying by instruments for extended periods of time, when there was no visual reference point, tricked the body into thinking that up was down and down was up or anywhere in between. In more modern terms, it is referred to as spatial awareness or spatial orientation. Pilots trained specifically to trust their instruments and not their own internal gyros, which could be misleading when flying in dark, hazy conditions. Assigned as a tanker that evening, 512 would have to wait for other planes to land before making his second attempt, but he wouldn't be the only pilot to suffer the effects of vertigo that night. The captain of the carrier, watching from the bridge, hoped the rest of the recovery went smoothly.

The F-18 Hornets were next to land. The primary Hornet, 301, had been keenly aware of the zero horizon and super-dark conditions from the start. The altitudes they were supposed to meet had to be elevated so they could get above the clouds— up to 2,700 feet. Coming back to the ship wasn't any better, with the final descent requiring a high degree of focus. This was not a night for nuggets!

2400 Central European Time, 6:00 p.m. Eastern Time

I was happy at dinner that night, and my girls picked up on their mommy's chipper mood. Hearing from Jon had been a breath of fresh air—something I greatly needed after enduring weeks of full-time parenting alone. From experience, I knew that once the letters started coming, they would keep coming. Sure, there would be delays now and then, but the first letter of the cruise was always a milestone to celebrate. Surely, Jon had received at least one of my letters by now. Hopefully, my letters would get to him as quickly now that mail drops were happening.

0045 Central European Time, 6:45 p.m. Eastern Time

E-2Cs were the first fixed-wing aircraft to take off on a mission and usually the last ones to land, but tonight an F-18 that had earlier been waved off its landing was returning behind the E-2Cs. The primary E-2C, Bear Ace 602, landed and proceeded out of the wires and to its parking place. Bear Ace 603 was just minutes behind 602 on its final approach.

"603, left one six zero," radioed Approach, giving 603 its proper heading.

"603," the copilot acknowledged.

"603, dirty up," Approach instructed, telling them to drop their landing gear and flaps, which would also slow down the plane.

603 acknowledged and continued course.

"603, fly the final bearing one eight zero."

Once again, 603 acknowledged Approach's instructions.

Watching the radar, the guys in Approach kept a close eye on 603's progress.

"He's not chasing his line at all," one operator said to another.

"You're right," the other agreed.

"He's got the straightest approach of anyone tonight."

As 603 got closer to the ship, the Final controller took over Approach's job and continued to give 603 the guidance it needed to stay on the glide path.

0051:40 Central European Time, 6:51:40 Eastern Time

With 603 seconds from landing, it was determined that there was a problem with one of the arresting wires.

"Foul deck," called the air boss over the flight deck's intercom system.

"Wave-off foul deck," instructed the LSO to 603.

The captain on the bridge watched Bear Ace 603 carefully and saw it perform a normal wave-off. Pilots were experienced with last-minute wave-off signals from a carrier in final landing approaches and were trained to climb out of a landing, circle the carrier, and come back in for a second landing after the flight deck was safe. Frenchy, 603's pilot, was no exception. However, with the harsh flying conditions that night, the foul flight deck added more stress in getting the crews back to the ship safely. The pilot of 301, the F-18 CO and lead pilot of the mission, had parked his plane and saw the foul deck lights, then watched 603 abruptly pull up and over the ship, as instructed, until he went out of sight. *It must be nice to have a second pilot to back you up on a night like this*, he thought to himself.

Mike, Jon's friend, was on watch, observing that night's plane recovery on a video system that recorded everything. He saw the wave-off lights and watched 603 climb out of its approach well and early at a good rate of climb. Mike walked over to his desk to check on some paperwork. The camera operator had been following Bear Ace 603 on its wave-off. He was ready to turn the camera around in preparation for the next plane to land, but something caught his eye. The E-2C seemed lower and slower than usual, so he kept the camera pointing toward 603 instead. The plane was now almost a mile off the ship's port side. To him, it looked like the plane was going into the water.

TR's captain, sitting at his station on the bridge, looked to see what the foul deck was all about. He glanced at his monitor when something in his peripheral vision didn't feel right. He looked out in front of the ship, on the port side, and saw a red, blinking, twirling light that was too low and was going lower.

Then it disappeared.

19

Bear Ace 603

Dinner dishes didn't take long to clean up those days, so I was done by 7 pm. I was looking forward to some me time once the girls were put to bed, especially since I finally had a letter from Jon to respond to. I could hear Jordyn playing with her Barbie dolls in the den. I wished I had half her energy, especially since I was living as a single parent.

"Hey, girls!" I called out. "It's time to go cut off another link from Daddy's chain and get ready for bed."

"And pray for Daddy," Jordyn called back.

"That's right, honey. It's time to pray for Daddy."

Plane in the Water

0052:47 CENTRAL EUROPEAN TIME
6:52:47 EASTERN TIME
USS THEODORE ROOSEVELT
IONIAN SEA
39°07'5" N, 18°25'8" E

"Did you see that—that blue flash?" said a flight deck petty officer to one of his mechanics.

"Yeah, like a camera bulb going off. Was it lightning far away?"

"I don't think so. Do you think the plane hit the water?" the petty officer asked anxiously.

"I don't know. It's weird."

One of the operators in Combat was still watching the video of 603. "Hey, do you see that? Something doesn't look right," he exclaimed.

Mike turned from his desk and walked toward the video monitor.

At the same time, the captain was calling Air Ops next door. "Are you talking to 603?" the ship's captain asked hurriedly.

The commander was taken aback. He didn't receive calls from the captain often. "I think so, sir," he answered unconvincingly.

"Are you talking to him now?" the captain yelled.

"Sir, let me check," said the commander nervously, realizing something was seriously wrong. The last transmission from 603 was at 0052:37. It was now 0053:52, well over a minute later.

"603, Approach, radio check," came the call out to the missing Bear Ace. There was no response. "603, Approach." Still no response. The commander immediately called the ship's captain. "Sir, no, we've called twice with no answer, and there's no radar squawk either."

The captain took in a quick breath and clenched his fists. His worst fears were confirmed. "Call a plane in the water!" the captain urgently ordered the officer of the deck.

Immediately, a blaring klaxon alarm went out over the intercom that covered every part of the carrier.

"Plane in the water! Plane in the water, port side! This is not a drill. I repeat: this is not a drill. Plane in the water, port side! Man all search and recovery stations."

Within seconds, waves of people began rushing onto the flight deck. Down below, every sailor, cook, janitor, nurse, enlisted man, and commissioned officer knew that one of their own was in peril. What affected one affected them all.

Approach continued to call out to 603, trying the guard frequency in desperation, but to no avail. "603, Approach on guard check in fifteen. Approach on guard out." Silence. "603, Approach on guard, acknowledge." No response. Nine times the call went out to Bear Ace 603, and nine times the result was the same: silence. Bear Ace 603 was missing.

The helicopter that was always operated to assist in these situations was vectored over the ship to search for 603. In a little while, two more helos were launched to search. Another warship in the battle group, USS Hue City, also joined the effort.

Up on deck, the Bear Aces' CO scrambled to the edge of the ship. He frantically shined his flashlight into the water, but it was no good. The night was as black as he had ever experienced, and his beam didn't even reach the watery depths below. It was a useless attempt, but what else could he do? He had a knot in his stomach as he rushed down to the ready room. He knew the cold temperature of the water. He knew all too well how difficult it was to navigate the tight, confined spaces of the Hawkeye's interior in good conditions, let alone in a plane that might be upside down and underwater with an injured crew. And that was the best-case scenario. His men were highly skilled, but no amount of training could overcome basic physics.

The ship's three chaplains sprang into action, with one reporting to the Bear Aces' ready room, one to the leadership of the air wing, and one below deck with the men who were anxiously standing ready to retrieve the missing crew as soon as they were found.

Within an hour of the disappearance of Bear Ace 603, USS *Theodore Roosevelt* transmitted a confidential notification through official navy channels:

```
603 E-2C BUNO 161549 CRASHED INTO IO-
NIAN SEA APPROX 1NM AHEAD OF CVN-71 AF-
TER FOUL DECK WAVE-OFF. FIVE SOULS ON
BOARD. SAR IN PROGRESS. COMMANDERS ES-
TIMATE:   ABLE    TO    CONTINUE    PRESENT
```

MISSION, PRESS INTEREST LIKELY, FIRST
REPORT THIS INCIDENT, AMPLIFYING INFOR-
MATION TO FOLLOW.

0200 Central European Time, 8:00 p.m. Eastern Time

Jordyn, freshly bathed and dressed in her pink pajamas, danced around the long, colorful paper chain as we prepared to cut off another link. At seven months old, baby Taylor was still too little to be much help, but her three-year-old big sister absolutely loved this nightly ritual. I wished I shared Jordyn's upbeat perspective on how many days were left in this cruise. After fourteen days, I didn't even have to prompt Jordyn on what to pray: "Dear Jesus, please keep Daddy safe in his airplane. Amen."

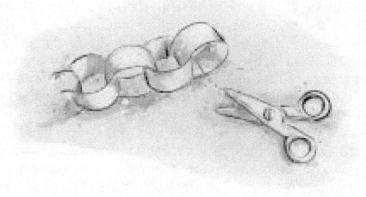

0218 Central European Time, 8:18 p.m. Eastern Time

SAR efforts were aggressive as the search for 603 intensified and more helos were launched. Searchlights from the surrounding ships scanned the water, but the only items found were a few floating charts and pieces of paper. The dark, hazy conditions worsened to the point that the helo crews' night vision goggles were useless. Until sunrise, visibility would be severely limited.

Mike, along with many others, was keeping up with the latest news. By this time, the video of 603's crash could be replayed, and everybody viewed it carefully and solemnly, looking for clues as to what went wrong. To Mike, it appeared the aircraft climbed out normally and then began to lose lift and settled into the water off the port bow about a mile ahead of the ship. The left wingtip caught the water first, which caused the aircraft to spin around. The plane's lights lit up the massive splash made on impact, explaining the bright blue flash that some on the deck had observed. After viewing the tape, hopes for finding the crew alive grew dim.

SAR had been going on for about an hour at this point, but little was being said officially. Mike figured surely Jon would know more than he did since the plane came from his squadron.

He got on the phone and called the Bear Aces' ready room to talk to the squadron duty officer. "Hey, this is Purcell down in Combat. Is Lieutenant Commander Rystrom around?" Mike asked gently, understanding that VAW-124 had lost one of their planes.

There was a long pause on the other end. "Uh, don't you know?" came back the answer in a hesitating voice.

"Know what?" Mike replied, with a growing sense of unease.

"Rystrom was on 603."

Mike's heart skipped a beat and he caught his breath. "I, uh, I didn't know. Sorry," and he hung up the phone in disbelief. Mike sat numbly in his chair soaking in the sad truth and then, overcome with shock, he left Combat and stumbled down to his own stateroom. Sitting at his desk, he dropped his head into his hands in despair. He tried to choke back the tears but couldn't do it; a hot mix of pain and anger had cut him in two. His mind flashed to Kris and the girls in front of their beautiful new home without Jon by their side.

"Dear God, why? How can this be!" Mike was a man of faith, but he felt shaken to the core. His mind went to Jon's wife back home. She would hear the news long before a letter from him could reach her, and she'd have to sort through the same emotions he was feeling. The Rystroms weren't simply another navy family; they were friends.

Mike got out pen and paper and let his fury out in an emotional letter. He saw his flight jacket hanging up in the corner and reached out to touch the TR patch. Tears filled his eyes again. It would take more than a patch to heal his broken heart. He couldn't even begin to imagine what it would take to heal Kris's.

> *Promise:*
> *"When you go through deep waters, I will be with you. When you go through rivers of difficulty, you will not drown. When you walk through the fire of oppression, you will not be burned up; the flames will not consume you. For I am the Lord, your God.... Because you are precious to me. You are honored, and I love you."*
> *Isaiah 43:2-4*

0400 Central European Time, 10:00 p.m. Eastern Time

The girls were sound asleep, and I'd been busy on the phone catching up with friends and family and planning different things, like the Sunday School potluck coming up on Sunday. Now it was time for me to relax and write to my favorite person in the whole world. Writing letters was much more fun when you could respond to each other.

Thur. 3/25

Hurray! My 1ˢᵗ letter came today! It only took 6 days! It was so great to get it. The funny thing is it was #5, so half the stuff you told me didn't make sense.

No flying because of "... x" and "being behind PIM"? "Sawed logs"—is that sleeping? I've never heard you say that before. ☺ "MSG #2"?

When I showed Jordyn your letter, she was looking for her name in it (all you said was "the girls"). So I would suggest writing her name in every letter even if it isn't one specifically for her, and print it, because she can recognize it if it is printed. Yesterday, she pointed out a little "r" to me—amazing!

We are still cutting a link off every night, but it doesn't seem to make a dent yet. But Jordyn has such a positive attitude. I'm not sure she can really relate the length to how long it really is. She just loves this big, long chain in the playroom. Hopefully, close to the end, Taylor can help take some links off. That will be the biggest change—she won't be much of a baby anymore.

I gave Jon a rundown of all the people I had called and the plans I had made. Keeping busy was one cruise strategy I had learned worked for me.

So you can see, between these calls, giving both girls a bath, and fixing dinner, I've been busy. Of course, Jordyn's 4-hour nap this afternoon helped. ☺ Even I took a good 2-hour one (I only had 5 hours of sleep last night thanks to "Munchkin").

Taylor is getting more and more vocal. She is starting to use the syllables "ba-ba." So I figure the "da-da" will be coming. I'll show her your picture when she starts.

Well, babe, that wraps things up today. I'm glad you are doing well and especially glad that the mail has started. I love you! Kris, Jordyn, and Taylor.

I made sure to print "JORDYN" in nice block letters to remind Jon to include her name in his next letters. Tomorrow would be a busy day with our needing to be out the door by 7:30 so that I could get Jordyn to preschool. And, hopefully, another letter or two would be waiting for me in my mailbox. I looked at the clock. It was getting close to eleven o'clock. Even with a nap that day, I needed to get some rest.

Tough Assignment

25 MAR 1993
2300 EASTERN TIME
VAW-124 BASE
NORFOLK NAVAL AIR STATION
36°56'23" N, 76°17'31" W

When Lieutenant Commander Rick Vanden Heuvel reported to the headquarters of Airborne Early Warning Wing, Atlantic, he knew something major had happened. Four other CACOs were there, along with several chaplains, the staff officers, senior officers' wives, and other personnel—about forty people in all. No one knew what was going on, but they'd all been called to the wing before midnight, and that was never a good sign.

Finally, the commodore, who was responsible for the training and maintenance of all the Atlantic Fleet E-2C squadrons, called everyone into the conference room. The mood was somber as he broke the news about Bear Ace 603 going down off USS *Theodore Roosevelt*. The SAR effort was officially continuing, but everyone there knew that the chances of the men being found alive were practically zero. The commodore identified the crew members and made the notification assignments as to which one of the CACOs would lead the teams to notify the next of kin. Rick and the other four CACOs sat down with the commodore and developed a plan.

The navy had a policy that prohibited waking up the next of kin before morning. One of the families had to be contacted in Baltimore while the rest were in the Norfolk area. The important thing was that all families be notified at roughly the same time. Rick was familiar with the "wife-net," where word would spread like wildfire before they could deliver their official notifications. Waiting a few hours would give time for all of them to be in place by morning.

The other consideration was that the loss of 603 was certain to make international news since it concerned Operation Provide Promise and the growing conflict in Bosnia. The press wouldn't want to be kept waiting to break the story, and no one wanted a family member to discover their loved one was lost by hearing it on the news. With Norfolk being a navy town, the local media would be all over the story.

This was the first time Rick had to carry out his CACO duties. He'd been trained on the protocol and how to guide the survivors through all the unavoidable red tape. But for him, as for most CACOs, it went a step further. Rick was making a personal commitment to walk by the side of the affected family not only for the next few days or weeks but for life. He considered it his duty to assist them in any dealings they had with the military now and in the future.

The commodore looked at Rick and told him his assignment was to notify Kris Rystrom, Lieutenant Commander Jon Rystrom's wife, of Chesapeake. He sighed when he saw that she had two little girls. This would be one of the hardest assignments he'd ever had.

Cheated

26 MAR 1993
0540 CENTRAL EUROPEAN TIME
11:40 PM EASTERN TIME, 25 MAR 93
USS THEODORE ROOSEVELT
39°24'5 N, 18°56'2" E

The early morning sun that rose over the chilly Ionian Sea couldn't penetrate the thick fog bank that hung in the sky above the *TR* or the grim mood that dominated the ship. Mike made his way to the bridge, high up on the ship's island, and found a pair of handheld binoculars. Someone else was already using "Big Eyes," the massive high-power binoculars mounted to the ship, and Mike joined him in scanning the vast gray ocean for any signs of life. Mike had been up for more than twenty-four hours at this point, but there was no way he could sleep. He felt helpless. He had to do something, even if there was little likelihood that the crew of 603 might be floating in a life raft somewhere waiting to be picked up.

As his eyes strained for any speck on the horizon, Mike could honestly say that everything that could be done was being done to find the crew of 603. And after watching the replay of 603's final moments, he felt that Jon's death would have been sudden and therefore painless. That was a small consolation considering the loss, but it was something.

Mike felt cheated. Cheated out of a good friend. Cheated out of all the fun hobbies and experiences they'd planned on sharing together after the cruise. Cheated out of getting to become close to one of the coolest people he'd ever met.

Mike was still scanning the ocean when the call came in from a helo that wreckage had been spotted not far from the original site of the mishap. Not surprisingly, it was the light-weight radome—or at least what was left of it—that was first seen. Other smaller pieces of wreckage were floating nearby. But only wreckage was seen—no bodies and certainly no survivors. Whaleboats were launched to begin the salvage process. As the tragic reality began to set in, Mike set the binoculars down. Looking further was futile now; his friend and the other four crewmen were gone.

Mike thought about the letter he'd written earlier that morning to his wife and decided it was best if he didn't send it. His emotions had been raw, and he didn't want his wife to have to process such volatile feelings. But if Mike couldn't find Jon, dead or alive, the least he could do was recount the events in detail so Kris would have some knowledge of the night's events. As hard as this was, Mike began writing every detail before his emotions took over. Kris would need to know the last moments of Jon's life.

As the few remaining pieces of shattered Bear Ace 603 were being plucked from the Ionian Sea, the chaplains of the *TR* were planning a memorial service for the five men to be held the next day. The crew of USS *Theodore Roosevelt* did not have the luxury of extended time to mourn the loss of their friends and crewmates, but the chaplains knew the ship needed an opportunity to grieve together before returning to their duties.

The thousands of people serving on the carrier were like one large extended family. Even enlisted men working below deck felt the pain of 603's loss. But the crew of the air wing felt it even more deeply. And the Bear Aces felt it most of all. Five of their close friends were gone. Suddenly. Forever. The Bear Ace squadron would be able to take a few days to deal with their grief, but then the responsibilities of Jon and his lost crewmates would be assigned to others, and the next mission would be planned and executed.

More Boxes

Even more difficult to bear was that the personal belongings of the lost airmen would have to be carefully collected from their bunk rooms and other shared places and sent to their grieving families. As boxes were packed with the men's clothing, pictures, flight suits, and personal items, the mourning squadmates who had to carry out the grim task were also packing up other boxes of their own.

Naval aviators and flight officers are trained to box up and compartmentalize their emotions. When the mission planning started and the flight suit went on, everything else had to be left behind. Marriage trouble, financial stress, grief, loss, anger—it was all to be put in a box, closed with a lid, and left untouched until there was time to open the box and deal with what was inside. During a mission, that box had to stay closed, because if you weren't totally present in the moment, your distraction could be deadly. The loss of 603 would require a large box. Operation Provide Promise had to go on. And Jon and his fellow crewmates on Bear Ace 603 would have expected nothing less.

VAW-124 Bear Ace 603

20

Lost at Sea

Life was good that Friday morning—filled with promise and hope. The girls and I were up early for our normal weekday routine—making breakfast, packing lunches, and getting dressed. Before we hopped into our minivan to drive to preschool, I made sure I put my letter to Jon in the mailbox. As I closed the lid, I imagined finding more letters from him that afternoon.

The late March skies were gray, and the air was cool. We were anxiously awaiting warmer days so we could enjoy the playgrounds and walking trails throughout our beautiful neighborhood nestled in the wooded wetlands of Coastal Virginia.

On my drive into Norfolk, I reflected on where my life was. At the age of thirty-one, I was living the perfect life. My Jon adored me and our girls. I was secure in his promise to write to us every day while he was deployed. We lived in our dream home. I was blessed during this season of our lives to be a stay-at-home mom with plans to pursue my doctorate degree in communications after Jon returned from his deployment. The rich relationships we had built with friends and families in our neighborhood, church, and the Bear Ace Squadron provided security for the girls and me while Jon was away. My world on Seagrass Reach was one of contentment.

While many navy marriages fall apart when a spouse is deployed, I took great comfort in knowing Jon was committed to our family and our marriage. We had no angst over finances or Jon's future in the navy. Jon and I shared a deep faith, and we rested in God's promise to take care of us. That morning on Seagrass Reach, I had no doubt my perfect life would continue its peaceful, predictable course.

After dropping off Jordyn at preschool, I planned the rest of my day. Once I got home, I would clean up the den of Barbie dolls and give Taylor a snack. In the afternoon, I would drive back to preschool to pick up Jordyn, do our nightly routine, and cut another link off Daddy's chain. Another ordinary day in the life of a navy wife.

The White Car of Dress Blues

26 MAR 1993
0730 EASTERN TIME
SEAGRASS REACH
CHESAPEAKE, VIRGINIA, USA
36°44'14" N, 76°16'19" W

Lieutenant Commander Rick Vanden Heuvel sighed as he pulled into the driveway of the Rystrom home and turned off the engine. With him in the white, official navy car was the rest of his notification team: the XO's wife and a navy chaplain. The officers were wearing their navy dress blues, and the mood was quiet and somber. As the CACO, Rick's responsibility now was to follow protocol and lead his team as they notified the next of kin. His team's duties would be over in a few hours, or maybe a few days, but his job was just beginning.

Rick knew that coming to the Rystrom home before 7:30 a.m. would be too early, but the pressure to notify all the families and release the media to break the news of the tragedy meant they needed to move quickly. Hopefully, Mrs. Rystrom wouldn't still be in bed.

"Any questions before we go?" Rick asked his team. Everyone knew what to do, though no one wanted to do it. As they exited the car, the men put on their navy covers (hats) as they all walked down the sidewalk; climbed up the curved, brick steps; and stood together in front of the large double doors.

Rick took a deep breath and rang the doorbell. No answer. Rick rang the bell again, but no one came. As he was peering through the glass inserts to see if anyone was inside, he heard a woman's voice calling out behind him.

"Hello, excuse me?"

Rick and the others turned around to find a woman running across the Rystroms' front yard with a look of concern on her face. "Are you Mrs. Rystrom?" Rick asked, as the woman reached the bottom of the stairs.

"Oh no, I'm Jennifer, a friend of hers from down the street. My husband is a navy officer," she explained nervously. "Please, sir, tell me why you're here."

This navy wife obviously knew why they were there, but he couldn't divulge any details. "We need to find Mrs. Rystrom, ma'am. Do you know where she is?"

"She left to take her daughter to preschool, but she should be home soon. Please, tell me, what's wrong? Has something happened to Jon?"

Rick could see the tears forming in her worried eyes, and there was no way to hide the grim truth that showed on their own faces. Rick tried to give her a polite smile. "I'm sorry, ma'am, but we really need to speak to Mrs. Rystrom first, before anyone else." Rick hoped that she understood his double meaning and wouldn't start the "wife net" before they had a chance to deliver the news.

"I understand," she replied solemnly, then turned and walked briskly away.

"Well," said Rick, as he turned to go down the brick steps, "I guess we need to pull around the corner and wait for Mrs. Rystrom to come home. We certainly don't want her to find our car in the driveway when she returns."

Going through a trial run didn't help to settle anyone's nerves. They all knew the next time they stood before those double front doors, there would be no turning back.

Rick and his team had a clear view of the Rystrom house from the side street less than a block away. Eventually, a minivan approached the home and pulled into the garage.

"Let's give her a little time to get settled," Rick said, and the rest agreed. After they waited a few minutes, the CACO team knew the dreaded time had come. Rick drove the car back to the Rystrom home and pulled into the driveway.

This time he didn't say a word.

Stripes by My Windows

As I carried Taylor into the kitchen from the garage, I considered which chore to tackle first. Maybe I'd start with picking up Jordyn's toy clutter. Taylor's fussiness interrupted my plans, and I knew I wouldn't get anything done until I gave her a mid-morning snack. Our nursing days were almost over; she was enjoying more solid foods, and I was enjoying the freedom her new eating routine gave me. A sprinkle of her favorite Cheerios would keep her happy. I sat her in the highchair and took the box from the pantry.

Max was waiting nearby, probably hoping for a treat of his own. As I leaned over the high chair to pour out some cereal on Taylor's tray, I heard Max begin to stir. When I glanced up to see what could be bothering him, I saw something unusual: stripes going by my dining room windows. Naval stripes. Stripes sewn on the sleeves of naval officers. Stripes on dress blues. Stripes like the ones sewn on Jon's naval uniforms hanging in his closet upstairs.

My first thought was, *Why are naval officers coming to my house on a Friday morning while Jon is at sea?* And then, in an instant, time stopped. The doorbell rang. I couldn't move. I tried to walk toward the front door, but my mind was frantically spinning. My body was frozen. Through the glass inserts of our front double doors, I could see the naval officers. There seemed to be so many of them. Jon had told me about this day. He had frequently joked with me that if I ever saw a group of naval officers wearing dress blues walking up to my door, they were coming to tell me he was gone. Jon had prepared me. God had prepared me.

As if in slow motion, I staggered through the hallway and toward the front door. I hesitantly opened the door and saw ... faces. Faces of strangers in dress blues. Faces with tears streaming down their cheeks. There were no greetings, no introductions, nothing but silence and tears. They didn't have to speak; I already knew. My eyes swept over these men in stripes until I found a familiar face. There stood my friend, the executive officer's wife. Her hands were covering her mouth while she wept.

My knees buckled, and I grabbed onto the banister to break my fall. In utter abandon, I threw my head back and wailed in anguish over the loss of my Jon, my beloved. Mournful screams—deep, raw wailings—erupted from the depths of my soul. Wails of despair hidden deep within me that I never knew were there. Screams of loss, of disbelief. This was not happening. My Jon, my precious love. Our life, our girls, our home. A perfect life shattering before me—shattering before these men in stripes. My life as a navy wife and a stay-at-home mom was suddenly thrown into the dark abyss. I was now a navy widow and a single mother.

I lifted my head and once again found my friend's face. Slowly and clearly, I asked, "Who else was on the plane?" Our squadron wives' group had become close, and my thoughts had turned immediately to these dear friends. I knew I wasn't the only one having men in stripes come to my door that day. The E2-C's crew is made up of five aviators. This meant there were four other men from Jon's squadron who had lost their lives. Oh, how I dreaded hearing their names.

The executive officer's wife took a deep breath and stammered as she began. "Frenchy," she whispered.

Oh no, not Shelly! She and Frenchy were newlyweds. Jon would always brag on Frenchy, a top-notch pilot. "He is the best stick in the Aces," I would hear him state many times with pride.

"Billy Ray," she continued slowly, as I began to sob again. I thought of Paola Dyer and their eleven-month-old baby,

Christopher. My tears and gasps were becoming more uncontrollable, but the dreaded list of names went on.

"Aardvark," she spoke softly. *Jon loved Pat Ardaiz.* Patrick was Jon's chess buddy. Thankfully, he didn't have a wife or children, but the loss was still deep. I couldn't stop the sobs. These sobs were now for my friends. Jon's friends. Our navy family.

One name remained. I shrank back anticipating the horror of hearing it. "Bobby," she finished, as she wept from the weight of delivering the tragic news. This name shocked me most of all.

"Bobby Forwalder?" I gasped aloud. My mind couldn't comprehend this one. *Not Bobby. Of all our guys, not Bobby.* Bobby and Katie were expecting their first baby any day. "What about Katie?" I cried. "Does she know yet? What about the baby?" My own loss was temporarily pushed out of my mind. I could think only of Katie and her unborn baby. There were no answers to my questions as my mind struggled to take it all in. Jon. Frenchy. Billy Ray. Aardvark. Bobby. What went wrong? "What happened?" I heard myself ask.

One man stepped forward and explained the situation. I couldn't process all he said, but the phrases "Operation Provide Promise mission last night," "foul deck wave-off," "went into the water," "plane crash," "missing plane," and "Ionian Sea" came through. I had never heard of the Ionian Sea.

"Where is my Jon?" I questioned.

"They've been searching with helos for hours now, and the search and rescue operation is ongoing, but so far no survivors have been found," was the solemn reply.

My mind exploded with a thousand questions: *What do you mean you can't find them? How do you lose an E-2C Hawkeye? How do you lose five men? What do you mean you don't know what happened? Who are you? Aren't you the navy? Aren't you skilled and trained for anything?* But I didn't ask any of these questions out loud. They had no answers.

They were telling me that Jon was missing—not that he was dead. But I knew. I knew they didn't send out these men in stripes to tell me Jon was missing; that would have given me hope, but my hope was gone. My hope was lost at sea. Jon's plane had gone down, and our perfect life had gone down with it.

A little squeal interrupted my thoughts as I was jolted to the present. Taylor! My sweet baby was still sitting happily in her highchair snacking on her Cheerios and completely unaware that her life was changed forever. One of the men, a chaplain, walked toward the kitchen to check on the baby.

My eyes drifted over to our den floor, scattered with Barbie dolls where Jordyn had been happily playing the night before. In my fog of shock, something told me that more uninvited guests would arrive. They couldn't find our home looking like this. I walked over to the den, bent down, and started to pick up the toys. The executive officer's wife knelt beside me to help. I turned to her and our eyes met.

"What am I going to do?" I whispered hoarsely. Her tear-stained eyes told me that she didn't have an answer. I looked back at the Barbies. In Jordyn's innocent world of make-believe, there was no sadness or tragedy. My girls were going to experience what little girls should never know: they were fatherless. No, it was more than fatherless. That term now seemed cold, heartless, and impersonal. No, my girls were left without their daddy.

I was still picking up the dolls when the doorbell rang again. One of the men in stripes opened the door and Jennifer, my neighbor, came running in.

"Kris!" she screamed in a desperate cry. I stood up and turned to face her.

"Jen, he's dead!" I cried out and ran to her open arms. "He's dead, he's dead, Jon's dead!" Jen held me close as I shuddered in her arms. I was saying these words for the first time, and they felt like knives slicing my throat. We clung to each other and wept uncontrollably.

"I am here for you, Kris," she kept saying over and over. "I will take care of Taylor—don't worry about her," she assured me.

And she did. She went to the kitchen, relieved the kind chaplain, lifted Taylor out of her highchair, and held her closely. Jennifer stayed next to me the entire day making sure tasks were carried out, phone calls were made, and Taylor was cared for.

At this point, the man in charge introduced himself and the other man with him, but I didn't want to know their names or who they were. I didn't want these strangers in my home—the home Jon and I had built together. Their news wasn't welcomed, and neither were they. I wanted them to leave and leave now! My mind was screaming at these men in dress blues, but my words were polite and respectful of their stripes.

I knew what their stripes meant. I knew that they didn't want to be there. To be given the orders to deliver news that would destroy my life must have been horrific, so I was polite to these strangers in my home—to the one in charge who told me to call him Rick. What I didn't know then was that this man would become my lifeline over the next days and months—a friend who would help me navigate my new life as a navy widow.

Everything was a whirlwind. I don't remember much of anything other than my mind racing with thoughts of how to tell my parents, Jon's parents, and most importantly, Jordyn. Having taken care of our home and family for years while Jon was at sea, my instincts took over. I wasn't processing as a woman who had learned of her husband's tragic death. On the contrary, I was thinking as a navy wife. There was a task at hand, and I was the one to do it. I remembered the words Jon had written to me in hundreds of letters: "You can do it, Kris. I have faith in you! I always have the utmost confidence in you."

Next of Kin

Immediately, I knew I needed to get word to Jordyn's preschool. I didn't want her coming home—not yet. The last thing I needed was my sweet three-year-old walking into a confusing group of strangers and complete upheaval in her normally quiet home. Arrangements were quickly made for her to spend the night with a friend.

Once I was certain Jordyn was in a safe place for the next twenty-four hours, I knew that my next task was to inform our closest family. I wished that I could protect them from hearing the heart-wrenching news! But I had to push these emotional thoughts aside and focus on the job at hand. Rick explained that we had to make the phone calls quickly. The media had already heard the news, and they were on standby waiting until the next of kin had been notified. Our family was now part of their news story. My Jon was getting ready to have his name and picture shown on news stations and printed in newspapers around the country. I had watched these tragedies over time—a pilot lost, a policeman killed in the line of duty, a family that had perished in a fire—but now it was *me*. It was *my husband* on the news. It was *our family* that was being labeled next of kin.

I started the painful notification with my parents. Oh, how my heart ached for my dad. He loved his son-in-law dearly, and Jon was more than a son-in-law; he was a good friend. I called my dad at work, and when I heard his voice, an overwhelming wave of despair came over me. I burst into tears as I tried to say the dreaded words. "Dad, something terrible has happened." I fought for breath through my uncontrollable sobs. "It's Jon," I struggled to continue. "His plane is missing. They can't find his plane. Oh, Dad, please hurry."

"Krissy, are you alone? Is anyone with you?" My father's first thoughts were to take care of me.

I told him the navy was with me and handed the phone over to Rick, who gave him the pertinent details. After the call to Dad was completed, there was a short sense of relief. My parents were on their way, and though they had a long drive to reach me, they should arrive that evening.

The next difficult call would have been to inform Jon's parents, but given their age and more delicate health, I didn't want to shock them with an unexpected phone call. I had Rick phone Pat, Jon's sister, instead. After he broke the news to her, Pat and I cried together over the phone. I told her not to give Mervyn and Jo any hope. I knew the search and rescue operation would be futile, and there was no way that Jon or the other men had survived the crash. I suggested that Pat go to a nearby town and find a reservist officer so she wouldn't have to give her parents the tragic news alone.

With the most important phone calls made, I got out my address book and gave orders about who else to contact and how. First, I asked Rick to call my pastor. He and his dear wife came over right away.

The men in stripes went into action and were respectful and efficient as they carried out their duties with military precision. As the hours passed, I learned that they weren't there to simply deliver the news; they were there *for me*. They were the navy, and they were there to take care of their own. I was one of them.

Life suddenly became chaotic—very demanding—as word of the tragedy broke and my home began to fill with people. Faces were everywhere. Faces from church, our Sunday School class, and choir. Faces from the neighborhood. Faces from the navy. So many faces. Faces of people I had never met. Women were in my kitchen making coffee. Women were putting food in the refrigerator. People were opening the front door. People were answering the phone, which would *not* stop ringing. Who were these faces?

I wanted to be nice. It felt like I was supposed to be happy with all these people in our home. The people were sad but busy. My mind was foggy as I sat at my kitchen island and watched them work. I sat. Numb. As each new person walked into my kitchen, the sobs would come again. All this food. All the pound cake. I wanted to visit with each of the faces. I wanted to thank them. Receiving all this attention was embarrassing. My desire was to let loose and scream and give full vent to my sorrow, but I couldn't. I didn't want to lose it in front of all these people. Sometimes I would run upstairs to my bedroom, close the door, and grieve alone for a few minutes. I would dry my tears and put on a brave navy-wife face before presenting myself again. All I could think about was Jon. My Jon.

> Promise:
> "Father to the fatherless, defender of widows—this is God, whose dwelling is holy."
> Psalm 68:5

Then a call came—the call that the men in stripes were waiting for. I already knew. Rick hung up the phone and sighed. As he slowly walked over to where I was sitting, the people filling my house grew quiet so that they too could hear the news. Rick knelt before me and stared me straight in the eye, making sure I would hear what he was about to say. His face was grim, and his words were measured and clear.

"Kris, the navy has recovered a few pieces of wreckage from the plane. They've discontinued the search and rescue operation, and the air crew has been officially declared lost at sea." Rick paused and then pointedly stated, "There are no survivors. Jon is dead."

My Jon was gone. My Jon was lost at sea.

5 fallen naval aviators mourned

Top: An honor guard performs a 21-gun salute at Norfolk Naval Base near the end of a memorial service held Tuesday for the five naval aviators who died Friday when their surveillance plane crashed in the Ionian Sea, east of Italy. The five were members of Norfolk-based Carrier Airborne Early Warning Squadron 124, operating from the USS Theodore Roosevelt.
Above: The wife and child of a deceased aviator leave service.   Photos by **Craig Moran**/Daily Press

21

Love Letters from the Grave

The magnitude of the tragedy still did not register in my mind. I couldn't understand anything. How did the safest plane in the navy disappear off a carrier? Did Jon try to get out? Did he know that the plane was going down? Did he drown? Was he trying to help the other guys escape? Jon was the senior officer on board and the mission commander, and I knew he would have done everything he could to save the other four crewmen before trying to save himself. All these questions, and the men in stripes couldn't tell me what my mind was screaming to know. Neither could the growing crowd of people in my home on Seagrass Reach. There were so many tears everywhere I turned. This wasn't happening to me, to my girls, to my Jon.

The continued blur of faces and tears and numbness was briefly broken that afternoon when President Bill Clinton came on television for a previously scheduled news conference. The strangers in my home anticipated that the tragedy of Bear Ace 603 would make national news, so they had the television on. I was never one to pay much attention to the news, but this time, the broadcast had my full attention. I didn't have to wait long to see if the president would acknowledge our loss.

> Good afternoon, ladies and gentlemen. Before we begin the press conference, I have a sad announcement to make. I have been informed that five United States servicemen onboard the United States Ship *Theodore Roosevelt* have crashed at sea within a mile

of the carrier. I want to express my deep concern over the accident.

Two weeks ago, I visited USS *Theodore Roosevelt* and met the fine sailors and marines serving their nation at sea there. I was profoundly impressed by their commitment, their dedication, and their professionalism. They made America proud. And I want to say that my thoughts and prayers are with the relatives and the shipmates of those five servicemen who are missing at sea.

Of course, we knew that Jon and the others had been declared lost at sea, and there was no chance of them returning to us safe and sound. The logical part of me understood that with notifications ongoing, these officials couldn't tell the whole truth of what was known about the mishap to the international news outlets. But his words reminded me that Jon and his navy brothers had died doing something noble. They died in service to their country. I couldn't help but wonder if Jon knew that his story was on the world stage and how he would feel about that.

The Rystrom Promise

That day, as the initial wave of shock subsided, and I began to interact more with all the faces in my home. Friends encouraged me to eat. I went to the kitchen and politely attempted to comply, but the few bites I managed to swallow were like sawdust in my mouth. My appetite disappeared completely. On the surface I was calm and controlled; underneath I was in a suspended state of grief.

Until the mail came.

Jennifer sat down beside me and handed me some envelopes. She whispered quietly, "Kris, I got your mail. There are some letters here—letters from Jon."

One glance at Jon's familiar scribbling of our address on the envelope of the carrier's official stationery and my frozen grief instantly erupted into red-hot tears and guttural screams. Everyone in the house could hear my cries, but I couldn't control my spontaneous outburst of despair. The letters! The letters that had once nourished my soul. That had filled me with such joy. That had sustained me through lonely months when Jon was at sea. And now that he was *lost* at sea, those same letters pierced my soul and left me shaking and wailing like a wounded animal.

And yet, as I grasped the letters in my trembling hands, I clung to them as though they were the only remnants of Jon's tender love and devotion for me. These were his last words—some of the final messages I would ever receive from my beloved Jon. Painful, yet precious. Wounding, yet healing. I rushed from the table, ran up the stairs, and retreated to the solitude of my bedroom so I could open them alone. I fell onto my bed and, after taking a few moments to allow my sobbing to subside, turned my attention to Jon's latest letters. They were marked with numbers "7" and "8." I opened No. 7 and pulled out a single page. He had written "Saturday night" but didn't give the date. It must have been written a couple of days after the No. 5 letter I'd received yesterday.

> Dear Kris,
>
> A lot better day...

He went on to describe some training and a briefing he'd attended and how he'd enjoyed pizza night. What he wrote next both cut and comforted me at the same time.

> But most of all, I realized how much I love you and miss family life. I have been writing the letters in bed usually, but a few have been at my desk. And as I write this letter, I look at your pictures and

realize how beautiful you are and how lucky I am to have you as my wife. Kris, never forget how important you are to me and how important you are to our children.

Jordyn is so cute. I look at her and all these memories flow through me.

We heard that an ex F-14 RIO from VF-84 never returned from a hop at Oceania. Did that make the papers? Lt. Cmdr. Fred Dillingham. A memorial service will be held tomorrow sometime. He left a wife and two kids. It makes one think.

He went on to ask about Jordyn's preschool, and then he told how they were heading straight for the Adriatic. He closed his letter with these words:

Well, kiddo, hug Jordyn and Taylor for me.

Love you, Jon.

Tears streamed down my face, knowing Jon would never hug his sweet girls again. I hadn't heard about Lieutenant Commander Dillingham's death, but it was clear that the wives of 603 weren't the only new navy widows in our area. How chilling to think that Jon received this news only days before his own tragic accident. Maybe God had been preparing him for what was to come.

I opened letter No. 8, but it was simply a brief note he'd written before the first COD of the cruise departed, asking me to mail him some paperwork. I was hit with the harsh fact that Jon—responsible, organized, detailed Jon—would no longer be handling the details of our family's finances and household. My grief was raw. In that moment, I couldn't begin to process all the troublesome ramifications of his death.

It was clear that when Jon wrote these letters, he'd yet to receive a letter from me. Had he received any of my letters before he died? I'd written faithfully—every day. But what if none of my letters ever got to him? I desperately hoped that was not the case.

What if the last thing he heard from me was that rushed goodbye on the morning of his departure? To know now this would be the last time I would ever see my husband is a sobering memory. Why didn't I cling to him longer? Why didn't I relish his touch? Why didn't I look him in his eyes and tell him how much I loved him? When we reflect on our past, we often regret the words not spoken or moments not cherished. But then I sometimes wonder if this is God's way of protecting us from the harsh realities of life and death. To relive that last moment with Jon would be such a gift. My thoughts now are that my husband knew he was leaving a family who adored him and that he would return to us again someday.

The daily mail would become a bittersweet ritual. The Rystrom promise had been kept, and now it meant more to me than ever. I read the letters again, and this one phrase stood out to me:

Kris, never forget how important you are to me and how important you are to our children.

Jon was asking me, as if from the grave, to make another promise. As I closed my bedroom door and slowly descended the stairs to rejoin the waiting crowd below, I hung onto Jon's words of encouragement.

Navy Proud

Surviving the upheaval in my home was my more immediate problem, as my house continued to fill with a never-ending stream of people. As hard as Jennifer and Rick tried to protect me, well-meaning friends kept asking me questions. It seemed that everyone wanted my attention. There was a constant tugging at me from all directions. The chaos around me shoved every thought of Jon into a painful void that I couldn't outwardly express.

As the hours ticked by, I found myself gathering strength I didn't know I had. Although the day's events were unplanned and clearly unscripted, I remained calm and controlled for the people around me. I could not and would not lose it. I resolved that I had to be like my Jon—strong. I could not give in to my spiraling emotions. I was a Rystrom. I had carried his name for seven years, and now I had to hold that name firmly in my grasp, being steady, level-headed, and methodical in every step.

The people around me would not watch me crumble. That was for later, in the silence of my own place—our place. I was an officer's wife, and everything I did in the hours to come would make my husband proud—would make the navy proud. I was, and always would be, the U.S. Navy, and this would not break me.

Jon's constant words of encouragement had filled a deep reserve within my soul—a well I would draw from for many years to come. A well of grace my Lord had prepared for me so that I could stand strong when my world came crashing down.

Afternoon turned into evening and people started leaving, going home to their perfect worlds, to their normal lives, to their families where death had not come to visit. The few friends who remained were waiting for the arrival of my parents.

Baby's Comfort

The one thing in that day of hell that gave me a smile was my sweet baby girl, Taylor. She smiled and cooed at every person who held her, loving the extra attention, hugs, and snuggles she received. My innocent baby was oblivious—she couldn't understand that her loving daddy was never going to hold her again. He wouldn't be able to tell her he loved her, laugh at her cute giggles, or read her bedtime stories. Seven-month-old Taylor would never know her amazing father.

These thoughts started to overwhelm me as I realized I needed my baby girl to comfort me. She and Jordyn were a part of Jon and made me feel even closer to my beloved Jon. I took my baby from a friend's arms, as Taylor rubbed her little eyes in exhaustion from the chaotic day. I carried her upstairs and slowly walked into the nursery, hugging her closer, as I softly began to weep. I breathed in the baby smell on her little neck while tears slid down my cheeks and landed on her precious face.

I quietly closed the door and sat down in the rocker Jon and I had painted for her, gently rocking her back and forth and singing softly to my baby girl. Her life and mine had made an unexpected and violent shift. With even more chaos to come, I made a difficult decision. As I rocked in the nursery Jon and I had planned and decorated together, I nursed baby Taylor for the last time.

Once Taylor was sound asleep in her crib, I was in no hurry to leave the solitude of the nursery. I continued rocking as my mind raced with many unanswered questions. The basic facts of Jon's mishap were still cloudy to me, but I knew for certain that his body wasn't found. I prayed that somehow the navy was wrong and that Jon and the rest of the guys had miraculously survived and would be spotted in a life raft once daylight broke over the ocean. Then Rick's poignant words came to my mind: "There are no survivors. Jon is dead." My mind couldn't shake the image of Jon lying at the bottom of the Ionian Sea, the final resting place of my precious husband. My Jon.

I kept thinking of the love of the ocean that Jon and I shared. A picture of Jon giving two thumbs up while deep underwater reminded me how much he enjoyed scuba diving. He never got enough of visiting the wonders of the underwater world. Now the depths of the ocean were his graveyard, and his beloved E-2C Hawkeye his coffin. I remembered the little bottle of oxygen Jon showed Jordyn's preschool class. Did he have time to use it? Did he panic when the cabin filled with icy water? Did he drown? Was he scared? Or did he even survive the impact long enough to know he was in trouble? Did he have time to think of us before he stepped into eternity? He was always at home in the ocean, and now it was his forever home. Or was it? Wasn't Jon in heaven now?

> Promise:
> "Remember your promise to me; it is my only hope. Your promise revives me; it comforts me in all my troubles."
> Psalm 119:49-50

My thoughts turned to much darker questions. Didn't God hear our prayers to take care of Jon? Didn't He hear Jordyn's prayers to "please keep Daddy safe in his plane?" Why would He allow this horrific tragedy to happen to us? Was God angry at us? It wasn't fair! Jon and I had gone to church for years, read our Bible, given faithfully of our time and money to our church. We were honest, God-fearing people. I had always believed the Bible and God's promises. What good were His promises now? I was questioning everything I had ever known about God.

I prayed alone in the darkness and pleaded with the God I had loved and served my entire life. *What have You done to my Jon? Why have You taken him? You told me You'd never leave me or forsake me! Where are You now?* I believed that God had turned His back on us, and I felt the ice-cold withdrawal of His protection. This sort of thing wasn't supposed to happen to good people like

Jon and me. I had checked all my boxes, and now my boxes weren't just empty—they were demolished.

Into Loving Arms

I heard a commotion downstairs and realized that my parents had arrived. All day long, I had been grieving with friends, but this was the first time I could grieve with my family. I hurried from the nursery and rushed into my parents' loving arms. The shock of Jon's death hit me afresh as we poured out our grief together.

My parents and I spent the late hours of that fateful Friday talking through all the details Rick had told me about Jon's mishap. My family was in total shock. I was still my daddy's little girl, and I knew he would do all he could to help me navigate this nightmare, but he was grieving too. He had lost his best friend.

My mom was crushed, but there was no question that she would comfort and care for her granddaughters and stand by me through it all. I wanted to assure my parents that the girls and I would be fine, but I really didn't know if we would be. My dad was so much like Jon with his analytic, discerning mind, and he would do his best to fill Jon's shoes.

However, now was not the time to dig into the harsh realities to come; my body was completely exhausted. With my parents' arrival, the brave navy-wife persona along with the adrenaline melted away and my energy came crashing down. Like it or not, I had to sleep, for tomorrow would be another day filled with more visitors, more phone calls, and more questions with few answers.

My parents would sleep in our playroom, where the girls' paper chain still hung in its place. Another wave of sobbing hit me as I realized no link would be cut off the chain tonight. There would be no prayers for Daddy's safety in the airplane. However, the worst part was yet to come. Tomorrow my little

Jordyn—Jon's Jordyn—needed to be told that her daddy wasn't coming home.

With tears in her eyes, Mom asked if I wanted her to stay with me in my room that night, but I knew I had to face my bedroom alone—without my beloved Jon. As much as I was accustomed to sleeping alone through Jon's many deployments, I always knew he would be coming home. Now I knew he would never be coming back.

As I opened the bedroom door, a rush of emotions overwhelmed me. Loss, loneliness, longing, fear, and hopelessness. Why was I not warned? How could life change in a second? What seemed to be a normal Friday spring morning with our girls had turned into pitch-black storm clouds, plunging my perfect life into a dark, hopeless abyss. My peaceful world was now devastated by frenzied chaos and my sheltered life catapulted onto a worldwide stage. In an instant—in one horrific, gut-wrenching second as I opened my front door to the men in stripes—my hopes and dreams lay shattered and scattered at my feet. Nothing prepared me as my heart, nurtured by Jon's tender love and devotion, was ripped to shreds. How I wished he could have been by my side today holding me close as I heard the news no wife ever wants to hear and breaking my fall as I crumbled to the floor in shock. Suddenly and so unexpectedly, an eruption of grief and devastation swallowed my soul and left me staggering and alone without my beloved Jon, without the love of my life, without my soul mate—forever.

As these thoughts consumed me, I ran to his closet and clutched the closest thing I knew would bring me comfort: his worn, brown terry cloth bathrobe. The robe he wore when he would get up with one of the girls in the middle of the night. The robe he wore when he would bring me coffee in the morning. The robe he wore the morning he rushed to get ready to leave for the ship—the day I said goodbye to my husband for the last time. I could still smell his cologne lingering on his robe.

I fell to the floor inside his closet. I couldn't stop the screaming. I muffled my screams with his robe. I finally could mourn for my husband: *My Jon, my love, how will I live without you?* I screamed and sobbed until I had nothing left. The questions I'd asked myself in the nursery kept repeating in my mind like a macabre carousel that I couldn't stop. Time stood still as I mournfully cried in the closet. At last, fatigue overcame grief, and I lay down in my cold, empty bed and drifted into a fitful sleep.

22

Is My Daddy Happy?

27 MAR 1993
1100 CENTRAL EUROPEAN TIME UTC+1
USS THEODORE ROOSEVELT
IONIAN SEA
38°31'45" N, 17°36'55" E

Nearly thirty-six hours had passed since the mis-hap, and the time had come for the crew of USS *Theodore Roosevelt* to mourn the loss of Bear Ace 603. The fo'c'sle (the forward part of the upper deck of the ship) was packed as service members of every rank—from the rear admiral commanding the carrier battle group to the lowest-ranking enlisted man—came together to honor the men. In the middle of a candlelit table was a folded flag surrounded by pictures of each man dressed in his flight suit. There were also five navy dress white hats. The scene was like the one Jon had witnessed six days earlier at the memorial service for Lieutenant Commander Fred Dillingham.

The three chaplains officiated the service of recognition and thanksgiving, which included prayers, readings from the Bible, and remarks from the Bear Ace squadron's commanding officer. Most touching were words of remembrance offered by the Bear Aces who had served alongside the lost men. Tears were seen in many eyes as each man was mentioned—Frenchy, Billy Ray, Bobby, Aardvark, and Rooster. Jon was described as a loving and faithful husband, a loving father, and a friend to the entire squadron: "the kind of guy you could count on when the chips were down" and who "always tried to do the right thing."

A poem written by an enlisted marine was read that put the feelings of everyone in attendance into words:

It was six in the morning when I first heard,
VAW-124 had that night lost a bird.
On its final approach the plane was waved off,
Did a quick flyby and started to loft.
As it rose up and banked off to the side,
For reasons unknown everything died.

The worst part of all was the five men aboard.
For them and their families our sympathies poured.
All through the morning we didn't know what to say.
The whole ship was depressed all of that day,
For airplanes can be bought with dollars and cents,
But you can't replace a person no matter how much
    you've spent.

It must be real hard to tell a man's wife
That the plane had crashed taking his life.
Or to see the little kids' tears start to churn
When they learn that their dad will never return.
Or to tell two parents of the death of their boy—
That they will never see their pride and joy.

Though we're not all Bear Aces, we still feel your
    pain,
For the whole ship's morale was sucked down the
    drain.
Where we used to see laughing and joking around,
People don't say a word and just stare at the ground.
But we must pull together through thick and thin
So this kind of thing won't happen again.

—by LCpl. Chris Anderson, VMFA-312

As the service concluded with the singing of the "Navy Hymn," a final prayer, and a trumpet playing "Taps," the CO of the Bear Aces knew that although the service was over, the grieving of his squadron was not. After taking off a few short days to pause and catch their breath, it would be time to get back to the business of flying. In the days and weeks to come, the CO would provide strong, calm, and much-needed leadership to help his squadron move forward and focus on the mission before them.

For the next several days a palpable sadness permeated the entire ship. An unusual quietness ruled conversations as men struggled to make sense of the loss of their navy brothers. In the air wing, everyone was thankful to be alive, yet they couldn't understand why a plane that seemed to be operating perfectly was flown into the water. For the men serving in the Bear Ace squadron, the tragedy created a deep sorrow that time would not erase. For decades, the loss of their friends would haunt them, bringing a lump to the throat and tears to the eyes at the mention of Bear Ace 603.

Having to pass by the few scraps of recovered wreckage down in the hangar bay, roped off and guarded by a lone marine, didn't help. In less than a week, a representative from the Judge Advocate General, or JAG, would come aboard USS *Theodore Roosevelt* and commence a thorough investigation into the mishap, including taking sworn statements, analyzing all the records and video footage from the evening, and carefully examining the wreckage. While such an inquiry was necessary, none believed it would bring any lasting resolution to affected families and friends.

Fog of Grief

The sun came up and another day began. My mind was awakened from the fog of sleep. Suddenly, thoughts of what had happened the day before hit like a shotgun blasting a hole into my soul. Jon was gone. The stripes, the plane, the people, the news— it all came rushing back into my memory and sucked the air out of me. My body went into spasmodic sobs as I grabbed my pillow to smother the sounds of my screams. A deep, sick, eroding ache in my stomach set in as the nightmare of my new reality picked up right where it had left off the day before. I didn't want to leave my lonely bedroom to live out this horror.

My rational mind took over—Taylor! I needed to check on Taylor. I threw open my bedroom door and ran into her nursery. She was still sleeping in her crib. Quiet. Innocent. Peaceful. This child would become my newly found source of serenity. She would help me breathe again. She would help me face each day.

Jordyn though–I wasn't ready. I wanted to keep her innocent of the news about her daddy for as long as possible. My parents and I had arranged for Jordyn to come home later in the afternoon. *Let her keep playing with her friend* was my thought. That reminded me of something Jordyn loved playing with—the paper chain hanging in the playroom. What once had been a symbol of hope and anticipation was now one that haunted. I walked into the playroom and sighed as I held the paper chain in my hands—fragile, light, yet so heavy. Here were all the special days we'd never celebrate together. No more links would be removed—the uncut links now stretched into eternity. I shuddered as I placed the cursed chain in a black plastic garbage bag and asked my dad to hide it in the attic.

By now, the news of the mishap had reached everywhere. As the morning hours passed, the phone resumed its incessant ringing and more people began to arrive at my home. Unlike yesterday, my parents were by my side. They provided a much-needed buffer for me, handling many details and decisions so I wouldn't have to, such as the arrangements for our relatives who were arriving from far away.

Through the efforts of so many, I saw God's people come to my rescue. Like a warm blanket, God was covering me with His love through His children. Wonderful women from my church became my lifeline—keeping everyone fed, washing dishes, answering the phone, recording sympathies, and maintaining household order. Multiple casseroles, plates of sandwiches, and an assortment of desserts kept appearing out of nowhere. Thoughtful friends brought paper products to make feeding the onslaught of family and friends easier. Jon would have been thrilled to attend the party that was being thrown for him.

My Church Family

Lieutenant Commander Rick Vanden Heuvel, my casualty assistance calls officer (CACO), had a mission of his own to perform, and while he was thankful the first difficult day was behind him, he knew many more painful days were ahead. Rick watched in admiration as my church family rallied around me, keeping my home running like a well-oiled machine. He was amazed that my pastor even took the time to personally minister to him. Reflecting on the love and generosity he'd witnessed in my church family, Rick told his wife, "Honey, if anything ever happens to me, call the Baptists."

For me, Rick was always there. I was learning to trust him and his calm, reassuring nature. Rick informed me that the navy had decided to honor Jon and the other lost crew of Bear Ace 603 on the following Tuesday in David Adams Memorial Chapel at Norfolk Naval Base. This service would follow navy tradition and would require little input from me—unlike Jon's personal memorial service, which our family decided to have the day after, on Wednesday, at First Baptist Norfolk. This was all new to me. Even though I'd been to many funerals, I never realized there could be a funeral when there was no body to bury. My pastor was gentle and kind in helping me plan a touching service that would have made Jon proud.

As the fog of grief loomed into another day, I was able to have more time alone thanks to my parents assuming my roles. Throughout the day, I would slip up to the solitude of my bathroom (my "cry room") and mourn the loss of my beloved Jon. The gut-wrenching questions, the disturbing images, the overwhelming fears, and the relentless sorrow were no less present than the day before. During one of these moments, I heard my mom gently tapping on my bedroom door. I opened it to see her holding the cordless phone in her hand, but the look on my face plainly told her that I didn't want to talk to anyone.

"Kris, I think you need to take this one. It's Olga Plautz. She lost her husband in the E-2C crash last summer." I gasped in shock. She knew. This woman on the other end of the phone understood exactly what I was going through.

I grabbed the phone from my mother's hand as if I were grabbing a lifeline to hope. "Hello, Olga?"

A soft woman's voice was on the other end: "Kris. Yes, I'm Olga, and I am here for you."

The two of us wept on the phone. This woman whom I had never met was reaching out to me in my grief. Nine months earlier, she had stood where I was standing now. I remembered how shocked Jon had been when he received the call about the fiery E2C crash that had taken the lives of five men. I remembered feeling sorry for the men's families, never knowing we'd suffer a similar fate. In Olga—a navy widow and single mother of a baby boy—I found a new friend. I was now a member of a new squadron: the navy squadron of wives left behind.

Later that morning, Jennifer asked me quietly what she and our neighbors could do to bless me. I knew Jennifer and Jon shared a love of landscaping, something Jon had not had time to complete, except for the planting of his precious rosebushes. With so many friends and family arriving, he'd be embarrassed to show off our gorgeous new home surrounded by a bare yard with mounds of dirt. We needed flowers, and we needed mulch. Jennifer understood completely, and she reassured me that she and our neighbors would be honored to accomplish this mission.

I was a little better prepared when the mail came that Saturday afternoon, but the sight of Jon's handwriting on another envelope was still painful to bear and reduced me to sobbing once again. I retreated to the quiet of my bedroom to process his latest letter alone. It was No. 6, written one week earlier on March 20.

Good morning sweetheart,

I hope today is better than yesterday. Yesterday sucked...

I couldn't get past those first few words without breaking down. What an understatement, yet Jon never knew the circumstances under which I would read his words. Obviously, the day before he wrote the letter had been a hard one for him, with some important message that didn't go right. The next paragraph was completely unexpected.

Guess what I need? My battery-operated squirt gun. Send it when you send my 1ˢᵗ care package. No hurry. I need it in a few weeks. It appears the new XO is into it and blatantly told everyone he brought his, and where's ours?

I couldn't help but smile through my tears. Oh, Jon, always the jokester. I could imagine him in a spirited water-gun fight with his squadron mates after a long day of flying.

I heard Nebraska lost—the turkeys. But Wake won, so it is Nebraska in football and WFU in basketball.

I wasn't up to date on college sports, but I remembered Jon writing me once that he had two great loves: me and college football, and in that order. I managed another weak smile.

*Still no mail. The COD had to turn back cuz of wx.
I think you will hear me talk or mention wx a lot.
The admiral is briefing us today at 1300. I bet it's
about our role in the Adriatic.*

*Love you, Jon.
Kiss my little sweeties, OK?*

The Adriatic must have been close to the Ionian Sea. No one would have guessed the consequences of Jon's role in that region and in Operation Provide Promise. What about my role? Now that Jon was gone, what role would I play?

"Kiss my little sweeties, OK?" This was a promise I would keep. *Yes, Jon, I'll kiss your little sweeties.* I could do that much to-day. As for the rest, I'd have to take it one day at a time.

A Little Girl's Heart

Jon's request reminded me that there was still one task I had to face—the one I dreaded the most. That afternoon Jordyn would come home, and I wouldn't be able to shelter her any longer from the cold, hard truth. My parents and I had discussed how best to break the news, and we had agreed that we would tell her to-gether. How do you tell a three-year-old that her daddy is dead? I only hoped I could find the right words.

When Jordyn walked through the door, she was thrilled with excitement to see all the people, including several church families with children. In her innocent eyes, it was a party. She was especially excited to see her grandparents from West Vir-ginia. After a few minutes of Jordyn getting settled, I asked her if she would come upstairs to the playroom; her grandparents and I had something important to tell her. Without hesitation, her little legs ran up the stairs. She wanted to return as fast as she could to play with the kids who were visiting.

Mom, Dad, and I sat down together on the bed in the play-room, and Jordyn stood in front of me. There was a solemn still-ness in the room. Jordyn didn't notice that the paper chain she had proudly hung around the room was missing. I took her lit-tle hands in mine and stared into her big, beautiful, hazel eyes.

"Jordyn, Mommy has some-thing very sad to tell you."

Jordyn became quiet. "What is it, Mommy?"

I started slowly and calmly. I spoke with no tears. I simply said, "When Daddy was flying in his plane last night, his plane broke, and it crashed into the wa-ter. Jordyn, Daddy died last night."

> *Promise:*
> *"In his kindness God called you to share in his eternal glory by means of Christ Jesus. So after you have suffered a little while, he will restore, support, and strengthen you, and he will place you on a firm foundation."*
> *1 Peter 5:10*

As much as I wanted to protect Jordyn's little heart from the reality of our tragedy, I couldn't soften the news. I didn't know how else to say it. As if she was trying to comprehend the words, I had spoken to her, her worried eyes met mine, and she asked, "Is my daddy ever coming home?"

The tears started creeping down my cheeks, and I said to my daughter for the first time, "No, honey, Daddy isn't coming home again."

She looked at me and then to my weeping parents and burst into tears. The wails from my sweet, innocent child on that day will never be erased from my soul. I watched my daughter's life be torn apart, like a link torn from her beloved paper chain. I held her close as we all mourned together. Suddenly, Jordyn stopped crying. There was a quiet pause. She looked at me with a pro-found question that I will never forget: "Mommy, is my daddy happy?"

In amazement at the words spoken from the innocence of a child's heart, I was able to smile. Perhaps my first real smile since I'd seen the stripes pass by my window. A calmness came over the room. With sober confidence, I answered, "Yes, Jordyn, your daddy is happy because he is with Jesus."

Jordyn smiled, wiped away her tears, and politely asked if she could go outside and play. To our amazement, Jordyn left her playroom with the satisfaction of knowing that her daddy was with Jesus. God brought the reality of eternal life into a little girl's heart that day.

Jordyn Rystrom at her daddy's Arlington National Cemetery
memorial marker, 1993

Jordyn's Life Verse:
"But those who trust in the
Lord will find new strength.
They will soar high on wings
like eagles. They will run and
not grow weary. They will walk
and not faint."

Taylor Rystrom at her daddy's Arlington National Cemetery memorial marker, 1996

Taylor's Life Verse:
"So don't worry about tomorrow, for tomorrow will bring its own worries. Today's trouble is enough for today."
Matthew 6:34

23

My Folded Flag

On Sunday, Rick drove me to the memorial service for Bobby Forwalder, the first Bear Ace to have his funeral. Getting together for the first time with Katie, Bobby's wife, and the other widows, Paola and Shelly, was intensely emotional for all of us. Naturally, we were concerned for Katie since she was due to have her baby any day. I couldn't imagine how distraught she must have been as she prepared for her firstborn under such trying circumstances. Bobby's service was a wonderful celebration of his life, but it was challenging for me to process the sudden death of five men along with my personal loss. The fog of grief was only growing thicker, and Bobby's service was merely a warm-up for the much larger navy memorial service to come.

On Tuesday, Rick took my sweet girls and me to the navy's tribute to Bear Ace 603. Everything about that service seemed wrong to me. I deeply appreciated the navy honoring my husband and the other men, but I walked through the events of the memorial as if they were scenes in a distorted nightmare. Pulling up to the gate at Norfolk Naval Base was wrong. Jon wasn't by my side, and he wasn't the one being saluted.

We had prepared that day as though we were going to church on a normal Sunday morning—the girls and I dressed in pinks. But this was wrong. Wrong that my family was going to a church on a naval base on a Tuesday. Wrong that we were going to a memorial service for my husband. Wrong that we were going to sit with three other widows. Wrong that four children were never going to see their fathers again.

As we made our way into the crowded David Adams Chapel, I realized that hundreds of people had already taken their seats. I carried Taylor and held Jordyn's hand as Rick escorted us down the center aisle between the rows of sorrow-filled faces.

Familiar, friendly faces of my choir friends, who had come to sing for the service at my request, greeted me from behind the pulpit as I got closer to the front. Dressed in robes and sitting in rows, the choir had left one chair empty save for a single white pillow in remembrance of Jon. What I wouldn't have given to see him wearing his choir robe and winking at me from the tenor section.

From their warm smiles, my eyes fell onto the somber stares from the pictures of five navy aviators' faces framed and displayed on a wooden table in front of the pulpit: Frenchy, Billy Ray, Bobby, Pat, and Jon. My Jon. In his flight suit. I took strength from Jon's beaming face and sensed my heart steadying as I met his photo gaze.

With fifteen years of service in the navy, Jon was one of the most senior officers in the squadron and was so proud of his Bear Ace patch. He was up for promotion to the rank of commander. But all this was insignificant as I stared at his picture. Now on display in a chapel packed with mourning friends, the crew of Bear Ace 603 could not have known they were posing for their obituaries when those portraits were taken. Everything was wrong.

Behind each picture was a folded American flag, one for each man who had given his life for a country he would never see again. A single ceremonial navy sword lay on the table. "Welcome to the navy, Mrs. Rystrom" flashed in my mind as the smack of the saber at our wedding had welcomed me. The sword that cut my wedding cake now proclaimed that I was a widow. Everything was wrong.

As I turned to find our seats, I looked at all the people sitting in the pews behind me; every seat was taken. I frantically looked around, realizing no one had saved a seat for my girls and me. In front of the packed crowd, I started to sob hysterically. I turned to Rick and cried out, "There isn't a seat for us!" This strong officer's wife, who was going to make Jon proud—make the navy proud—had a meltdown in front of hundreds of people. Rick jumped into action, and front-row seats were quickly cleared. My girls and I sat down in silence. It was wrong.

The navy memorial service honored Jon and the crew of Bear Ace 603 well. Stripes were everywhere as hundreds of naval officers had come to pay their respects. I quietly sang along as our choir performed familiar songs, ones that Jon and I had once rehearsed together. As a navy chaplain spoke words of comfort, my eyes were glued to Jon's framed photograph. Even through tears of loss, I was still being comforted by him from the grave. Our love was so deep that even death could not destroy it.

As the service ended, a sobering military tradition began. I watched as one naval officer walked to the memorial table and picked up one of the five folded American flags. He stepped over to Aardvark's mom, Sheila, and softly whispered something to her. With reverence, his white-gloved hands gently placed the folded flag in her frail arms. Next was Katie, then Shelly, then Paola. I watched each of my friends receive their flags one by one as each naval officer continued in silent procession. Then it was my turn.

One of Jon's closest friends and a fellow navy officer picked up the flag, neatly folded into a triangle behind Jon's picture. He turned from the table and bent down to me and whispered in my ear as he wept. "Kris, on behalf of the president of the United States and the chief of naval operations, please accept this flag as a symbol of our appreciation for your loved one's service to this country and a grateful navy." He gently placed the flag in my hands.

I clutched the folded fabric and pressed it close to my chest as I sobbed in my friend's arms. With no body to bury, the flag had now taken the place of my Jon.

The service concluded with a silent procession to a court-yard outside in front of the chapel. I held Jordyn's hand as we gathered around our family. Throughout the service, Mom had held Taylor, and she was content to stay with her. While we waited, I noticed an army of camera crews and reporters from the local news stations. This was a national news item, and they didn't want to miss the chance to tell the world their story of five more fallen heroes.

As we waited for the rest of the mourners to congregate outside, Jordyn's preschool teacher knelt and presented my daughter with a pink peony. During such a somber moment, my daughter was being nurtured through the tender gift of a flower, something Jon loved dearly.

A single trumpet filled the air with the familiar sound of "Taps," followed by a 21-gun salute—seven rifles shot three volleys into the air. Each blast shook me to the core. Then, in the distance, I could hear them coming: the familiar and distinct hum that I heard every day over my house—the hum of an E-2C Hawkeye. But this hum was different—much louder than I'd heard before. People all around me started scanning the sky.

What happened next was a moment I will never forget. I looked up and saw five E-2C Hawkeye planes flying toward us in a single "V" formation, their hums growing louder and louder. The deafening roar took over my mind as they flew closer. Suddenly, one E-2C banked hard to the outside and flew up and out of formation, a reflection of the lost crew. The remaining planes continued flying overhead in a missing man formation.

As the one plane flew out of the pattern and the others continued, I frantically ran to the open grass. Wails erupted from deep within my soul as I dashed toward the planes. Running for my Jon. In the solitude of my bedroom, I had painfully imagined Jon's terrible plane crash many times. But as I watched in horror as the missing-man formation flew over my head, it was as though the terrifying crash was happening before my eyes.

I clung to my flag, to my Jon, as he was lost forever in front of me. My friends, my family, and my daughters watched in anguish as I screamed in despair. I didn't care that hundreds of people were watching me lose control. I didn't care that the camera crews were taking videos and pictures of this officer's wife lamenting the loss of her husband. I didn't care anymore. I couldn't stop the screams. That was the day I said goodbye to my Jon forever and became the young navy widow on the front page, clutching my flag, my moment of heart-wrenching grief frozen in time for all to see.

> Promise:
> "All praise to God, the Father of our Lord Jesus Christ. God is our merciful father and the source of all comfort. He comforts us in all our troubles so that we can comfort others. When they are troubled, we will be able to give them the same comfort God has given us."
> 2 Corinthians 1:3-4

Flight Suit On

Two surprises awaited me when I returned home from the navy memorial service. While we were gone, our sweet neighbors had lovingly transformed our barren yard into a splendidly landscaped lawn complete with colorful pansies and boxwood hollies. After the emotionally draining service, it was a blessing to be greeted by a vivid reminder of life, beauty, and the kindness of dear friends. Jon would have been proud.

The earthy smell of fresh mulch filled the air as I went to the mailbox and found my second surprise—another letter from Jon. My heart always skipped a beat, and that now-familiar internal ache intensified whenever a letter from Jon arrived. I held onto each letter as if I were holding a priceless diamond. In the privacy of my bedroom, I opened his latest message. This one was dated Monday, March 22, at 12:11 a.m. I tried to smile at how detail-oriented he was and realized he had written this letter just past midnight.

> My wonderful bride,
>
> Finally, 3 letters, I really should say wonderful feelings and informative pieces of art.

At last, Jon had received my letters! I was so thankful he had heard from us before he died and saw his Jordyn's precious pictures one last time. He wrote that he'd enjoyed a letter from our Sunday School class as well. I wish Jon could have seen the way those same people rallied around me in the days after his death.

> I fully understand what you said about not crying. I fully believe that, because of our faith and our love, our bond is closer than most couples.

I had shed buckets of tears over the last several days, and it took a moment before I remembered what Jon was referring to. I'd written him about how I hadn't cried this time when he deployed. I'd sure made up for it since then. That close bond built on our faith and love now felt shattered, yet I found myself drawing strength from his words.

> Do the shrubs look nice? Did Jordyn have fun with playing in the dirt while you planted the shrubs?

If only Jon could see our yard now with all the new flowers and mulch that enhanced his rosebushes and the shrubs I'd planted before the "storm of the century" blew through.

> The paper chain is a great idea and, yes, it probably is 183 days in all.

Could Jon see from heaven that the paper chain was discarded in a black garbage bag in the attic?

> I pushed the issue of no training on Sundays and the XO and CO bought off on it. I attended a memorial service for Lt. Cmdr. Dillingham. The chaplain from our church presided over the memorial.

Jon had grown in his faith over the years. I cried to think that he had attended a memorial service only a few short days before his own. I remembered that this chaplain's wife was one in the army of women who had selflessly served our family. This same chaplain would have helped conduct Jon's shipboard memorial as well.

> CO and I attended a full ops brief given by the 6th Fleet people about the Med. No new news. We expect our first full day of flying tomorrow. I am writing this in the ready room as I wait for an airplane. It is past midnight. I expect to get to bed about 2.... Well, sweetie, the airplane has arrived, so kiss my girls and I miss you, Love, Jon.

His plane had arrived, but there was never a guarantee that it would bring him safely home. Jon's love of flying was something we didn't share, and now his love had cost him his life.

"Kiss my girls." Another promise I would keep. I knew more letters were to come, but one day the letters would stop. What would I do then?

Exhausted with the emotions of the day and knowing tomorrow was Jon's memorial service at First Baptist Norfolk, I went to bed early that evening and attempted to get some rest. Late that night, I heard voices downstairs and knew Jon's family had arrived from Nebraska. With my heart heavy and my body spent, I knew I could not face them yet. In the morning, our welcomed embraces would be replaced with yet another anguished round of grieving.

Jon, the girls, and I had visited them only a few weeks earlier when we attended Mervyn and Jo's fiftieth wedding anniversary celebration in Nebraska. I was so thankful we had made the effort to attend, not knowing it would be Jon's last visit with his family. How would my sweet, elderly in-laws who lived such a simple, Midwest life ever recover from the tragic death of their beloved son Jonny? As much as I dreaded grieving with Jon's family, I was relieved that we would be together to celebrate Jon's life the next day.

Every detail of Jon's service had been planned as if Jon himself were watching me from heaven. In my mind, I kept asking him, *Jon, what do you think of having the choir sing this song? What about having our Sunday School teacher give your eulogy? How about Dad sharing some words?* I knew this was probably silly, but I kept imagining that Jon was cheering for me as I carried out my newly assigned duties, not as a navy wife but as a widow planning his funeral. Although I was still emotionally raw from the navy's memorial service, tomorrow's service would be for Jon alone, and I would be strong for him—for my precious love. I would make him proud.

First Baptist Norfolk was overflowing with people. This was more than a church—for Jon and me; this was home. Our Sunday School class was our family. We'd sang in the choir together, shared Wednesday dinners in the fellowship hall with friends, taught Mission Friends, and studied the Bible under Dr. Record's teachings each Sunday. I remembered only a few months earlier when we dedicated Taylor to the Lord in the same sanctuary where we were now remembering Jon's life.

The Rystrom and Windham families, along with the other widows from 603, sat in the front rows as Jon's celebration-of-life service began. I smiled through tears as we sang songs reflecting on our Savior. The death and resurrection of Jesus was now personal. Eternity became part of me because my Jon was experiencing it himself. Jon was living with Jesus, and I would see him again. I prayed that Jon and the angels were watching the service. How many times had we stood in this sanctuary side by side worshipping our King? Now I worshipped alone. Nevertheless, I worshipped with the blessed image of my Jon surrounded in God's welcoming glory.

Our Sunday School teacher shared a warm eulogy, including the reading of several excerpts from Jon's most recent letters. Dr. Reccord gave a heartfelt sermon that comforted my soul, but what touched me most of all was a poem that my dad—and Jon's best friend—wrote for the occasion. Tears were in his eyes as he read it, but his voice was strong, and his admiration for Jon was evident.

Jon Alvin Rystrom
Some of us called him Commander;
Others of us called him Jon, some Jonny;
Some affectionately called him Jonathan;
Others, Brother; others, Uncle Jon.
Two of us called him Son;
One of us called him Daddy,
But I called him My Friend.

He was all of these to each of us,
But first and foremost he was a teacher.
Each and every one of you that knew Jon
Learned something from this Teacher-Man.

He may have taught you guys how to throw and catch a
*   ball;*
He may have even taught you a game or two,
*   Or even an evening prayer.*
For us who are navy, a button or a switch on an E2,
Or lever on the Dog Machine at the Mess Hall.

Some of you, I know he taught you how to
Smile and to laugh.
Two of you I know he taught how to love.
Me, he taught me how to hug another man.

But today he taught each and every one of us
How to die...
You die with your Flight Suit on!

—Chuck Windham, March 31, 1993

I know Jon would have been humbled by all the kind thoughts shared, but the words from Jon's "friend" would have impacted him deeply. He would also have been touched by the outpouring of love for his two daughters. In lieu of flowers, an educational fund for Jordyn and Taylor was started, thanks to the generosity of others.

With the funeral behind me and the goodbyes said, our friends and family returned to their lives, but my nightmare continued.

Rick and my dad helped me begin the process of working through the mountains of red tape that Jon's death had caused. Several important decisions were made right away. In deciding where to live, I considered the loving network that surrounded me—especially my church family and fellow widows and the access I had to military benefits—and decided to remain in our home. Memories of Jon were all around me here. My mother decided to stay with me for the next several weeks while I tried to piece my shattered life together.

Jon's Nebraska family wanted to hold a memorial service in mid-April in his hometown of Stromsburg, and I knew Jon would have approved. So I would have one final funeral to endure, but I knew this would be a crucial step in his family's grieving.

Mixed Emotions

As days passed, my mailbox filled with sympathy cards and letters from friends and family far and wide, including a formal letter of condolence from President Bill Clinton. Sorting through them was a mixed pleasure, as I enjoyed hearing from old acquaintances, but instead of sympathies, I wished they were Christmas cards.

Mixed in with these cards were priceless letters from Jon. Each day the mail came, I would search the stack of envelopes anxiously looking for Jon's familiar scribble. One day soon—very soon—my last letter would arrive. The last letter from my beloved Jon.

The next letters I received from Jon were from the first days of his cruise. Jon had kept his promise and written every day but getting the letters so far out of order meant I had to piece together his last days like a puzzle. His No. 1 letter from the cruise was dated March 13, the first full day he was gone.

> My dear, wonderful wife, beautiful daughters, and mighty protector, Max. Well, it is finally for real, deployment to the Med ... We are hearing rumors already that the first several port calls are in jeopardy and we are heading directly for the Adriatic Sea, between Italy and Yugoslavia, Bosnia and Serbia ... The weather is really bad. We couldn't fly today cuz the seas were too rough. I heard most of the storm missed Norfolk ...
>
> Now to the only part of the letter that really matters. I love you and miss you like crazy. Tell Jordyn that Daddy misses reading stories to her at nite. And give Taylor a big smooch for me. I

want to get this in the mail in case a COD flies off tomorrow by chance. I LOVE YOU.

Jon missed me like crazy, and he'd only been gone twenty-four hours. How was I going to live without him?

His next two letters were written while the storms were at their peak. He even included a picture from the *Rough Rider*, the *TR*'s newspaper, which showed a blast of saltwater spray from waves that rose more than eighty feet, soaking the parked planes on the flight deck. Had I known how intense the storms were, I would have feared for Jon's safety much sooner.

For the first time, Jon mentioned Operation Provide Promise and needing to prepare a brief on the flights where C-130s dropped MREs in Bosnia-Herzegovina. Knowing my lack of knowledge when it comes to geography, he had marked the Adriatic Sea for me on the blue map located on the back of his official *TR* stationary. Even in the everyday things he mentioned—who he ate meals with, what reports he had to prepare, when he moved their clocks ahead as they headed east, or who swore off dog (the ice cream machine) until he lost some weight—I treasured the glimpses into Jon's final days on earth.

The letter he wrote on St. Patrick's Day, March 17, was filled with comments that seemed somewhat strange and ironic.

We have onboard a satellite phone called INMAR-SAT and when we are in satellite range, we can call home. It is for anyone. It costs $35 for 5 minutes. So if I call you and say Kris, this is an INMARSAT call, you will know it is only going to be 5 minutes in length.

I remembered how in our San Diego days we would stress over the long-distance phone bills whenever Jon would call from overseas. I'd give anything to talk to him again.

Uncontrollable sobs were now part of my days, and they began once again when I read his closing paragraph.

> *I pray everything is going OK. I love you, Kris, and*
> *really miss our little girls. Is everyone healthy? I*
> *guess I worry about that the most. I love you and*
> *miss you. Jon.*

No, Jon, everything was not okay. And I wasn't sure it ever
would be again.

The next envelope I received from Jon was a tape. He labeled
it No. 10, and he recorded it over two days, ending the night of
Tuesday, March 23—two days before he died. Hearing Jon's
voice was gut-wrenching for me, though I had to smile when Jon
asked about the pilot light in the gas fireplace and whether we'd
had an explosion as a result.

My tears wouldn't stop when he talked about the paper
chain and how hard it would be to get to the end of it. He talked
more about Operation Provide Promise and how on March 25 he
planned to visit Dave, our friend from church who was serving
on USS *John F. Kennedy*. I'd almost forgotten about Dave, who
was due to come home any day now. I wondered if he and Jon
had met on that fateful day.

The rest of the tape was almost too painful to hear. I let
Jordyn listen to the other side for her final bedtime story from
her daddy. Jon's made-up story had a moral that was hard for
me to swallow:

> *So, Jordyn, remember to always be a good little*
> *girl, love God and your parents, and nothing bad*
> *can ever happen to you.*

*Something bad had happened to Jordyn—to all of us. Was it some-
how our fault?* This tape would not be something I could listen to

repeatedly. Jon's voice stirred too many deep emotions in me. After playing it through and sharing Jon's story with Jordyn, I tucked it away and out of sight but never forgotten.

Kris at Norfolk Naval Base Bear Ace Memorial Service
March 1993, The Fly-Over

24

The Last Letter

Finally, it came—Jon's last letter. I was going through the daily mail as always, and there was letter No. 11, postmarked March 25. I knew there would not be another. I decided to leave the girls with Mom and take a private stroll around our quiet neighborhood to savor Jon's final words to me. Perhaps I was trying to avoid another meltdown, which by now I should have known I couldn't always control, but also, this beautiful neighborhood was an extension of our home—the home Jon and I had chosen together. It seemed fitting to carry his words around the familiar streets for a final walk together. I gently opened the envelope and found five pages dated the morning of Thursday, March 25.

Hey woman,

It is 0830 on the twenty-fifth. I was up to 0300 planning a brief for Carrier Group 8 and the admiral. Then it is up at 0700 to get on a helo for the JFK. I'm getting too old for this stuff.

Well, the die is cast. The 0-5 board ended yesterday. We should know our future in 6 to 8 weeks. I keep thinking that I should have done something differently, but then I realize I need to eliminate "I" and put my faith and trust in God. It is hard sometimes, but God will take care of me.

I have you, two healthy wonderful children, I am healthy. When I think of all of this, I realize how insignificant making O-5 really is. I know I would trade making O-5 in an instant if you, Jordyn, or Taylor were not healthy. I thank God for the great life He has given me.

When it comes to the girls, Kris, I trust your judgment. Do what you gotta do. How is the blue shelving paper project coming? Are you planning just the kitchen? Have fun with your friends! I hope Jordyn is good for you. I figure she will come in every nite that she wakes up. You are her security while I am away.

I have an appointment to get my teeth cleaned on April 10, so life does go on. I love you Krista and miss you. Kiss my 2 babes! Love, Jon.

P.S. Doing the tape was tough this time. When you send a care package, include several thin books for Jordyn so I can read them to her. I should have brought some. Jon.

This was a letter written by a man at peace. At peace with his wife, at peace with his life, and at peace with his God. I read the letter a second time and realized Jon's final words to me were an indescribable gift. Jon always marked the back of his letters with a dot where the ship was located on his stationary map. As I turned the letter over, I saw a small ink dot where he had placed it that morning. The dot was in the Ionian Sea, the final spot my beloved Jon was lost forever.

I looked at the time he'd written the letter and remembered that he almost never wrote me in the morning. What If he'd waited until he came back from his mission to write me as he usually did? Was God at work behind the scenes to coordinate this last treasured letter I held in my hands? My fingers touched these precious written words that I would recall in the days, weeks, months, and years to come.

It is hard sometimes, but God will take care of me.

Kris, I trust your judgment. Do what you gotta do.

You are her security while I am away.

So life does go on.

I love you, Krista, and miss you. Kiss my 2 babes!

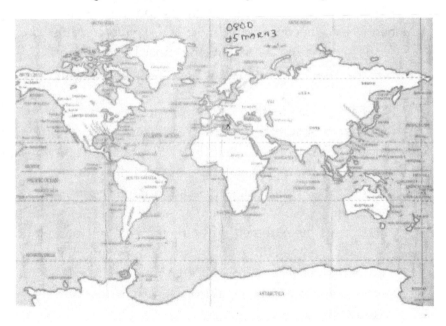

In his last letter, Jon hand-marked the location of the Ionian Sea, near the boot of Italy 38.50.72 N 17.60.58 E, not knowing this would be the final resting place for him and the crew of Bear Ace 603.

A Little Strength

Getting the mail would never be the same again, but a ray of sunshine soon found its way into my mailbox and took me completely by surprise. The same week I received Jon's final letter, I found an unexpected envelope in the daily stack of sympathy cards, bills, and junk mail. I was shocked when I saw the address: Kennebunkport, Maine. The name? President George H. W. Bush. I ran inside and opened the envelope to find this typed note inside:

> April 5, 1993
>
> Dear Kris,
>
> I was so very sorry to get the news about your husband, Jon—a courageous man who gave his life while serving his country in the most honorable of ways. I want to wish you and Jordyn and Taylor well.
>
> One of the great joys of my presidency was seeing, from time to time, the courageous navy pilots to whom I felt so close. I didn't know Lieutenant Commander Rystrom personally, but what I do know is that he was a wonderful person serving our country with honor.
>
> It must be extremely difficult for you, but perhaps you can get a little strength from knowing that a lot of people are thinking about you. Barbara joins me in conveying to you and yours our most sincere condolences.
>
> Sincerely,
> George Bush

I was stunned. Oh, how I cherished this letter from former President George H. W. Bush. Though he had never met President Bush, Jon served him during his tour at NEACP in Nebraska, and it was our next-door neighbor in Bellevue who had written the former President about my husband's death. President Bush was also a naval aviator who had survived being shot down and bailing out at sea. He understood Jon's service and sacrifice as few leaders did. Knowing he and his sweet wife were thinking of us meant the world to me.

A few days before the girls and I flew to Nebraska for Jon's final memorial service, I received another surprise. Dave, our friend who had served on USS *John F. Kennedy*, returned home from his cruise and came to visit me. I was comforted to find out that Jon and Dave had indeed met, and we hugged each other and wept, knowing he was the last friend from home Jon ever saw. I was thankful Jon had taken the time to make that connection happen.

Dave told me Jon had basically passed the baton to him, saying he had looked after Dave's wife and kids, and now it was Dave's turn to look after the girls and me. And he did. Dave, along with other men from our Sunday School class, faithfully helped mow my yard, and he and his wife included my girls and me in many of their family outings.

Dave's return from his cruise reminded me that USS *Theodore Roosevelt* was still at sea. I had no contact with anyone from the ship, and while the squadron wives were still supportive of me, now that I was a widow, my connection to the navy was shifting.

Scuttled Wreckage

16 APRIL 93
0700 CENTRAL EUROPEAN TIME UTC+1
USS THEODORE ROOSEVELT
ADRIATIC SEA
42°40'18" N, 16°42'89" E

During the days after the mishap, a JAG representative came onboard the *TR* to conduct a formal investigation. He carefully reviewed all the records, interviews, and evidence from the event. After reviewing more than thirty sworn statements, he would soon complete his exhaustive final report.

While it was too early to make a final determination of the cause of 603's crash, one decision had already been made: the scuttling of the wreckage into the sea. Over eighty pieces of wreckage had been salvaged—multiple pieces of the light-weight radome, shattered sections of the fuselage and wings, two helmets, headrests, a carpet piece, navigation chart, and more, including multiple "possible" pieces that couldn't be accurately identified. Very little was recovered. After close examination, it was determined that the leftover fragments should be discarded into the sea.

No one would miss having to walk past the grim reminder but scuttling the wreckage did not remove the wounds from the hearts of those who knew the men of Bear Ace 603. The ship and her crew had moved on, but they had not recovered.

Hometown Hero

In April, the girls, my mom, and I made the trip to Nebraska for Jon's final memorial service. As much as I dreaded having yet another service, I knew that this was a special way for the Rystroms and their friends to honor Jon.

The drive to Stromsburg through the endless acres of prairie farmland took me back to happier days when Jon was serving with NEACP and we'd make regular trips from our home in Bellevue to visit his family in Stromsburg. As we drove by the old town square, usually festooned with multiple Swedish flags during the annual summer festival, my heart was touched to see an ocean of American flags instead—a beautiful tribute to my husband. Their hometown boy was now a hometown hero, and the entire town proudly displayed their appreciation of his sacrifice.

Jon's family organized a beautiful service, including several personal stories shared by Jon's childhood friends and close relatives. The service was followed by another 21-gun salute, and the sounds of the rifle shots still pierced my soul. His family had a memorial headstone erected, and a college scholarship was set up in Jon's memory to benefit graduates of the local high school. Although I was grieving deeply, Jordyn was thrilled to play with her Nebraska cousins. I had to remind myself of some of Jon's final words: "So life does go on."

Yet Another Box

We returned to Seagrass Reach, and I attempted to go on with my life, but unpredictable reminders kept coming that made even simple tasks challenging. Jon's letters had stopped, but the mail hadn't. One day an envelope arrived with familiar handwriting on it: my own. This was the last letter I wrote to Jon, postmarked March 26, 1993.

I knew what was inside, but the outside of the envelope was a revelation. On the back, I found where I had labeled the letter No. 14, but next to it I saw where the *TR* had processed it on April 9. On the front, the envelope was stamped "Return to Sender" and marked "Unclaimed." Then below the address, another stamp marked the reason for the letter's return: "Moved, Left No Address." The words cut at my heart.

Not long after that, I came home to find a large box left on my front steps. This crumpled box was addressed to me. It was from USS *Theodore Roosevelt*. The box was heavy, but I managed to bring it into the house. This curious package had obviously experienced significant wear and tear to reach me. *What could possibly be inside?*

As I opened it, a shockwave of despair hit me once again. For inside this crushed box were all of Jon's personal possessions from his stateroom onboard the ship. Why I thought his things would stay on the ship until the squadron returned home from their cruise in the fall, I don't know, but I was completely blindsided by this Pandora's Box that landed unannounced on my front steps. Processing one letter at a time was hard enough. Facing a mountain of memories in an instant was overwhelming. I was completely undone.

My intense reaction was a complicated mixture of anger, confusion, sorrow, and comfort. I felt anger because it appeared that Jon's precious things had been thoughtlessly dumped like leftover trash into a flimsy box. Whoever cleared out Jon's things might have carried out the dreadful task with the greatest of care and respect, but after travelling for thousands of miles across the ocean, it appeared the tattered box, which should have been labeled *Fragile: Handle With Care,* had instead been marked *Fragments: We Don't Care.*

I felt confusion because there had been no warning, no heads-up, no instructions to prepare me for its arrival. Why had Jon's things been handled so poorly?

Sorrow came with every item I found inside: his extra flight suits, his precious flight jacket with patches reflecting the ships and squadrons he'd served on over the years, his worn leather Bible, his leftover toiletries, family pictures he'd displayed on his desk, letters from me, socks, shoes, and so much more. One everyday item touched me in particular. It was a tear-away calendar filled with sports trivia. It stopped on March 25.

I also had deep sadness about one item I knew I would never find in this box: his wedding ring. That had gone down with him into the depths of the Ionian Sea. I took comfort in knowing the golden symbol of our marriage would stay with him in that cold, dark, lifeless place. I also took comfort in having at home the last things Jon saw with his eyes and touched with his hands, but the painful memory of finding that crushed box on my doorstep haunts me to this day.

> *Promise:*
> *"He will wipe every tear from their eyes, and there will be no more death or sorrow or crying or pain. All these things are gone forever."*
> *Revelation 21:4*

USS Theodore Roosevelt CVN-71

Hey woman   *25 AM*

    It is 0830 on the 25th I was up to 0300 and planning a brief for C 68 (ADR Johnson, cags Direct Boss) then it is up at 0700 to get in a helo for the JFK. I'm getting to old for this stuff.

    Well the dye is cast, the O-5 board ended yesterday. We should know our future in 6 to 8 weeks I keep thinking that I should have done something differently but then I realize I need to eliminate I and put my faith + trust in God, it is hard some times but God will take care of me. I have you, two healthy wonderful children, I am healthy, when I think of all of these I realize how insignificant making O-5 really is. I know I would trade making O-5 in an instant if you, Jordyn or Taylor were not healthy. I just thank God for the great life he has given me.

    We are making history today. The Germans and French are also flying today. 1ST time. CO in the 1ST F-2 I in the second.

Jon's last letter he wrote to Kris the morning of his death
March 25th, 1993

25

Wreckage in My Hands

When my first summer as a widow arrived, I was still in the winter of grief. So for the first time since Jon died, I wrote a letter. Letters had been an integral part of my life for many years. I had met Jon through a letter, our relationship had been nurtured through letters, and letters contained the last words we would ever say to each other on earth. Months later, I was finally ready to turn the page and write letters again.

This letter I wrote was to President George H. W. Bush, who was known to be a letter writer. I wanted to let him know how much his kind words had meant to me so soon after Jon's death. Along with my handwritten letter to him, I included snapshots of our family. Perhaps it was silly, but there was a yearning inside me to communicate to this leader how much I admired Jon for the honorable man that he was. I was thrilled when President Bush responded with this short, handwritten letter:

August 3, 1993

Dear Kris,

After reading your July 27 letter, written from the heart, I know that your abiding faith will carry you and those kids forward into a life of new happiness.
Jon must have been a great guy.

Love from the Bushes,
George Bush

When I sent my letter, I was not sure he would respond, and I never dreamed he'd write me a letter with his own hand. This sprinkle of sunshine soon joined the other framed letters proudly displayed in my home.

One Woman's Story

One of my friends thought this was the kind of story worthy of the local news and contacted WAVY-TV. Terry Zahn, a respected news anchor and journalist, reached out to me and asked if he could feature my story. I was surprised but agreed. The news coverage at the time of Jon's death had featured my agonized re-action to the missing-man formation. I was looking forward to showing the world a much calmer and dignified widow who had her act together. More importantly, it was an opportunity to honor Jon.

Terry Zahn and his crew taped footage of my girls and me eating ice cream, me singing in my church choir, my framed let-ters from the presidents, and a meeting of the Wids support group at my home. The piece was aired in late August, and Terry's lead-in was perfect:

> Whenever there's a military air crash, we tell you about it. We tell you about who got killed. What we don't tell you about is the struggle for those left be-hind. How do they cope? How do they survive? To-night, one woman's story of tragedy, healing, and hope.

Terry proceeded to tell the basic facts of Jon's death, and I didn't mind them using footage from my meltdown at the navy memorial—not when the next scene showed me smiling and singing "I Must Tell Jesus" in the church choir. After featuring a few members of our Wids support group, I shared a final thought with a sweet smile on my peaceful face:

I feel that I am going to see him again one day, and I want him to look at me and say, "You did a good job, Kris. And I'm proud of you," because he was such a special guy.

The report created a wave of positive responses from viewers, and I decided to send a copy of the video to President Bush as a thank-you for sending me his handwritten letter in the first place. I was pleased with the serene, peaceful persona that I presented, and it seemed to me to be an accurate reflection of my inner world. I still had sorrow, but I was making it. I was strong. I was stable. I was confident. I didn't need counseling like some grieving people because I was healing fine on my own. Or so I thought.

Nowhere to Hide

Hardly a week after the WAVY feature aired, USS *Theodore Roosevelt* was scheduled to come home. The squadron wives invited me and the other 603 widows to attend the celebratory fly-in, but we weren't sure how to respond.

In the months after Jon's death, the guys from the squadron had been silent; they were focusing on their mission. Now that they were returning home, we didn't know if we should be there to greet them, or if our presence would only be a tragic reminder on what should be a celebration for them and their families. In the end, I decided not to attend. I knew the sights and sounds of the planes flying in would be more than I could stand, and I didn't want a meltdown from me to spoil their reunion.

Any time a ship and an air wing came back to port after a cruise, the event would receive extensive coverage from the local media. I decided that, until it was all over, I would escape to somewhere peaceful to have fun with my girls. My chosen destination? A beachside hotel where my girls could enjoy the ocean and play in the sand.

The day of the fly-in for the Bear Ace squadron arrived, and I was relieved to be away from Seagrass Reach and out of the daily flight path of military planes. We were settled in our hotel room suite several stories high with a gorgeous view of the ocean from the balcony. I was in the bedroom getting ready for the day when I heard a sound. My heart seemed to stop beating as the sound grew louder. No. It couldn't be. That old familiar humming was the unmistakable sound of an E-2C Hawkeye. This couldn't be happening.

I ran out of the room and onto the balcony, where my nightmare was confirmed. Soaring over the ocean and toward land in perfect formation were four E-2C aircraft. They were flying in the missing-man formation. Surely, they would turn. Surely, they were headed somewhere else. I willed them away, but it was no use. Our hotel was in their direct flight path.

I stood frozen in panic, my hands gripping the balcony's railing much as I had gripped the spindles of my stairway when the stripes were at my door. A tsunami of anguish, horror, and despair engulfed me. The deafening noise of the Hummers shut out the sound of my wailing as the Hawkeyes passed directly overhead. They were so close I could see the black and red Bear Ace insignias painted on their sides. It seemed as if I could reach out and touch them. They were so close, I feared the aircrew could see me standing there howling on the balcony: Jon Rystrom's widow, distraught and alone, consumed with grief.

The band-aid of denial I had carefully applied to my grieving heart was ripped off in a single moment. Any pretense I'd embraced that Jon was still at sea, that I was living the navy-wife life, and that nothing had truly changed was shattered into a million tiny fragments.

The strong, stable, confident widow with her calm, peaceful smile, who had appeared on television a few days earlier was now reduced to a quivering and wounded wretch lying in the fetal position on the balcony floor. One reality reverberated in my soul: *Jon is not coming home*. For the first time, this reality hit me, and it hit me hard. There could be no more make-believe, no more denial, no more head in the sand. The time had come to face the facts at last.

What was I thinking—trying to escape to the ocean, at a beachfront hotel, nonetheless? I knew the ocean was a trigger for me. How could I have forgotten such pertinent information? But I knew this moment was arranged for me. God was telling me, "You have to face this. You can't run from reality anymore." As exceedingly painful as this moment was, it was also the turning point that exposed my wounds so that my grief could be expressed and my healing could begin.

> *Promise:*
> *"Trust in the Lord with all your heart; do not depend on your own understanding. Seek his will in all you do, and he will show you which path to take."*
> *Proverbs 3:5-6.*

My poor girls didn't know what to think of their sobbing mother. After several gut-wrenching hours of trying to regain control, I finally called a friend who lived nearby and arranged for us to go to her home so I wouldn't be alone and my girls could be looked after.

In the days that followed, I found a qualified therapist and started regular counseling. Clearly, I was depressed, a common condition for any widow. Any pride I'd had about not needing outside help had evaporated, and I willingly accepted a prescribed antidepressant. When I hear people say that counseling is not necessary, that "Jesus can heal you, and you don't need that stuff," I like to ask them what they would do if they had a broken arm. Would they hesitate to go to a doctor and have it set? Why should a broken heart be any different? Yes, Jesus can heal you, but in the same way, He often uses doctors to heal our bodies, He can use therapists and counselors to help heal our brokenness.

Mishap Mystery

With the Bear Ace squadron back from their cruise, the commanding officer invited the widows of 603—along with Mrs. Ardaiz, the mother of the only unmarried victim—to his home for a meeting. This was our chance to hear a firsthand account of what had happened on the evening of the mishap. The CO was calm and understanding, but he didn't mince words. He said that night was the blackest he'd ever seen. There was no moon, a hazy cloud cover hung overhead, and there was no visible horizon. He told us the mission was a simple one, and even though 603's radar wasn't working, they were still a valuable player in the mission.

His plane landed right before 603 approached the ship, and because he was exiting his aircraft, he didn't see them hit the water. He had viewed the camera footage of the accident, and with the knowledge he had of what other pilots had experienced that evening, his best guess was that either the crew experienced vertigo, or there was some unknown distraction in the cockpit, or the plane had a mechanical failure. To him, every piece of evidence seemed to point to a normally functioning aircraft, and the cause of the mishap was a mystery.

This wasn't what we wanted to hear. We thought the Commanding Officer who was flying that night would have answers. Not knowing why the plane crashed and being unable to find answers was difficult. Tears quietly streamed down our cheeks as he continued. He went on to describe what the flight surgeon had told him. The speed the plane was traveling when it impacted the surface of the water was equivalent to a car hitting a brick wall at 180 miles per hour. The crew's necks would have snapped immediately, and they wouldn't have known what hit them.

Hardly any wreckage was recovered, but among the pieces salvaged were two flight helmets. The CO couldn't tell us who they belonged to, and since they were a part of the forensic investigation and would be studied to see how they withstood the impact, they would not be returned. But he did have something he could give to us: small pieces of the shattered plane—two for each family. My hands shook as I received what was left of my beloved Jon. Wreckage. Wreckage that I could hold in my hand. This man whom I loved had given his life for our country, and all I got in return was wreckage.

My Husband's Coffin

Still holding the pieces of jagged metal, we asked the CO if we could memorialize our guys by visiting one of the E-2's from the Bear Aces. As unusual as this sounded, we wanted to go inside one of the planes and sit in the seats where our loved ones had died. Hearing the horrific details of the mishap was heart-wrenching, but somehow sitting in an E-2 could possibly give us the emotional resolution we so desperately needed. While frustrated and angry at the lack of information we'd received, we knew we couldn't demand answers. The CO, however, was eager to help us gain the closure we needed and planned our visit to the Bear Ace hangar a few days later.

Our CACOs joined us for this grim tour, and my heart clenched in grief as we stepped out onto the tarmac to see a single E-2C Hawkeye awaiting us. The CO allowed us to enter the plane alone. We silently walked through the door on the port side, with Shelly and Paola walking up the narrow passage to the cockpit, while the rest of us scooted toward the rear. I sat down in the middle seat between Mrs. Ardaiz and Katie. The experience was painful—like returning to the scene of a fatal accident. I was sitting inside my husband's coffin, my husband's final resting place.

I was struck by the tight confines of the space; ejection could not have been an option, even with parachutes attached to the seats. I could not imagine Jon squeezing out of the narrow hatch at the back, especially in a time of crisis. Remembering what the flight surgeon had said, I realized that none of our guys had a chance to even try. I held the cold, heavy-duty buckles of the seats in my hand. Surely these would have held him in place when the plane hit the water but there was no way to know for certain. At least, I could remove the tormenting picture of Jon drowning as he struggled to escape the wrecked plane. I decided to hang on to my image of him sitting in his flight suit, surrounded by the fuselage of his beloved Hawkeye and resting in the company of his navy brothers.

The seat I was sitting in represented the culmination of Jon's fifteen-year naval career. Jon loved being a CICO, playing the role of a quarterback in air missions, running the E-2C's advanced radar systems, and passing on his considerable expertise to junior officers. Jon and I shared many things, but much of his navy life had been a mystery to me. I now had a better understanding of the world he loved.

Six Hundred Fifty Pages ... for What?

The navy's final report from the JAG investigation was released a few weeks later. Rick helped me request my copy, and I was floored when more than six hundred fifty pages arrived. I didn't have the mental energy to dive into the endless pages of sworn statements, maintenance and safety records, radio transmission transcripts, pictures of some of the wreckage, ship's log, and much more.

What little I did read made me angry. The report mentioned that Jon hadn't flown in a few weeks, but how could he with all the bad weather they'd experienced? I wasn't sure that a few touch-and-go landings in advance would have made any difference on the night in question, not with Jon's years of experience and the fact that he wasn't flying the plane. The report also brought up "crew coordination," the idea that everyone on board had the responsibility to keep an eye on the altimeter and speak up if something seemed amiss. I knew Jon took his role as the senior officer seriously, and Frenchy was perhaps the best pilot in the squadron. How could five guys have been asleep on the job at the same time? It didn't make sense to me.

The official conclusion of the JAG investigation was like the CO's: "The exact cause of this mishap is not known." The report pointed to the theory of vertigo as the most likely explanation. The JAG investigation did recommend several changes for the VAW community, including crew coordination, refresher training, and altimeter alarms. The navy was diligent in attempting to increase the safety level of the E-2C fleet and doing everything within its power to ensure that this sort of mishap never happened again.

I should have felt some kind of honor in Jon's sacrifice, but instead, I was consumed with sadness. Sad that Jon was gone, sad that this was how his life had ended, and sad that our girls would never know their daddy. The crew of Bear Ace 603 were now looked upon as American heroes, and the families left behind were considered survivors. Survivors of a tragedy with no known cause, and survivors who would carry the wreckage of Bear Ace 603 forever in our hearts. As I closed the pages of the JAG report, I sat in silence, mentally dismissing it. I saw no purpose in its conclusions, for nothing anyone could say would ever bring back my beloved Jon. There will never be answers to all the questions. Somehow, I had to come to the place where I could live with never knowing.

The wreckage from Bear Ace 603

26

How Do You Get Through?

When someone hears my story for the first time, they often ask, "How did you get through it?" The next two chapters are designed to help answer that question. Everyone grieves uniquely, but many of the emotions and experiences I endured are common to all who have suffered significant loss. My hope is that if you are walking through grief, whether it's fresh or something from your past, these topics will help you on your journey. And if you aren't grappling with grief, these pages will give you the understanding to support those around you who are.

Unwanted Companion

The memorial services were finally behind me, and I refused to have a fourth when Jon's headstone was placed at Arlington National Cemetery. While I'd had enough of funerals, the grieving had only begun. The time had come to move on, but I felt like a rudderless ship adrift at sea.

I had no idea what grief was before Jon's sudden death. Being young, my friends weren't dealing with grief, and the only losses I had experienced were that of my grandparents. Even after becoming a widow, grief was something I wanted to escape, deny, and avoid. That, of course, was impossible to do. Grief became an unwelcomed and constant companion, sometimes hiding in the shadows and at other times throwing me down the stairs or slapping me repeatedly in the face.

Grief was more than an emotion. Grief ate away at my soul, kept my mind in a fog, and interrupted my life at the most inconvenient and unexpected moments. As painful as the depths of grief were to experience, it was a necessary part of my healing. To be honest, grief never completely goes away. The journey does change over time as the sun comes out, the flowers bloom, and joy returns, but in the beginning, walking through grief is grueling, demanding work.

Sanctuary

Having a private, safe place to grieve is critical for anyone who has experienced loss. As agonizing as it can be to mourn and face tough questions, healing won't come if grief can't be released. My bathroom became my crucible of grief. I called it my *cry room* because it was the one place where I could be completely alone, with no distractions and no fear of my sweet girls hearing the release of my intense, gut-wrenching wails.

When planning our dream home, Jon and I chose a lot with no neighbors behind it and a beautiful view of pine trees and the wetlands beyond. We designed the grand bathroom in our second-floor master suite to take advantage of this vista, creating an intimate oasis to enjoy together. With a large, palladium window over the jacuzzi tub, a spacious double vanity, and luxurious, emerald-green and burgundy ornamental wallpaper, our bathroom resembled a model home's showroom display. This private sanctuary that Jon and I had envisioned being our decades-long honeymoon suite took on the morbid atmosphere of a funeral parlor.

Everywhere I looked, I saw Jon. The vanity held his personal toiletries, like his razors and cologne. The view from the large bathroom window not only gave me a glimpse of the tall pine trees lining our backyard but also the fence that Jon had built and the swing set for the girls that he'd installed. Right off the bathroom was his sizeable walk-in closet filled with clothes that brought back special memories.

The most precious article of his clothing wasn't a navy uniform or one of his silk suits from our time in Hong Kong; it was his old bathrobe. Whenever I hugged it close and buried my face in its soft folds, it was as if Jon himself were standing next to me wrapping his strong arms around my trembling soul. Sometimes I would retreat to his closet, turn off the light, close the door, and cling to his bathrobe.

During those lonely times in the dark, I would weep with deep, heaving sobs of sorrow. Surrounded by his clothes, I would return to those equally dark questions, the ones that came in the first days after his death, that seemed to have no answers. Did Jon feel the impact of the plane when it hit the icy water? Could he unbuckle from his seat in time? Did he try to swim? How long until he couldn't breathe? Were there screams? Did they even have time to cry out? To pray?

The image of Jon lying at the bottom of the ocean wouldn't leave my mind as I replayed the crash—at least how I envisioned it—over and over. I had spent time at the bottom of the ocean myself. Though my dive wasn't even close to the nearly mile-deep water where Bear Ace 603 had crashed, I knew something about the cold, dark, lifeless places of the deep. My one comfort was that there were no sharks living at those depths to disturb his body.

Being in our bathroom wasn't always torturous. I could go about my daily routine, putting on my makeup or brushing my teeth, and the emotions wouldn't hit me. At other times, though, the painful feelings would flood in and I could hardly breathe, or a deep sadness would permeate the room and my soul.

These episodes were an amplified version of what I had experienced early in our marriage when Jon was deployed. Living alone in San Diego in an empty house with an empty bed had made me feel as if I were married to a man who was never present. I remembered going through his closet and putting on one of his shirts so I could feel close to him. That response was merely from a temporary delay in receiving his daily letters. The heartache I'd felt in San Diego was genuine, but nothing compared to the agony of knowing my husband would never return.

Crashing In

Grief would hit me out of the blue, crashing in like a rogue tsunami. I remember being at the kitchen sink while the girls were sitting at the center island eating dinner. Suddenly, the pain of Jon's death hit me like a freight train out of nowhere. I tried to hide my grief from the girls, but as my shoulders began to heave, they couldn't help but notice. I turned around and told them I was feeling sad about missing Daddy. At times, I would be having fun playing a game with my daughters when a wave of grief would wash over me, swirling my emotions into a riptide of sorrow. Almost as suddenly as these waves of loss hit me, they would retreat. Minutes later, I'd be back to doing the dishes, the laundry, or playing with my girls. Over time, the monstrous waves that had tossed me to and fro weakened and grew farther apart, gently rocking my world.

The day finally came when I realized I hadn't cried in the last twenty-four hours. Then a few days went by, then a week, and so on. It takes time. For the sake of my girls, I didn't wait until the waves were rare occurrences before returning to my regular life. I was proactive in making sure they had a semblance of a normal life on a regular basis.

As a navy wife, I'd handled many boxes in my life, and eventually grief transformed from a wave into a box, something I felt I could handle much easier. There were times I had to put my grief box on the shelf so I could focus on the task at hand, be it household chores or dealing with financial matters.

No one in mourning needs to feel guilty for setting aside grief for a season in order to focus on other things. When life was less hectic, I could take the grief box off the shelf, open it up, and deal with what was inside. To help me deal with my grief box, I would imagine Jon was watching me—cheering me on, and I wanted to make him proud. He wouldn't want me to wallow in grief and sorrow, yet I often couldn't help it. Sometimes unannounced, my grief box would come tumbling down and spill its painful contents all over the place. I had lost so much. The loss was real and so was my grief, but what a beautiful gift I had in the tender words my beloved Jon wrote to me in his letters.

At the beginning of our first cruise, I didn't realize how much our letter writing would mean to both of us. I never dreamed, as I started collecting Jon's letters in shoeboxes, that the love captured in their pages would continue to minister to our daughters and me after his death. The letters not only sustained us in our months apart but also provided a history of our relationship and a legacy for my daughters today. How glad I am that I kept them all these years tucked away out of sight, waiting to be rediscovered—waiting to unlock their enduring messages of devotion, faithfulness, and affirmation.

Our world today is so different, with our instant gratification of text messages, emails, and social media posts. We rarely invest our time to physically write a letter or repeatedly check our mailbox, longing to hear from a distant loved one. Our electronic messages so easily slip through our fingers and fade away. If a letter could be written to someone you love, not a text, not an email but a handwritten letter— what a precious keepsake it would be.

Nighttime

During the day, I focused on my daughters and made their joy and happiness my priority. Once they were put to bed and nighttime permeated the house, I would grieve—especially in my cry room. Friends encouraged me to journal but writing down my thoughts seemed like a horrible reminder that my daily letter writing to Jon was over for good.

One thing that brought me solace was talking on the phone with my widow friends. Olga, the pilot's wife who had called me after Jon died, was one of them, along with the other widows from Bear Ace 603: Paola, Shelly, and Katie (who was now the mother of a healthy baby boy). Late at night, we knew we could reach out and hold each other up in our times of weakness. An unbreakable bond was made with these women, and I will always cherish them as my soul sisters.

Till Death Do Us Part

When I lost Jon, I felt as though I had lost everything. In the seven short years that we knew each other, Jon had become my best friend, my lover, my encourager, my biggest fan, my provider, and the father of my daughters. I never stopped being married to him. We had vowed "till death do us part," but even death could not break my commitment to Jon. He was not my ex; I still carried his name. I was mothering his children and carrying on his legacy.

Loss of identity was one of my greatest struggles. That point was driven home when my CACO took me to the naval base to change my military ID card to show that I was now a URW (unremarried widow). I had no desire to embrace my new identity. I felt like I had a large "W" plastered on my forehead, and I tried in vain to hide it. I kept attending the married Sunday School class at church, and it took some time before I moved to the singles class. I didn't fit in there either. I didn't fit in anywhere.

In the first several months after Jon's death, when faced with the fact that I was a widow and a single mom, I told myself that it didn't matter because Jon would have been at sea anyway. I was living the navy-wife life. Nothing had truly changed. I loved being an officer's wife—being saluted when we drove onto the base. That salute still came because of the tag on my car, but I knew my Jon wasn't there to receive it.

One bright spot after Jon's death was when news came of his promotion. Jon never knew that days before he died, the promotion board had approved him for the rank of commander. I had the additional stripe added to all his uniforms and the golden oak leaf embellishments to his covers (hats).

Losing Jon also meant losing my financial security and many of my dreams for the future. I was thankful that he had increased his insurance policy and that I wouldn't have to sell our home. By no means was I set for life; I would need to reenter the workforce at some point. Jon had always been adept at handling our finances, and I had never bothered to learn much about how he did it. I wish I had. Dreams of him retiring from the navy and starting a new career were over. My own dreams of earning a doctoral degree seemed meaningless. Dreams we'd shared of traveling, seeing our girls go to college, and becoming grandparents had all disappeared in one awful moment.

> *Promise:*
> *"I tell you the truth, if you had faith even as small as a mustard seed, you could say to this mountain, 'Move from here to there,' and it would move. Nothing would be impossible."*
> *Matthew 17:20*

I wasn't the only one suffering loss. My girls had lost their father, though it would be many years before they could comprehend what that truly meant. Some losses were immediate. Jon wouldn't be home by Jordyn's birthday like he'd promised. He wouldn't join her for rides at Disney World in the fall. He wouldn't teach Jordyn's Mission Friends class again. Other losses were long term. Jon would never teach his girls how to ride a bike or how to drive a car. He'd never watch them go on their first dates, see them graduate from high school, or walk them down the aisle on their wedding days. Their daddy was gone forever.

I felt this "daddy loss" most acutely at church, of all places. There I would watch other fathers with their daughters and feel the pang of knowing that my girls were missing out on their dad's affection and presence. While these families would go home after church to a nice Sunday roast and houses filled with happiness, we went to a house filled with silence.

Being jealous of those who weren't suffering like me was a constant temptation. My Jon was a good and honest man, and it didn't seem fair that men of far less character seemed to be living a charmed life. Feeling like a victim was easy, but making the choice to be thankful for what I had — even the small things — was the path to wholeness.

True Blues

God brought people into my life to help fill the void in my heart through their love for my girls and me. Many answered the call to be a defender of the widow and to reach out to the broken-hearted. I learned to embrace close relationships and not journey through grief alone.

My close relationships were what I liked to call "true blues," amazing friends and family who walked alongside me. Jon and I had always prioritized relationships, and that choice paid off when my world shattered. My church family mobilized into a loving army who became the hands and feet of Jesus. They covered practical needs — like mowing my lawn for the first year, doing household repairs, or watching my kids — as well as meeting emotional needs, like making sure I wasn't alone on special days and including me in family gatherings. My network of widow friends was a constant source of mutual support as well.

Nothing compared, however, to the sacrifice my parents made for me. My sweet mother stayed with me for the first month, and before the first year passed, my parents had retired, sold their home, and taken a detour to their beach-house retirement in order to be close to the girls and me. They were on a mission to rescue me and their granddaughters from this horrific tragedy, and their love and support were beyond measure. Now I had a Sunday roast to come home to, and their presence helped fill the void of Jon's death that we all felt.

Beyond my inner circle, other kind people reached out to offer their sympathies and concern, like neighbors, friends from across the country who heard the news of Jon's death, and former college classmates. However, another class of people came into my life, and they were not my true blues.

Pound-Cake People

In the days and months after Jon's death, everyone brought me food, including people who didn't really know me. Because they brought me food, some of them felt validated to get into my business and give their opinions on how. I should be living my life. Mom and I came up with the term *pound-cake people* to describe these well-meaning but nosy, pushy individuals.

I imagine that their motives were with good intention, but these people who barely knew me were pressuring me to live up to their expectations and ideas. I was told when to go through Jon's things, when to take off my wedding ring, when I should or shouldn't date, and how to raise my daughters. Not only was I told that I should move but also when, where, and how I should do it! They didn't truly understand my situation or the fact that grieving had to be done on my schedule, not theirs.

Some of these pound-cake people had no clue what I was going through. I remember one situation where a woman asked me to pray for her because they were putting a pool in their backyard and had issues with the company installing it. The workers were late, which was a bother to the family, causing them undue stress. I wanted to grab her by the shoulders and shout, "You're stressed about a pool while my husband is dead at the bottom of the ocean?! Do you realize that I'm struggling to keep my head above water? Really!?!"

As difficult as it was to receive the pound-cake people with their desserts and casseroles, they helped feed my family, and I appreciated their love and concern. Eventually, they did leave, and a year later when they were gone for good, I did miss them a little. I learned that you can't live your life trying to meet everyone's expectations. Listen closely to your true blues and simply smile and say thanks to the pound-cake people.

Dead Books

Mom and I created another term to describe the stacks of books I was given after Jon died. We called them *dead books*. In no time, I accumulated a massive library of books on grief, death, and dying. I couldn't read them at first. These dead books made me sad. I wanted joy, encouragement, happy thoughts, and laughter. I wanted to keep pretending that Jon was still at sea and that this nightmare was temporary. Some dead books came from pound-cake people, along with their casseroles; others came from true blues. Regardless of who gave them to me, I hated them.

Not all widows shared my distaste for dead books. One widow friend of mine read all her dead books, and they were an immense help to her. Sometimes it's more a matter of timing. I'm glad I didn't toss my collection because as time passed, I found some of them meaningful in ways I couldn't have at first. No matter the book, I always received the love intended when it was given, and that was a great comfort. (I find it ironic that having avoided dead books in the past, I now have written one myself.)

I have to say though, that the greatest book of all on grieving is not a dead book—it's God's Living Word, the Bible. As the shock of Jon's death softened, I began turning to the Scriptures looking for answers, guidance, and comfort. What I found most comforting were God's promises. I found multiple verses that talked of God caring for the widows and the fatherless. When I read the Scripture about the sea giving up its dead at the resurrection, I took great comfort in knowing that verse applied to Jon.

However, some people had a twisted view of Scripture, and they weren't hesitant to share their warped theology.

Stupid Things People Say

Sometimes the pound-cake people were guilty of making hurtful and insensitive comments. Whether it was distorted opinions or inappropriate questions, here are some of my infamous favorites:

"God needed another angel in heaven."

"This was God's will. He's in a better place now."

"You're lucky you didn't get his body back after his awful accident."

"You should move back home with your parents."

"Are you going to remarry?"

"What are you going to do with Jon's car?" (This really meant "I want to buy it" even though it had only been a few weeks since his death.)

"I think that losing your husband to death must be easier than being in a miserable marriage like mine."

Some of these statements had elements of truth in them. It was difficult to respond, however, realizing that these comments were not meant for harm but for sympathy and advice.

Loss, death, and devastation are different for everyone. How I chose to live my life with my girls was for me alone to decide. Navigating the waters of grief and despair is a new experience to anyone, especially one who is young and living a life of anticipated fulfillment and promise. When well-meaning people said Jon was in heaven, that it was a far better place for him, and that he was with Jesus, I was somewhat reassured, but even more so, I was disturbed, knowing that my precious husband died at the age of thirty-eight, leaving me a young widow and two little girls fatherless. Losing the vibrant, loving, and passionate relationship Jon and I shared was nothing short of devastation, and I didn't understand why people felt the need to give out powerless, and sometimes insensitive, platitudes.

People will always say stupid, inappropriate things—it is inevitable. What I did with these words was my choice. Letting their careless words float away into a supersized word vacuum that was sealed for eternity was somewhat entertaining and at times comical. To be able to create healthy boundaries, to understand their innocent ignorance, and then to extend grace to the clueless people who said such things kept me in a much healthier place.

Routine

Life needs rhythm and purpose. Caring for my two daughters helped me keep living and moving forward. I couldn't crawl into my bed, hide under the covers, and check out when they needed to be fed, bathed, and, more importantly, nurtured and loved. Once the memorial services were over, my daily routine was not much different than before Jon died. Unfortunately, this enabled me to live in denial of his death.

Daily tasks provided structure and a sense of control and accomplishment. Did I make my bed today? Check. Did I get the garbage out? Check. Did Max get fed and does he have fresh water? Check. The mundane chores of life kept me sane and propelled me forward.

My church involvement and my goal to make life as fun and normal for my girls as possible got me out of the house and into the community. But the fatigue of grief meant that I couldn't burn the candle at both ends as I had in the past. I had to extend grace to myself and take things one day—or sometimes one hour—at a time. There were days when even my best efforts at keeping a regular routine got derailed by a new enemy: triggers.

27

From Triggers to Moving On

Triggers are sensations or events that instantly—
and often unexpectedly—throw you into an unplanned eruption
of grief. The best way I can describe it is to imagine you live near
a Corvette dealership that only sells red cars. People are test-
driving them all the time, traveling down your road daily. Your
spouse loves the sight of these gorgeous, crimson Corvettes and
decides to take one for a spin. Unfortunately, your spouse
crashes and dies as a result. Still every day, the red Corvettes are
driven down your street. You can pull the curtains, but you can't
shut out the sound of the supercharged V8 engines.

You pass the dealership filled with red sports cars every
time you leave your house. Whenever you see or hear one of
those Corvettes, you instantly relive the loss of your spouse.
Even when you go on vacation, a red Corvette unexpectedly appears in a parking lot, on the interstate, or at a stoplight. Can you
see how hard it would be to escape the constant reminder of your
grief?

Triggers set off flashbacks. Some were a one-time occur-
rence, like when I received Jon's personal items in the crumpled
cardboard box on my front steps, but most of them were recurring. The unique, humming sound of an E-2C flying over my
house every day was one of those triggers. What had once filled
my heart with pride and joy now unleashed a torrent of sorrow,
pain, and uncontrollable tears. Being saluted at the gate whenever I drove onto the Norfolk Naval Base to shop at the commis-
sary was a trigger. Once I walked into the navy grocery store,

triggers were everywhere: aviators in their flight suits, officers in dress blues, and Jon's favorite vanilla sandwich cookies on aisle four. All these sights brought me to tears.

One embarrassing incident happened when my parents and I decided to take the girls to enjoy the public beach at Dam Neck Naval Base. Of course, this was also where we had our wedding, but months had gone by since Jon's death, and I thought I could handle it. However, once on base my mind was distracted, and I didn't pay close attention to my speed.

A military police officer pulled me over and asked for my ID. The sight of his uniform and being in such a memorable place, combined with the stress of getting a speeding ticket, instantly did me in. I completely lost it. I was sobbing and screaming so hysterically that the officer had no idea what to do with me, so he called the paramedics. My parents and my little girls were helpless in managing my meltdown, and what was supposed to be a fun beach day for the girls turned into a torturous embarrassment. All because of triggers.

College football, one of Jon's greatest loves, was another trigger. So was anything Nebraska: football, basketball, or a license plate. Our house was perhaps the biggest trigger of all. When I looked out the window over our kitchen sink, the sight of our fence or our sprinklers would bring up the image of Jon in his familiar, worn overalls working in the yard. As we had designed our home together, every tile, every piece of molding, and every door could trigger an episode of grief. Even though reminders of Jon surrounded me, I didn't want to leave the home we had built together.

Some triggers were smells. Fresh-baked chocolate cake reminded me of when Jon would bake in the kitchen after a hard day at work. The smell of mulch still takes me back to when we returned home from the navy memorial service and my neighbors had planted flowers and mulched our yard. Even now, I can recall the smell of Jon's favorite cologne that I bought for him.

Special days were triggers, such as the anniversary of our first date or our wedding anniversary. Movies were triggers too. After twenty-five years, I still can't watch *Top Gun* or *An Officer and a Gentleman*.

The ocean and the beach also sent me into sobbing hysteria. Living close to the beach and having kids meant this wasn't a place I could avoid. The ocean was Jon's grave, and the beach reminded me of special memories such as our wedding, living in San Diego, and tropical vacations we enjoyed together.

Over time, some triggers can take on dual personalities—painful *and* comforting. Max, Jon's Norwegian elkhound, was like that. On the one hand, this lovable, fluffy dog that lay at our front door to protect us and allowed the girls to use him as a pillow was a tremendous source of happiness. There were other times when his presence would remind me that he'd never see his master again. Other memories that used to bring a tear eventually brought a smile. I eventually found that time, counseling, friends, and prayer helped me work through my grief, or triggers could have kept me trapped and isolated in a pit of despair.

Triggers cannot be avoided. And sometimes they shouldn't be avoided. When you know they are coming, you can be prepared to deal with them. But when they take you by surprise, cut yourself some slack. There was so much I had to process during those dark days, and triggers often led to other issues.

Mind Games

When trying to find your footing, you go through mind games to help you cope. By far, denial was my most unhealthy coping mechanism. I still fantasized that Jon and the guys had been picked up by a boat and that they were on a little island somewhere waiting to be found. One minute I'd be mourning Jon's death, and the next minute I'd be asking God to quickly bring him home. Since Jon would have been at sea five more months after the time of his death, this denial was convenient to maintain.

I also denied the reality of how he died and what had happened to his plane. Knowing his plane rested in waters nearly a mile deep, I imagined that he was protected by his aircraft. Surely, no marine life would disturb his body at such depths. Surely, he and his navy brothers were still buckled in their seats peacefully at rest. As Jordyn began asking more questions about where her daddy was, I came up with a unique response. I told her that he was "down deep, deep, deep where the sharks don't go." This was true and seemed to give Jordyn some peace.

Faith

Before the mishap, I had been coasting through my navy-wife life naively unaware of much of the pain, suffering, and conflict in our fallen world. As a person of faith, I wore my relationship with God like a lucky rabbit's foot, expecting protection from "undeserved" calamity. A false sense of security had led to my arrogant belief that because I had my *Christian* box checked, I was immune to life's heartaches. I now was living my darkest nightmare, and what was I going to do with God? Where was my lucky rabbit's foot now?

Being slapped with sudden grief often caused me to face my struggles with faith. Gone was the box-checking religious life I had lived before. There was no faking it now—no glossing over any of my doubts or faults. I was raw, real, and desperate, but it took time before I was ready to dig deep and find real answers to my hard questions.

At the beginning of my grief, I didn't immediately reach out to God. My anger at Him caused me to turn to the one thing I had depended on for years—myself. I wasn't reading the Scriptures for solace or hope, and I wasn't praying for guidance and healing. The difficult questions I asked God in my first months of grief were questions I continued to ask, not expecting any answers: *Why did this happen? Was it my fault? How can You take away the dad of these precious girls? Are You punishing me? If You're such a powerful, loving God, why did You allow this to happen? Don't You care? Do You even hear me?*

In the first months after Jon's death, I didn't read the Bible much at all. I would open it at church, but it gathered dust otherwise. Yet God found a way to still minister to my wounded soul. Christian music became a lifeline for me because while I wasn't willing to meditate on Scripture, I was willing to listen to music. I rejoined my church's choir and listened to music at home. Songs filled with words of hope and encouragement gradually brought the light of God's love to my dark, bitter soul.

During the dark lonely nights of grief, I found that music ministered to my heart. While it reminded me of my childhood memories of Southern Gospel sings with my parents, it also took me to a place of sweet peace of simple worship. I would cry as I listened to the melodic lyrics written to my Savior, and I found myself praying. My prayers were often small and selfish, but faith was slowly awakening in my grieving, hopeless soul.

On Sunday mornings while singing in the choir, I would look up at a stained-glass image of Jesus holding His outstretched hands to the congregation below. In my heart, it was as if God was whispering to me, "I held out My arms to Jon and welcomed him home. Kris, he is here with Me, safe and loved for eternity."

The powerful messages from the hymns and praise songs our choir rehearsed and sang each week were like a healing salve gently massaged into my wounds of loss. Through the safe place of my church family and the sounds I surrounded myself with at home, God was restoring what Satan intended to destroy. He was gently revealing His deep love for me through the gift of music, releasing sprinkles of sunshine into my bleak winter of grief.

I spent time in prayer, but I wasn't listening for a response — not yet. I would pour out my heart, but in my anger at God, I wouldn't reach out to Him. The one thing I could do was keep the promises Jon and I had made when we dedicated our daughters. We had promised to raise them in a godly home, to keep them connected to a church body, and to encourage them to have their own relationship with God. Like a plane flying by instruments, faith kept me on track. Even in my doubts, deep down I knew God was real. And in this dark season, He kept me out of the ditch as I limped along with Him supporting me.

Sometimes, in prayer, I'd pretend I could get messages to Jon. I'd cry out to Jesus and say, "Can you please tell Jon that I love him? Can you tell him that I miss him?" or "Can you wish Jon a happy birthday for me? Asking hard questions is important. God can handle every painful, bitter, hateful question we throw His way. During confusion and sorrow, keep looking for His goodness. In time, you will see it.

Sprinkles of Sunshine

During the darkest days, God will give you *sprinkles of sunshine* to brighten your path, to lighten your load, and to remind you that He is there. He gave me plenty, such as when my neighbors landscaped my yard and when I received letters from Presidents George H. W. Bush and Bill Clinton. I had them framed and hung them on my wall.

Some sprinkles were tied to specific dates. On the date of our wedding anniversary, the check from Jon's life insurance policy arrived. It was like a warm embrace reminding me of Jon's love. My first Mother's Day without my beloved Jon was the day the first rose bloomed on one of the bushes Jon planted right before he left. Don't tell me that was a mere coincidence. At first, seeing those rosebushes after his death was a thorn of grief in my soul, but this transformed that Mother's Day. It was like Jon was sending me his rose from heaven.

Other sprinkles God sent was through the people surrounding me. A few friends hid two hundred strips of paper with the words from Isaiah 43:2 everywhere in my house: in a box of pasta, in my deodorant, under my towels, in drawers, in the girls' rooms, etc. To this day, Isaiah 43:2 is my favorite scripture. Little did my friends know that their sweet gesture would impact me for the rest of my life. The constant—and sometimes humorous—reminders to not fear, that God was with me, and that He wouldn't let me be overcome by tragedy gave me hope.

The Mission Friends class planted a beautiful dogwood tree and installed a plaque in Jon's honor at our church. Since we had no grave to visit, this special tree became a living memorial for my girls and me. We would decorate its branches on major holidays.

The wives of the VAW-124 Bear Ace squadron had helped establish a VAW scholarship fund for the children of downed Hawkeye and COD aviators and created cookbooks as a fundraiser for it. They proved their motto was true: "Once a Bear Ace, always a Bear Ace."

Sprinkles of sunshine will come, but you can miss them if you aren't looking. Expect them, remember them, and they'll give you the grace to get through.

> *Promise:*
> *"Then Jesus said, 'Come to me, all of you who are weary and carry heavy burdens, and I will give you rest. Take my yoke upon you. Let me teach you, because I am humble and gentle at heart, and you will find rest for your souls. For my yoke is easy to bear, and the burden I give you is light.'"*
> *Matthew 11:28-30*

Decisions

When you get past all the triggers, dead books, pound-cake people, loss, hard questions, and more, you still must handle the everyday practical things of life and work through the nitty-gritty details and decisions after losing someone you love. As a navy wife, having to make decisions in Jon's absence wasn't a new experience, but now that he was dead, *every* decision had to be made alone. My guiding principle in decisions, big or small, was *What would Jon do? What would make him proud?*

I knew the adage about not making any major decisions for the first year after losing your spouse, but there was still a myriad of decisions that couldn't wait. Once I'd worked through the initial financial and living issues, I was thankful for men in my Sunday School class who helped me sell our two vehicles and purchase one car that was more appropriate for a single mother with two daughters.

Some decisions were small, yet important. I bought a new comforter set for my bed to give me a fresh start now that Jon would never share that intimate space with me again. Curtains were hung, which was one of the items in our new home that we hadn't finished. My widow friend, Olga, gave me the idea to buy a glass curio cabinet in Jon's memory to display his navy medals, cover, white gloves, NFO wings, and more. I took her advice, and the girls and I would lovingly look at this beautiful memorial in our home.

For me, what to do with Jon's clothes was one of those practical things. I didn't rush to clear his closet, and I often took comfort from his racks of clothing. But once I was past the denial and accepted that Jon was never returning, I was ready to part with his clothing. I put on my navy widow hat, took the grief box off the shelf, and did what had to be done. I was on a mission. How could I distribute Jon's items to bless others?

I enlisted a trusted friend to walk beside me in the process. Jon's khaki uniforms went to a navy chief whose house had burned down in a fire. His casual clothes went to his nephews. Dress clothes and his hand-made silk suits from Hong Kong went to our Sunday School teacher. Through the sorting process, I was stoic and methodical. For once, I didn't break down.

Firsts

There are many firsts in that initial year of grieving: first anniversary, first birthdays, first time to church alone, first Christmas, and on and on it goes. You can't avoid all the firsts; somehow you must get through them.

The first Father's Day was difficult, but I was determined to honor Jon and find a way for my girls to show love to their daddy. I decided to try an idea that a friend shared with me—attaching handwritten messages for a departed loved one onto helium balloons then releasing them to float up to heaven.

Jordyn drew a picture for Jon, and I wrote down what she wanted to say to her daddy. Taylor was almost one, so I wrote a note from her and one from me. Since Daddy was buried in the ocean, my girls and I went down to the beach to launch our balloons. We said a simple Father's Day prayer: "Dear Jesus, please tell Daddy Happy Father's Day and we love him. And Jesus, please take care of him in heaven. Amen." Tears filled my eyes as Jordyn jumped up and down and we waved goodbye to our heaven-bound love notes. I kept thinking: *Does Jon see us? Does he know his little girls are sending him their love? Is he receiving our messages?*

That first summer after Jon's death, Jordyn swam for the first time, and in the fall, Taylor took her first steps. Many of these events were bittersweet, but these firsts were my sprinkles of sunshine all the same.

When Jordyn's fourth birthday rolled around, I didn't want her to remember Daddy's broken promise that he would be home by her birthday. I overcompensated in a big way by ordering multiple large inflatables, booking a puppet show, and inviting every child we knew. I succeeded in creating a grand extravaganza that the kids would never forget, but no amount of games or parties could ever erase our loss.

The first Christmas was tough. I missed Jon's and my Rystrom tradition of decorating our tree together. Friends from church came over and put up the tree, and I didn't mind because I wanted Jordyn and Taylor to have a proper Christmas. However, as soon as presents were opened Christmas morning, I took the tree down and put the decorations away. The sight of it all and the associated memories were too painful to bear.

As difficult as it was to get through that year of firsts, I found that the second year was even more difficult. When the second wedding anniversary or Christmas comes, you realize it will be this way forever; your loved one is not coming home. Many of those friends who helped pull you through the first year have returned to their own normal lives in the second year, and you are left to face the emptiness alone.

Although I missed Jon terribly, I'm glad I didn't stop celebrating and remembering life's precious moments. Jon would want me to be happy, and my girls didn't need to miss out on the joy of special days. Make plans to not be alone and find ways to remember sweet memories of the past while making new ones for your future.

Wids

Thankfully, I wasn't alone on my grief journey. My sweet friends and sister widows from Bear Ace 603 grew into a much larger group of military widows living in our area. Years before Jon's mishap, several navy widows formed a support group called the *Wids*. It had become inactive over time, but after the tragedy of Bear Ace 603 hit the news, a lady from the original group contacted several of us and urged us to restart the group. She was certain that we weren't the only widows out there, and she was right.

That summer, as word spread, widows came out of the woodwork. Soon there were almost twenty women interested. I was saddened to see so many women like me, young widows with children. We'd meet in someone's home, keeping our time together informal and laid back. We'd share our struggles and our questions.

In this group, you could be gritty and honest. You could say, "I wonder if the fish have started eating my husband's body yet" or "I wonder if my husband screamed as he burned to death." We would also discuss practical things such as when and how to go through our husband's clothes or how to deal with the navy bureaucracy. We understood one another in ways that no one else could because we shared such similar stories. Eleven of the widows were there as a result of navy mishaps.

Lt. Cmdr. Fred Dillingham's wife came to one of our first meetings. When she said her husband's name, I gasped in shock. I remembered from Jon's letters that he had attended her husband's memorial service on USS *Theodore Roosevelt* only days before his own death.

We didn't limit our group to only navy or military widows. When a news report shared the story of a local man lost at sea in a tragic boating accident, I invited his wife to come. When a commercial jet crashed in Pittsburgh and it was reported that a local man had lost his wife (a flight attendant) in the accident, he accepted the invitation to join our group. Regardless of how our spouses died, we helped one another on significant days. We even had a Santa party for our kids at Christmas.

Later, I contacted another navy widow to come and talk to us. Her name was Jane Smith Wolcott. Her late husband was Michael Smith, the pilot of the doomed space shuttle *Challenger*. The loss of *Challenger* and her crew years earlier had shocked the nation as her explosion was broadcast around the world only seconds after liftoff.

NASA had such an outstanding safety record that successful launches and recoveries were taken for granted. Everyone was stunned that something like this could happen, and I could only imagine the pain and suffering the families of the seven astronauts were experiencing—especially when their grief was on public display.

I never dreamed I would meet the wife of the pilot and certainly not under such difficult circumstances. There were many tears shed as Jane openly shared her journey through grief. Her smile and reassuring words, however, gave us hope that we would find joy again. One day our paths would cross again.

Wids didn't only meet in homes and mourn together; sometimes we would go out and have fun. I remember one time when we all went to see the movie *Sleepless in Seattle*, in which Tom Hanks plays a widower who is struggling to open his heart to love again. What was intended to be a fun night of entertainment resulted in a cryfest—a row of sorrowful, hurting widows. We were connected through tragedy, and ours was a precious, unbreakable bond.

The counseling we received from one another was never scripted or in any way academic; it was merely encouraging, heartfelt words from one another that spurred us on to continue living life. Over time, we would celebrate whenever one of us found love again. Without exception, we could always count on a group of Wids being at our weddings.

At least a year after the mishap, the original Wids of Bear Ace 603 went to the Bahamas to celebrate making it through our first year. On that trip, I dusted off my scuba diving skills and, leaving my non-diving widow friends behind, enjoyed some time exploring underwater. I had chosen a group dive to a sunken ship. However, unbeknownst to me, our boat was being diverted to an alternate site. When the dive master told us we'd be seeing a downed plane instead, I went numb. Even on vacation, I couldn't escape triggers.

I knew that my random dive buddy wouldn't want to hear my sob story, and I determined that I wouldn't have a meltdown thirty feet underwater. As we swam toward the small, private plane, I got an eerie picture of what it was like for Bear Ace 603. The magnitude of that moment was even more powerful than what I had experienced at the navy memorial service.

Hundreds of people had viewed the missing-man formation that day, but this moment was custom designed for me alone. When I returned from my dive, I shared with the other widows what I had seen and how God had orchestrated that unique moment to help me heal and gain some much-needed closure.

Bear Ace 603 "Wids." L to R: Katie Forwalder, Kris Rystrom, Shelly Messier, and Paola Dyer, the Bahamas, 1994

I don't know how I would have made it without the support the Wids provided. Today, there are many support groups and wonderful counselors who provide effective therapy to assist the grief-stricken in working through loss. Finding what fits your situation is worth the effort and will be a tremendous blessing on your road to healing.

Moving On

These topics cover many of my experiences as a new widow, but my grief journey was by no means over. My path was still foggy and filled with sorrow and pain, and sometimes I felt that for every step forward, I took two steps back, but in the middle of the journey, you rarely can see your true progress of discerning divine guidance. In moments when I felt abandoned and alone, Someone was carrying me on the road to healing. That's what I had to trust as I continued moving on.

28

Hello, Mr. President

While I had to accept the fact that I would never have concrete answers to the circumstances surrounding Jon's death, there were deeper spiritual questions I had to settle if I ever hoped to heal. My pastor, Dr. Reccord, was aware of my struggle and called me one day to see how I was doing. He told me he'd recently read a new book entitled *When God Doesn't Make Sense*. The author, Dr. James Dobson, a well-known Christian psychologist, had lost several close friends in a tragic plane crash, and the book explained how to hold onto faith during the difficult trials of life. Dr. Reccord thought it would be a significant book for me to read.

My stack of dead books looked overwhelming to me, but I trusted Dr. Reccord and took his advice. Hesitantly, I went to our local Christian bookstore and picked up a copy, the first dreaded dead book I had bought for myself. As I read through the pages, a light bulb switched on inside. Though I had sat in church and done Bible studies for years, I'd never had such a clear explanation of our fallen world and God's role in it.

Dr. Dobson explained that God did not cause the suffering in our world: the wars, disasters, crimes, accidents, diseases, and heartaches. He created the world without fault, but when man gave in to Satan's temptation, sin came into the world as a result. The world is evil, not God. Man has a free will, and God does not stop people from sinning, nor does He stop every consequence of living in a fallen world.

He explained that "most of us seem to be protected for a time by an imaginary membrane that shields us from horror," most often when we are young and life is easy, but "without warning, the membrane tears and horror seeps into a person's life," creating a crisis of faith if the person isn't rescued. This results in "anger and a sense of abandonment" and eventually estrangement from God for those who cut themselves off from Him.

Dobson went on to say, "Pain and suffering do not cause the greatest damage. Confusion is the factor that shreds one's faith." I was certainly confused by Jon's death, and I didn't know how to handle the life-shaking questions it caused. Dobson wrote that while sometimes God does miracles for us, other times, "when nothing makes sense, when what we are going through is 'not fair,' when we feel all alone in God's waiting room—He simply says, 'Trust Me!'"

> *Promise:*
> *"Therefore, we who have fled to him for refuge can have great confidence as we hold to the hope that lies before us. This hope is a strong and trustworthy anchor for our souls. It leads us through the curtain into God's inner sanctuary."*
> *Hebrews 6:18-19*

He also shared that often, "too much confidence is placed in what people feel and too little on the promises of God." I began to take Dr. Dobson's advice:

> In your hour of crisis, don't demand explanation. Don't lean on your ability to understand. Don't turn loose of your faith. But do choose to trust Him ... The only other alternative is despair.

Choosing to trust is possible because of what God chose to do: He sent his perfect Son to die in our place so that we could live forever. God can make all things work together for our good. Not that He causes the hard things to happen to teach us a lesson, but He transforms our pain and sorrows if we turn to Him. Because of Jesus, death has no sting. He never leaves us or forsakes us. He is a father to the fatherless and a husband to the widow.

I had a choice. I could harden my heart to God and blame Him for Jon's death, or I could run to Him, hand Him my pain, and receive His comfort and healing. My heartache could be used for His glory. And as heartbreaking as my grief was, I knew that Dr. Dobson's observation was true: "Nothing is equal to the agony of a shattered faith." Opening my heart to God was not easy to do; it was a process that took time, but thanks in part to Dr. Dobson's book, my healing process turned a corner.

God Nudge

The one-year mark of Jon's death was approaching, but one significant first remained: Valentine's Day. Being the day on which Jon proposed to me, the holiday was packed with triggers, so my therapist made sure to schedule an appointment for me on February 14. When the girls woke up that morning though, Jordyn had a fever. She couldn't go to the babysitter now.

Later that morning, Taylor, who was now an active toddler, discovered a way to crawl up the steps, find a bottle of my red fingernail polish, and drop it from upstairs to the tile floor below. The bottle shattered and red polish went everywhere, even onto the nearby carpet. I broke down, hysterical as I attempted to clean up the mess.

Taylor was simply being a toddler, so I couldn't be angry with her, but my grief was always hiding under the surface waiting to be triggered. Like the broken bottle of nail polish, my hope was shattered. I was still on my hands and knees trying to wipe up the remaining nail polish when the phone rang. A church friend was calling.

"Hey, Kris, I just dropped off my kids at school. Could I come by and make some Valentine's Day cupcakes with Jordyn and Taylor?" Words cannot describe what a tremendous blessing it was to have my friend come to my rescue without me even having to ask. This sprinkle of sunshine arrived at the perfect time, and I was able to see my therapist as planned on that difficult day.

If a person in need comes to your thoughts, that may be a God nudge. Don't dismiss those nudges. Someone needs a sprinkle of sunshine, and that sprinkle could be you!

Please Hold

This was the first time since I left home at 17 to attend Wake Forest that my parents were a part of my daily life, and their comforting presence was a blessing. In early 1994, Mom had read an article in the local newspaper about former President George H. W. Bush giving a speech in Norfolk in a few weeks.

In the fall when I'd sent him a copy of the WAVY-TV piece, he'd sent back a lovely note of thanks. Since we had established a sweet pen-pal relationship, I felt the urge to invite him to my home to meet me and the other military widows in our area. I knew that we widows held a valued place in the heart of this former President and naval aviator. What did I have to lose?

I didn't receive a response, which was not a surprise, but I wanted to hear his speech and see him in person. For the occasion, I decided to wear a custom-made suit from my Hong Kong trip with Jon. I proudly displayed my Gold Star widow pin and Jon's gold navy wings on the lapel. Not long before I left for the drive into Norfolk, the phone rang, and a man's voice that I didn't recognize was on the other end.

"May I speak to Mrs. Rystrom, please?"

"This is she," I replied, having no clue what this was about.

"Please hold for President George Bush," he responded, and I was shocked beyond words. My mother was nearby, and she saw the surprised expression on my face. I whispered to her that President Bush was calling me, and we were both floored. My heart was racing when only moments later the president's familiar voice came over the phone.

"Kris, this is George Bush."

"Hello, Mr. President." I didn't know what else to say.

"I wanted you to know that I got your sweet invitation, and if I had fifteen more minutes in my schedule, I would be sitting in your kitchen having a cup of coffee with you."

"I understand completely. I'm looking forward to hearing you speak tonight." At least, I had calmed down enough to carry on a conversation.

"You're coming?" he asked, sounding pleased.

"I wouldn't miss it." I paused and worked up the courage to ask him, "Would there be an opportunity tonight that I may get a chance to meet you?"

"Absolutely," he quickly replied. "Find a Secret Service man, tell him your information, and he'll direct you to where I am before I speak."

I expressed my thanks, and we exchanged goodbyes. I hung up the phone and looked at my beaming mother and said, "I'm going to meet the president!"

Jon, Can You See This?

As I drove to Chrysler Hall, I was excited and proud. Jon had given his life for the freedom of our country and was a hero in the eyes of President Bush, who cared enough for me to honor us both. I walked into the hall with my head held high.

I followed the president's instructions and found a Secret Service agent in the auditorium and asked to see the president. He confirmed my information and asked, "Does the president know you're coming?"

"Yes," I proudly answered. "He called me at home about an hour ago."

The agent led me through a sea of people and behind the stage to the green room where the president was waiting before he faced the crowd. When I entered the room, I saw him dressed in a tuxedo, standing with his back to me. I was struck by how tall he was.

As I walked up to him, he turned to face me, and I held out my hand. "Mr. President, I'm Kris Rystrom," I explained.

Instead of simply shaking my hand, he took it and pulled me into a warm embrace. He kissed me lightly on the cheek and looked me in the eye with a gentle smile on his face. "How are you and your girls doing?" he inquired.

I was touched by his genuine concern.

"We are doing well," I replied with a smile. "We are making it."

"I would like to introduce you to the people here," he said and turned to the other dignitaries in the room, including former high-ranking officials from the navy. Even at the highest levels, navy guys were still brothers.

We were all chatting when another lady walked into the room. I recognized her immediately. It was Jane Smith Wolcott, the *Challenger* pilot's wife, who had spoken at our Wids group.

"Hello, Jane," said President Bush warmly and greeted Jane with a hug.

"Hello, Kris," Jane said to me, as we greeted one another.

"You two know each other?" the president asked, surprised.

"Yes, Mr. President," Jane responded with a smile. "We navy families stick together."

Jane didn't say "we navy widows" but "we navy families." To the navy bureaucracy, I was officially a URW (an un-remarried widow), but to this band of brothers and sisters, I still belonged in the navy family. I was honored by the entire experience. As I sat in the audience later and heard the president's powerful speech, I was starstruck. I thought to myself, *Jon, can you see this? Can you believe I met the president? Do you know that he appreciates your sacrifice?*

Not long after meeting President Bush, the girls and I traveled to Nebraska to visit Jon's family on the first-year anniversary of his death. As usual, Jordyn and Taylor loved playing with their cousins, and I was thankful to have such wonderful in-laws in my life. With my year of *firsts* behind me, I wasn't excited about facing my year of *seconds*.

GEORGE BUSH

November 26, 1993

Dear Kris,

Your good letter and the videotape were waiting for me when I returned to the office today following two weeks abroad. I leave again Sunday for four days in London, but soon, when my schedule is less hectic, I will view the tape. I'm looking forward to seeing it and appreciate very much your sending it along.

I hope everything is going well for you and your beautiful family. Barbara and I send you our warm wishes for a joyous holiday season.

Sincerely,

Mrs. Krista K. Rystrom
724 Seagrass Reach
Chesapeake, Virginia 23320

A personal letter from President George Bush, November 1993

Kris with Jordyn and Taylor, Chesapeake, VA, 1993.

29

Balloons to Heaven

Spring was turning into summer, and that meant our second Father's Day without Jon was approaching. I was over it: all the grieving, the crying, and trying to keep special days special, but I knew the girls needed to continue the tradition of launching balloons to Daddy in heaven. Therapy and antidepressants were helping, but I was tired and drained and needed to keep things simple. There was no way I would allow myself to be triggered by taking Jordyn and Taylor to the beach again that year. I decided to do the launch in our front yard instead.

When the girls and I went to buy our Father's Day balloons, we picked out three shiny Mylar ones. One was round, and said, "You're the Best." The other two were heart-shaped. One said, "Thinking of You," and the other one said, "You're So Special!" and had flowers and butterflies on it. As the gal behind the counter filled the balloons with helium, she looked at my girls and grinned.

"Someone is going to be surprised," she said in a cheerful voice. I didn't want to ruin this kind lady's day by telling her where the balloons were really going. My unusual story seemed to suck the breath out of any innocent bystander who heard it. Jordyn looked up at me and I winked back. Even at age four, Jordyn knew that not everyone wanted to hear about how her daddy was dead at the bottom of the ocean, so we politely nodded.

When we got home, we drew pictures, wrote love notes, and attached them to the three balloons. Camera in hand, we stepped out into the front yard.

Taylor and Jordyn, Father's Day 1994
Jon planted the rose bushes in the background.

That Sunday was sunny with a bit of a breeze. We said our Father's Day prayer: "Dear Jesus, please tell Daddy 'Happy Father's Day' and we love him. And Jesus, please take care of him in heaven. Amen." We released the balloons to float up to the sky. The girls were so busy jumping up and down and waving to heaven that they didn't notice when one of the balloons went off course and ducked out of sight behind the house. The other two soared higher and higher, getting smaller and smaller, until they disappeared completely from view.

Where was the other balloon? I did a quick search and looked up to see the errant balloon caught in the top of one of the tall pine trees in our back yard. I was frustrated, but if the girls didn't notice, it wouldn't matter. I figured there was no need to worry. A helium balloon should work itself free and float away, especially if the breeze picked up.

On Monday, I got up early, as usual, threw on a pair of jeans and a t-shirt, and prepared to start another exhausting week in the life of a navy widow. While I was brushing my teeth at my bathroom sink, something caught my eye out the large window over the Jacuzzi tub. I hadn't realized the day before that my cry room window perfectly framed the view of the trapped balloon, its silver Mylar surface reflecting the morning sun and the ribbon string with notes attached gently swaying in the breeze. I couldn't have positioned it better if I'd tried.

My heart sank. The balloon hadn't worked itself free as I'd hoped. What if the girls saw this? They would be so disappointed that Daddy didn't get all his messages of love. Thankfully, they rarely came into my bathroom. The balloon was far enough away that I couldn't tell which of the three balloons it was. It was caught in branches so high—higher than our two-story house—that there was no way I could bring it down. The only choice I had was to hope the girls wouldn't see it. If they did, I'd have to come up with a creative explanation so they wouldn't cry.

Tuesday came, and the balloon was still stuck. Wednesday came. Then Thursday. Friday. Saturday. Still stuck. Every time I looked out my bathroom window, it was there. Every time I backed out of our driveway, I could see it "mocking me" from the top of the pine tree, barely visible over the peak of our roof. Another week went by. The balloon remained. Summer thunderstorms blew through our neighborhood, but the balloon hung on. A month went by and the shape looked more deflated, but the shiny surface glimmered in the sun.

I had avoided doing the Father's Day launch at the beach to sidestep getting triggered by the ocean. Now I had a disturbing and daily reminder of Jon's death in the form of an entangled balloon residing outside my cry room window. My only consolation was that the girls couldn't see the misplaced balloon from their wooden playset in the yard below.

Facing Faux Pas

Not long after that, I was thrilled to see a moving van down the street with two pink bikes in the front yard. Immediately, I thought, *Playmates for my daughters*! The next day, we walked over to welcome our new neighbors. The sweet woman who answered the door and invited us in had two little daughters of her own.

As the girls went off together to play, I gave my friend an overview of our neighborhood, telling her about the retired couple who shared their pool and the pediatrician who lived down the street. She leaned in close to me, lowered her voice to a whisper, and said, "I heard that there is a young widow who lives here who lost her husband in a plane accident."

Without missing a beat, I leaned in and whispered, "Yes, that's me."

A look of horror came across her face. "Oh no! I'm so sorry!"

"It's okay." I laughed. "I'm used to it." I felt bad for her, but this little faux pas didn't keep us from becoming the best of friends. While I was finally acknowledging my widow identity, I didn't look the part to most people I met.

I wasn't the only one who had to face surprising comments. One day I overheard Jordyn as she dealt with a more difficult comment. She had a new little friend over, and the two of them were making cookies. While I was busy stirring the cookie dough at the counter, the girls were behind me sitting at our kitchen island and sorting through our collection of sprinkles.

"So your daddy died?" the friend asked innocently.

"Yes, he sure did," Jordyn replied without hesitation.

This wasn't the kind of little-girl talk I was used to hearing. I found myself stirring the dough a little faster, nervous about where this conversation could be headed.

"Did he get eaten by a shark?"

My heart froze as my grip on the spoon tightened, and I vigorously stirred the dough in anger. What was this kid thinking? How dare she ask such a heartless question! How would Jordyn handle this? Should I step in to protect her? As much as I wanted to turn around and strangle that insensitive child, this was an opportunity to hear Jordyn's reaction.

"No," Jordyn said matter-of-factly, "'cause my daddy is down deep, deep, deep, where the sharks don't go."

I was proud of Jordyn's confident response, but it pained me to know that this was how my daughter would live out the rest of her life. Her little friend wasn't trying to be mean; she was asking an honest, childlike question. Friends at church were sensitive to Jordyn's situation, but she would have to face hard questions on her own as she got older.

Still Stuck

As summer progressed, I was thankful that my parents were around to support and encourage us, but I knew their heart was to retire to their beach house in North Carolina. As much as I valued their companionship, I didn't want them to feel obligated to delay their retirement indefinitely. I began to entertain the idea of selling our dream home and moving on.

In the meantime, I was trying to move on emotionally, but one thing made that difficult to do: that infernal balloon. For weeks now, it had hung there tangled in the pines. As I tried to go about my daily routine, the balloon peeked at me when I pulled out of the driveway and mocked me whenever I entered my bathroom. While I was well into my second year of widowhood, my cry room was still a quiet place to release deep grief and offer desperate prayers. Jon's closet was mostly empty, but I still clung as stubbornly to his old brown bathrobe as that deflated balloon clung to the pine tree's branches.

August came and the balloon remained. September arrived. The balloon hung on. Jordyn started preschool, but I struggled to return to regular life. On the surface, my normal appearance fooled most people around me, but inside, I was aimless and drifting and lonely.

Remember Your Legacy

My church offered me a part-time position as a communications director, and I jumped at the chance to get out of the house and earn some extra money. Working on the same days that Jordyn was in preschool was the perfect arrangement, and because most of the staff knew my situation, this was a safe, small step into the outside world of employment for me. My coworkers were supportive and understanding, especially if I encountered an unexpected grief slap across the face and had to excuse myself to deal with a possible torrent of tears. Our church had a large staff, but the halls of my church home were a place of comfort.

One day Dr. Reccord asked me to come see him. I was honored that with his busy schedule, he would take time to talk with me.

"How are you doing, Kris?" he asked, with a slight smile on his face.

I nodded. "I'm doing okay."

But we both knew that I wasn't, and he hadn't called me in for a shallow, feel-good conversation. He was genuinely concerned about me.

"Kris, I want you to remember your legacy." He looked at me with kind eyes, but his words were firm and to the point.

Perhaps my internal struggle was more obvious to others than I'd thought, at least to those with the wisdom to discern it.

His wise words reverberated in my heart. My dreams had died when Jon's plane went down: to have a career, to earn my PhD, to travel and experience the world, and much more. I had always been a high achiever, and now my greatest accomplishment was taking out the trash on time. There was nothing wrong with being a mom to my daughters, but my life was stuck in a rut and heading nowhere fast. My greatest barrier was that I was still shackled to my grief.

Picture Imperfect

When I picked up Jordyn from preschool later, my grief seized the opportunity to kick me down the stairs and slap me in the face in front of all the other parents. In that day's class, the children had drawn pictures of their families, and the teacher was handing out the artwork to the parents waiting in the hallway.

I looked forward to seeing what Jordyn had drawn, but when the teacher handed me her picture, I felt like a knife stabbed my heart. She had drawn me, Taylor, herself, and Max. But not Jon. Tears poured down my face, and the teacher gave me a box of tissues while she finished handing out the rest of the pictures.

Few of the other parents knew who I was, and between my uncontrollable sobs, I attempted to explain the situation to them. How embarrassing. It wasn't Jordyn's fault though. What she drew was accurate and real; I was the one refusing to accept our new reality.

When we got home from school and I went upstairs, the sight of the deflated balloon did me in. How much more could I take? I was trying to move on, but much like the spiraling branches that kept that balloon tangled in the tall pines, the constant triggers I continued to encounter kept me tangled in grief.

A chill filled the air as fall turned into winter. As leaves fell from the trees and color fled the landscape, the despised balloon stood out even more. Now, months after its capture in the pines, its Mylar material was wrinkled and shriveled, and the ribbon string with its notes of love was reduced to shreds. Storm after storm had blown through the tall trees, yet the balloon stuck like a leech.   I began battling with God every time I saw the cursed reminder through my bathroom window.

"God, I'm trying to move on. Why are You reminding me that I have a dead husband? You allowed this stupid balloon to get stuck in this tree. I get it. I'm not in control. But You are. What are You doing to me?"

There was no reply.

The Loneliest Season

The second winter after Jon's death was the loneliest season of my life. The Wids weren't calling one another as they once had. Everyone was moving forward, moving on, or moving away. With my "firsts" behind me, I was facing the "seconds" alone, and I was joining my married friends and their families less often. As much as I loved Jordyn and Taylor, they couldn't fill the gaping holes in my heart. My depression deepened as the gray, dreary days grew shorter, and the damp, frigid air grew nearer. Winter and grief came hand in hand and loomed over my house like a dark cloud.

Somehow, I managed to hang on through Thanksgiving and Christmas. So did the balloon. New Year 1995 came, and something had to give. I couldn't face another year of grief in this house. My soul was empty and raw, and the constant view of the horrid balloon was like pouring salt in the wound. I cried out to God, "You put this wretched balloon in the tree. Can't You take it away?"

One day soon after, I was backing out of the driveway with the girls to run some errands. I glanced up at our house and suddenly realized something: The balloon was gone. I put my foot on the brake and strained my eyes to make sure, but there was no mistaking it—the stubborn balloon had blown away.

For the first time in ages, a spark of joy entered my heart. I smiled as I backed up and turned onto Seagrass Reach. Finally, after nearly seven months of torture, the cursed balloon was out of my life forever! I began an internal conversation with God. *So, God, are You saying that I can move on now? You got rid of the dreadful balloon for me? It took You long enough, but thanks. I'm glad the miserable thing is gone!*

I cheerfully turned the corner and continued making my way out of our neighborhood. After stopping at an intersection before heading onto the main highway, a glint of sunlight caught my eye. I instantly glanced up and my heart stood still. There was the cursed balloon stuck high up in yet another tree! I sat there for a moment in disbelief as resentment flooded my soul.

I was glad Jordyn and Taylor couldn't hear my angry dialog with the Creator of the universe: *Really?? Seriously?? You've got to be kidding me! Is this a sick joke? Is the balloon going to start following me around now? Is there anywhere I can go and NOT be reminded that Jon is dead?*

On the next morning's commute, I discovered that overnight it had disappeared for good. Perhaps the balloon from hell had made it to heaven at last. I didn't care where it was if it was far away from me. I sighed with relief, but my mind was made up. The tenacious claw of grief would not let go. All attempts to break free were useless. I couldn't escape its relentless grasp if I lived here. I would put my house on the market, and my parents and I could move on to a new chapter in our lives.

Once the "For Sale" sign was displayed in the yard, the reality of what I was preparing to say goodbye to hit me like a ton of bricks. Over the next few weeks, as winter's grip persisted, the grip of grief was more than I could stand. So many losses: Jon, my lover, my best friend; my girl's father; my status as an officer's wife; my security; my dreams; and now, to top it all off, my precious home Jon and I had built together.

No Response

One cold, rainy night after I put the girls to bed, I entered my cry room, turned off the lights, and succumbed to overwhelming anguish and sorrow. Sobbing uncontrollably, I grabbed Jon's soft, brown bathrobe and his worn leather Bible and clung to them as I dropped to my knees in despair and bowed my head in mourning toward the cold bathroom floor.

I had to stop the unrelenting pain; I couldn't take the torment any longer. The only imaginable way to remove my intense suffering would be the miraculous return of my beloved husband. Heaving with bitter grief, I tearfully screamed out to God, "Bring him home! Bring him home! God, please! Let him come home!" This was my darkest hour. Many hopeless hours had passed since Jon's sudden death, but this one was by far the worst—the rawest and the hardest. My heart had never ached for Jon as much as it did in that wretched moment.

I waited woefully for God's reply. There was no response. I wasn't delusional; I was desperate. Of course, Jon wasn't coming home. And I knew that even when the house was sold and the girls and I had moved away, the crippling grief that clung to me like a cancer would follow me into my new life. There

> *Promise:*
> *"Then call on me*
> *when you are in*
> *trouble, and I will*
> *rescue you, and you*
> *will give me glory."*
> *Psalm 50:15*

was no easy escape. There was no reason to hope. Not if I had to face the dismal future alone. My Jon could not help me, but what about my God? A great, deep sadness settled into my soul, and I screamed out one last time in desperation, "Do You hear me? Do You know I'm here? Please, tell me that You hear me!"

In His Word, God repeatedly says that He loves the widow, and He promises to be a faithful husband to the husbandless. Surely a loving God would swiftly answer my urgent cries. In the gloomy darkness, I anxiously waited on the cold, hard floor expecting and yearning to hear the audible voice of God.

There was no response.

I don't remember how long I lingered there in the pitch blackness. Eventually, with a crushed spirit and an exhausted body, I stumbled to my empty bed, crawled under the chilly covers, and while clutching Jon's Bible and bathrobe, cried myself to sleep.

The morning sun streamed through my bedroom curtains and woke me from my fitful slumber. As my foggy mind gradually cleared, I remembered the agony of the hopeless night before. I sighed in deep disappointment as I realized that even my most desolate cries had brought no response from my Heavenly Father.

The last thing I wanted to do was face another wearisome day, but I had two little girls who needed their mommy. Jon had told me I was their security when he was away. I had to keep my promise to take care of them. I slowly crept out of bed and, with my mommy hat in place, deliberately put one foot in front of the other.

As I prepared cereal for the girls and put on their favorite children's TV show, my mind reflected on how drastically my life had changed. This wasn't how it was supposed to turn out. Instead of the glamorous California days of advertising, high-priced linen suits, and newlywed bliss, life had taken a sudden detour to mournful days of changing diapers and living in dirty t-shirts and jeans.

I noticed the calendar and groaned when it reminded me that today was trash day. *Oh, joy. Time to gather up the trash.* I went into task mode and mindlessly collected all the trash in the house. I passed through the kitchen lugging my large bag of refuse behind me and wearily walked through the door leading to the garage. I shuffled past my vehicle and unlocked and opened the side door as I had countless times before. I took one tiresome step outside into the crisp, morning air and looked down to see something odd lying at my feet.

It was the balloon.

30

My Letter from Heaven

There it was, lying before me—the old, wrinkled, dirty, withered, heart-shaped balloon—on the ground next to the garbage can, right side up, with its faded, yet clearly visible printed message facing me: "You're So Special!" I couldn't breathe. Not for a few moments at least. I silently stood there in the early dawn, in the stillness of the damp morning—the trees dripping with rain from the night before—and I stared in disbelief at the tattered balloon resting at my feet.

"You're So Special!"

How could this be? My baffled mind tried to process what my eyes were plainly seeing. Where did it come from? How did the balloon get inside the little privacy fence around my garbage can? And how did it land right side up, facing the side door, as if someone had precisely placed it there on purpose?

Wasn't this the same balloon my girls and I had purchased more than seven months earlier? Wasn't this the same balloon that was released with two others but went in a completely different direction? Wasn't this the same balloon that got tangled in the pine trees outside my cry room window? The same balloon that mocked me for months on end, piercing my heart with the daily reminder that my Jon was dead? Wasn't this the same balloon that blew a half a mile away, landed in another tall tree, subsequently disappeared for weeks, and then, on this particular morning, greeted me at my garbage can after a fierce night of wrestling with God, crying out in despair, and fervently asking

Him, "Do You hear me? Do You know I'm here? Please, tell me that You hear me!"

He responded. His answer was lying at my feet: "You're So Special!"

I dropped the bag filled with trash. I dropped my bag filled with grief. I instantly raised my hands toward the morning sky and lifted my head toward the heavens. Tears filled my eyes, but this time they were tears of joy. Light and peace and love saturated my broken heart as the oppressive weight of grief and my thick, gray cloak of despair dissolved in the glorious presence of my precious Savior.

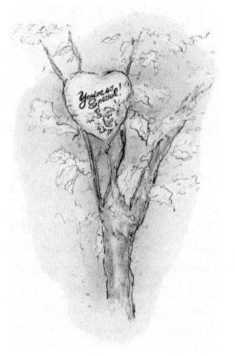

"Thank you for hearing me, Jesus! Thank you for answering my cries!" I exclaimed as tears of rapture streamed down my beaming face.

He heard me! I was special!

What was meant to help two little girls show love to their daddy in heaven was used by God to show His infinite love to His cherished daughter on Seagrass Reach. He allowed the heart-shaped Mylar balloon to be stuck in a pine tree outside my cry room window through June, July, August, September, October, November, and December. In January, He took the balloon on a journey, and where He had kept it during the weeks it vanished, only heaven knew. But one day, in His perfect timing, He did a reverse balloon launch and sent a life-changing message of love to me.

Stripes at my front door had ushered a torrent of grief into my life, but a Man with stripes on His back came to my side door and released a flood of hope into my grieving heart. He didn't meet me at a magnificent palace, on a majestic mountain top, or even in a soaring cathedral. He met me in a grimy, mundane, nitty-gritty moment with an everyday, ordinary object.

Just as I Am

Many of us are like that old balloon. We start off shiny and new, boldly proclaiming an uplifting message of promise, but inside we're puffed up with air. All is well until an unforeseen gust of wind blows us off course, and we find ourselves hopelessly tangled in the branches of our own bad choices, the hurtful actions of others, or the unavoidable sufferings of life. We're stuck in our past, paralyzed in our present, and unable to move on. The air slowly leaks out of us, leaving us deflated and empty. We think we're set free only to be entangled anew in another trap of our own making.

One day our Savior encounters us when we're tattered and wrinkled and worn, and He carries us gently in His nail-scarred hands. He lovingly transforms us into a new creation, freely breathes His eternal life into our spirits, and we rise again, victorious, to live out our true, God-given destiny, empowered by His measureless love.

For years, I searched for significance in what I could achieve in my own strength. My hunger for control resulted in an eating disorder that I battled for years. I hid my true needs from the people around me and even from myself. My relationship with God was all about following a religion and checking off the boxes, and while I believed in God to save me from my sin, I didn't know Him as a friend. In truth, Jesus had been with me all along, but in my brokenness, I didn't recognize His presence. After He met me at the garbage can, my eyes were opened, and my relationship with Him grew into an intimate friendship that filled my life with a new sense of hope, joy, and peace.

Jesus doesn't expect us to have perfect lives. We don't have to exaggerate our accomplishments, pump up our abilities, or reach the highest rungs on our ladders of success. We don't have to cover up our faults or hide our weaknesses. Whether we are struggling with addictions, crippled by fear, incapacitated by grief, overcome with remorse, enslaved to sin, or mastered by insecurities, Jesus wants us to come to Him as we are— dirty, wrinkled, raw, and real. That's the only way He can begin to heal us.

> *Promise:*
> *"And we know that God causes everything to work together for those who love God and are called according to his purpose for them."*
> *Romans 8:28*

That was the way He began to heal me. Something precious was lost from my life, and I searched diligently until I found it again. The whole time, God was searching for me, desiring not only to regain our relationship but also transform it into one of tender intimacy, abiding love, and lasting joy. For me, that was at a garbage can, and I was forever changed.

Often, amid our suffering, we expect Jesus to come charging through the front door to rescue us from our crisis, and there are times when He will. In other seasons, He will come in a way that we least expect, quietly and gently slipping through the side door to meet us at the point of our greatest need.

Fingerprints of God

I would be a liar if I told you that my life was all rainbows and butterflies from that moment on. I still had to take out the trash. I still had to clean up after my girls. I still had to sleep in an empty bed and face the future without my beloved Jon. Some nights I cried. Some days I was triggered. And many of the questions that had troubled my heart were never fully answered.

But now I had Him, and He had me. I could trust Him with the unknowns, I could trust Him with my future, and I could trust Him with my heart. To make me whole, I didn't need another man to love me and take Jon's place. Jesus was the lover of my soul. I was finally complete, more complete than I was when Jon was alive. It was me, the girls, and Jesus—all that I needed to make it through.

Looking over my life with Jon, I can see the fingerprints of God from the beginning: how He guided our paths and brought us together, how He freed me from my eating disorder and healed Jon of his broken heart and restored his faith, how God transformed both of us, how He taught us about true significance, and how He blessed us with two amazing daughters. Jon's last letter to me demonstrated the depths of that transformation when he said:

> I realize I need to eliminate "I" and put my faith and trust in God. It is hard sometimes, but God will take care of me ... I realize how insignificant making O-5 really is ... I thank God for the great life He has given me.

What a contrast from the lonely, drifting man I met on a blind date in Virginia Beach!

Thinking of letters, I cherish the treasure contained in the letters Jon and I wrote to each other. How thankful I am that I kept them all these years through multiple moves. Their powerful words still minister to me today, and by changing the words ever so slightly, the messages of love from Jon now reflect the relationship that I enjoy with my Savior. These are Jesus' messages of love to us all. Can you imagine the Savior writing these words to you?

First off, I love you!

I never want to lose you. My child, never forget how important you are to Me.

When you told Me how you felt, My heart wept when you did. I could feel the same emotions that you were feeling.

I am so glad you are finally getting My messages. As you can see, I have been speaking every day. Oh, how I love you.

I have gained so much in our relationship through your prayers. I can feel your pain, your hurt, your joy, your intense desire to please Me. When I hear your prayers, I read between the lines and marvel at what an incredible person you are. My child, from before I made the world, I chose you as my beloved one and you are not a disappointment to Me in the least. My love for you cannot be measured, and you care for Me more and more every day. I love it!!!

You realize that the more you like yourself and believe in the person I've created you to be, the more of you that you can give Me.

Always remember, you never—I repeat never— will be without My love.

Now, can you imagine those same words of love I wrote to Jon being shared with our Savior as though they were written to Him?

What I read in Your Word today are the warmest, most love-filled words that You have ever given to me. I will cherish them for the rest of my life. Thank you, Jesus, for loving me; that has made my life fulfilled because You have made my life complete! You are my world, and I will do anything for You, always and forever.

I love you, Jesus, more than I could ever express. I think about You constantly. I give You the best that I could ever give. No conditions, no demands, no expectations ... just me, with all my faults and flaws, the entire package ... And it is all Yours forever.

I thought of You all day today, knowing that because of You, we can celebrate freedom every day. Thank you for allowing me to have freedom, Jesus. You are so special and honorable to give so much for Your children ....

You changed my life and taught me how to live it. Thank you, Jesus. I will love You for eternity.

You are the only One in this universe that makes me feel alive, special, and loved. I want to go everywhere You go, do everything You do, be everything You are, and never, never be without Your love.

Of course, Jesus has written special words to each of us in His Word, the Bible. On my journey from grief to hope I traded in Jon's letters from the sea for a beautiful letter penned thousands of years ago from our Heavenly Father. Needless attempts were being made to find intimacy with Christ through church activities and the pages of dead books, but it was the Bible, with its letters of truths and promises, that began to heal my bleeding soul. It seems simple and obvious, and it is. God's divine Word is a healing salve for the hurting.

I had memorized Scripture when I was a child. I had opened the Word my whole life for Sunday School and church, but as I worked through my grief, I opened the pages for hope. Perhaps for the first time in my life, my Bible was my lifeline for redemption. There was nothing else. We can fill our lives with busyness and stuff, but for pure healing, the Great Physician has written His prescription within the pages of His Holy Word.

For some of you, this book is your balloon. Having this book in your hands is not a coincidence. He has been speaking to you through its pages, and He is reaching out His nail-scarred hands to inject life into your hopeless situation, to shine His light into your darkened spirit, and to release joy into your afflicted soul. You can stay stuck in the darkness or step out into the light. The choice is yours.

Twenty-five years after Kris received her folded flag.

31

H.O.P.E.

What is hope? As Andy Dufresne says in the movie *Shawshank Redemption*, "Hope is a good thing—maybe the best of things—and no good thing ever dies." As I stumbled through my valley of grief, my one constant, nagging question was how do I find hope again? The Bible says that hope anchors the soul. But how do we have an expectation of good happening in the future when our "anchor" is lost at the bottom of the sea?

I desperately wanted hope—hope for joy again, for a life fulfilled. Hope for answers and for finding purpose. Hope for laughter again. For real laughter—the kind that makes your sides hurt and tears of joy come spilling out. Hope for a happy life for my girls—that this tragedy wouldn't define who they are. Hope that one day my grieving heart would heal. Hope was out there. I didn't know where to find it, but the hope of finding hope gave me a reason to breathe again.

Faith is defined as believing in things unseen (Heb. 11:1). I always had faith that God would take care of Jon when he was flying. I had faith that our perfect life would continue its predictable path. When that path took a shocking detour, faith suddenly became something different—much deeper. Faith was no longer about checking boxes and what *Kris* wanted in life. Faith was now about eternity. Could faith be the vehicle to drive me to finding hope? Despite my questions and anger toward God, I realized that my faith in a loving God was still there. It was a tiny ember, but it was present.

Where do you find hope again after you have experienced a crisis of belief? How do you put one foot in front of the other after tragedy? Perhaps you have not lost a husband in a plane crash but have had other losses. We all lose. There is no way to avoid it in this world. We live in a world that suffers loss—loss of a marriage, loss of a business, loss of a relationship, loss of health, loss of dreams, or even loss of hope—but you can win in the end. God wins in the end, and we can experience the victory He offers to us.

After a loss, many believers choose to run from God in anger and bitterness. I would imagine that in heaven tears are shed when God's children turn their backs on the One who loves them deeply with an everlasting love. No, we don't have answers, and perhaps we'll never know why we suffer in our fallen world, but we have two choices, and the choice is ours to make. Our choices are to live for ourselves in bitterness and despair or choose hope through the One who offers it freely. I chose hope.

After Jon's mishap, I learned to live by four simple truths that gave hope to my hurting soul. My prayer is that these truths will offer you hope as you wrestle with your questions and travel your own path in finding hope after heartache.

HOLD onto God's promises.

OPEN your heart to others.

POSITION yourself for obedience.

EMBRACE the past and face the future.

HOLD onto God's Promises

Promise: God loves you.

God loves every part of you. He knows your pain. You can rest knowing that He gets down in the dark hole of grief and loss along with you. A natural question is, *If God loves me, how could*

He allow such a tragedy to take place in my life? This is a question we may never know the answer to in this life.

I had to remember that God didn't create the Bosnian conflict; man did. God did not create wars; man did. God did not create heartache; man did. Death is a result of the fall of man, but God sent His only Son, Jesus, to die in our place and rise again so that we too can have victory over death. In the battle between life and death, God wins; Satan loses. Satan was defeated at the cross, so why would I let him win the battle he was waging in my life? I am loved by the King of Kings, and I am more than a conqueror through Christ (Rom. 8:37)!

> I have loved you even as the Father has loved me. Remain in my love. When you obey my commandments, you remain in my love, just as I obey my Father's commandments and remain in his love. I have told you these things so that you will be filled with my joy. Yes, your joy will overflow! (John 15:9-11)

> But God is so rich in mercy, and he loved us so much. (Eph. 2:4)

Promise: God will never leave you or forsake you.

God wraps Himself around our hurts so that we can rest in His arms. Scripture tells us that He will never leave us or forsake us. Over and over, His Word tells us that we are to rest in Him. He will not turn His back on His children. Jeremiah 29:11 says He promises to give us a hope and a future. Know that we have our Comforter opening His arms to give us the rest we desperately seek.

> Do not be afraid or discouraged, for the LORD will personally go ahead of you. He will be with you; he will neither fail you nor abandon you. (Deut. 31:8)

> This is my command—be strong and courageous! Do not be afraid or discouraged. For the LORD your God is with you wherever you go. (Josh. 1:9)

In Jon's letters to me from his time at sea, he constantly told me to "be strong; you can do it." Now God speaks those words to me. He is always there for me, promising to take care of me.

Promise: God is your Provider.

God is Jehovah-Jireh (Hebrew meaning "God who Provides"). Worries and stress can overtake us, but God cares about our every need. According to Philippians 4:19:

> … God who takes care of me will supply all your needs from his glorious riches, which have been given to us in Christ Jesus.

Like Operation Provide Promise, which was an allied led mission to provide provisions of food and medicine to the refugees of war-torn Bosnia, our loving Father provides mankind with His provisions of love, mercy, grace, forgiveness, and eternal life through Jesus Christ. Scripture is filled with evidences of God providing for His children. We don't always see His provision immediately. Sometimes we don't know that He has already taken care of our needs; we are unaware of His hand in our lives, but we can rest in knowing that the Creator of the universe cares about our every need. He will provide.

Promise: God is a Father to the fatherless and a Husband to the husbandless.

As I searched God's Word for answers, I discovered a recurring theme: God takes care of widows and orphans. He treats us differently. He treats us with gentle care, and He commands others to do this as well.

Father to the fatherless, defender of widows—this is
God, whose dwelling is holy. (Ps. 68:5)

I believe God's promise to be a protector of widows applies
equally to those who have lost a husband to physical death as
well as to marital death, and in today's world, many children are
left fatherless. Find comfort, my friend, in knowing that your
Heavenly Father is there to be the father to your precious children.

But you see the trouble and grief they cause.
You take note of it and punish them.
The helpless put their trust in you.
You defend the orphans. (Ps. 10:14)

Promise: God carries you through your storm.

In the first days after the crash, my Sunday School teacher and
his wife hid strips of paper with the Scripture reference Isaiah
43:2 all over my house. I had never read that passage. Curiously,
I opened my Bible to see why this Scripture was so important
that this couple felt it necessary to fill my house with it. What I
read has carried me every day for the past twenty-five years and
has become my life verse:

When you go through deep waters,
I will be with you.
When you go through rivers of difficulty,
you will not drown.
When you walk through the fire of oppression, you
will not be burned up. (Isa. 43:2)

Crying was all I could do at that time. The tears were constant, the sobbing exhausting. I spent my days and nights in a
perpetual fog of numbness. Grief is the hardest emotion you will
ever experience. In addition to the verse in Isaiah, I found some

comfort in the sweet scripture of Psalm 56:8. It tells us that God collects our tears in a bottle. When you weep, He sees every tear that you shed. In fact, He weeps with us! I often cried out in my anger, *"How could You, the Almighty, possibly know how this feels or understand this pain?"* Suddenly, I would be reminded that He does know how this feels. He gave up His Son for mankind. He watched His only Son be murdered on a cross. Yes, my Lord does understand your pain. He grieves with you as He holds your weeping soul in His comforting hands.

Promise: God draws near to those who draw near to Him.

One final promise that needs to be emphasized is the subject of prayer. God wants to have a relationship with you, and prayer makes it happen—yes, prayer (having a conversation with God). "Come close to God, and God will come close to you" (Jas. 4:8). I realize you may not want to have anything to do with prayer, but trust me—He can handle your frustrations, your pain, and your needs. He is God, and He made you.

Praying became part of my everyday conversations. I prayed out loud. I prayed in the car. I prayed everywhere I went. These were not eloquent, fancy words. I talked, yelled, cried, and whispered my every thought. If I was going to be friends with Jesus, then we were going to talk—and talk a lot.

OPEN Your Heart to Others

Grief pushes us down into a hole and covers us in loneliness. The temptation is to keep our head in the hole while life passes us by. If you live with the attitude, "Let others live their lives; mine is ruined," you will find yourself falling further into the pit of self-PITy and despair. Let people into your world; others want to help you in your time of need. Pound-cake people will be around only for a season, but the true blues will walk with you every step of the way. They will help you find wholeness and wellness again, and God will use their love to throw you a lifeline. When you least expect it, your cries will be replaced with smiles.

The Bible tells us in 2 Corinthians that we are to help others as we have been helped:

> God is our merciful Father and the source of all comfort. He comforts us in all our troubles so that we can comfort others. When they are troubled, we will be able to give them the same comfort God has given us. (2 Cor. 1:3-4)

Life hurts, and the world is full of hurting people. Opening your heart to them brings an opportunity of healing for you and them, as there is a healing of your soul whenever you minister to others. To listen to them, cry with them, and sit beside them while they cry are all steps to making *you* stronger. When you open your heart to others, you will be a much different person than you were before your loss.

Having suffered greatly, I find that I have more empathy for others who are suffering. While most people feel uncomfortable talking with a friend or family member who has experienced loss, I now have courage enough that I could even sit in a room with a friend while her husband breathes his last breath.

I call my widowed friends my soul sisters. We are the body of Christ, and when there is a hurting part, we come together and help heal the part that needs healing. In the same way the Wids help one another, you can look for people who are hurting and offer help in their storms. God will gently bring blue skies to your cloudy days as you allow Him to use you to be a ray of sunshine in someone's life.

POSITION Yourself for Obedience

Obedience is to hear, trust, submit, and surrender to God and His Word. For me, that included honoring the promises Jon and

I had made to each other and to our daughters. At Jordyn's and Taylor's baby dedication services, we made a covenant with God to raise them under His authority. After Jon's death, I didn't get a pass just because he was no longer around to hold me accountable. My covenant was a promise to God, and I would continue to submit to His authority whether I felt like it or not.

Some days out of anger toward God, I had no desire to step foot in church, read the Bible, or sing any song of worship. The act of worshipping with other believers and being in fellowship with God's people was a step of obedience. Obedience doesn't always feel good, but it isn't about feelings; it is about promises and commitment.

For a single mother of two small children, going to church on a Sunday morning or a Wednesday night was no easy task. It included diapers, bottles, and snacks. It took planning and work; at times it was overwhelming. Sometimes I wanted to keep my sweet little grieving family at home, sleep in, make a big breakfast, go to the beach, watch cartoons all day, and forget that we needed to go to church. That would have been the easy way out.

Now that Jon was gone forever, would I continue to follow the path of obedience? The choice was mine, and I chose to position myself to obey and to submit to authority. I was frail and fragile, but my Savior was strong and able. I rested in knowing that if I submitted to the authority of Jesus, He would lead our family on the path of His choosing.

> We know we love God's children if we love God and obey his commandments. Loving God means keeping his commandments, and his commandments are not burdensome. (1 Jn. 5:2-3)

Being obedient to my God-given role as mother meant being obedient to the nurturing of and provision for our daughters, including even the most boring and mundane tasks. Bills, doctor appointments, car maintenance, and even taking out the trash were some of the ways I was obedient. As we walk in submission to God through our everyday jobs—no matter how insignificant they may seem—He finds joy in blessing us because we are His children.

EMBRACE the Past and Face the Future

To move on, there must be an acceptance of what has been in the past, but while embracing the life you once had, understand that there is a future in front of you. I have always loved the quote from the movie *Shawshank Redemption* when "Red" Redding states, "Get busy living or get busy dying."

I didn't die in that plane, and neither did my girls. What a wasted sacrifice Jon would have made if, when he died providing freedom for us, I chose to throw his sacrifice in his face by giving up on life. No, I chose to live life to the fullest and to search for joy in the living. A golden sunrise, a blooming flower, Max's soft fur, a sappy movie, and the giggles from my girls were freely given to me. Life was good and God was good. Finding the good can be easy with a grateful heart, and I, like Jon, was grateful for the great life God had given me.

We all have a choice to make: what do we do with the bad stuff of life that we've been handed? Striving to find hope in your world of grief does not make you forget the person you have lost. It doesn't mean you have stopped loving that person. I have told my girls that I will always love their daddy, and he will always be my husband, but there is a season for everything. There is a time for mourning and a time for love and life.

Throughout years in ministry, I have met people who stay stuck in their grief and never move past it. They let it define who they are and who they will be for the rest of their lives. They miss that there is a beautiful life in front of them. God has many people and places for you to discover.

God is our Master Weaver, and He is making a beautifully woven life for us. We can't see the threads interweaving or the design He is creating, but He is making something beautiful. We know that in making a woven piece of art, there are knots, tears, and ugly spots on the back. While we traverse our own knots and tears in life, we must trust His hand, as He sees the big picture and is creating His masterpiece in us.

In your future is joy, which is a fruit of the spirit. Though it may seem hard to believe, you will experience joy again. You must be ready to take those first steps into a new future. Start with trying something new: take a class, join a gym, or attend a book club. Consider making small changes. Buying a new comforter set for our bedroom was a small change, but it was a huge accomplishment for me at the time.

As I began making little changes to my surroundings, they became personal to me. These were not decisions that Jon and I had made together; they were decisions I made on my own. It felt good. Making individual decisions led to a sense of accomplishment and independence. I was doing it. I was living without him and doing it well. Yes, friend, life is good, and God is good.

A Lasting Hope

If you have read through the book, thank you. I know my journey through grief was difficult to experience, and perhaps you shed a few tears as you turned through these pages. Many tears were shed by all involved throughout the process of writing this book but reliving those moments and conveying those emotions were vital if we were to provide promise to you.

Lasting hope is available to everyone. I'm not telling you that if you get on your knees tonight and cry out to God for a balloon that you'll find one on your doorstep tomorrow, but I can promise you this: God answers the cry of every seeking heart. You will encounter Him in an extraordinary way that is unique to you. He will meet you where you are—perhaps when you least expect it. God knows how you are knit together, and

He knows exactly what you need and when you need it. He will come.

Isabella, Jon's granddaughter, honors Daddy Jon on the 25th anniversary of his death, Norfolk Naval Base

Conclusion

Life Does Go On

On the twenty-fifth anniversary of the loss of Bear Ace 603, former squadron mates of Jon, Frenchy, Billy Ray, Aardvark, and Bob gathered from across the country to join the widows, survivors, and their families and friends for a memorial remembrance weekend in Norfolk, Virginia. This was the first time since the tragedy that we had come together to honor and remember the fallen crew. We toured aircraft carriers, visited the Bear Ace hangar, observed a remembrance dinner, and held a special memorial service at the David Adams Memorial Chapel at Norfolk Naval Base, the same chapel where the navy honored Bear Ace 603 a quarter-century earlier.

As a representative of the widows, I shared a few words. Standing before the assembled crowd in the same spot where my Jon had been honored many years ago, the significance of this full-circle moment was not lost on me. I could see the aisle that my daughters and I had walked down together and the front row where there hadn't been a seat for us.

I stood on the same stage where my church choir had previously gathered behind a table that once displayed the photographs and navy covers of the lost Bear Ace 603 crew. Outside the chapel door was where I had been slammed with grief when the Hawkeye missing-man formation flew overhead.

On this day, though, crippling grief did not rear its head. For though my heart still ached over the loss of my beloved Jon, I was a far different person at that moment than the mournful widow I was then. As I stepped behind the podium, I looked over the congregation and smiled. These were my friends, my sister Wids, my navy family, and my personal family. I was honored to be in that sacred place and to share words of encouragement for us all:

Twenty-five years ago, there were five families who sat in these rows right here in this chapel, and they received a folded flag. To most Americans, a folded flag stands for honor, service, and sacrifice. For the five families from Bear Ace 603, our folded flags represented love lost, families ripped apart, and dreams and futures completely shattered. My family was one of those families.

So what do you do when your whole life completely crumbles before you? What do you do with your faith? What do you do with your whys: Why us? Why our guys? Why our families? And certainly, why our children?

Anytime you go through any type of devastation, loss, or grief, you can't help but ask those "why" questions, especially if you believe in a God who loves and cares for you. You go through a crisis of belief beyond anything you've ever experienced before.

On Thursday night, March 25, my girls and I began our nightly ritual: Jordyn, Taylor, and I went into the playroom, and we cut the link from our paper chain that we used to count down the days until Daddy got home. And like we did every night that Jon was deployed, my daughter Jordyn prayed. And she said, "Dear God, please protect my Daddy as he flies in his airplane."

So how do you tell a three-year-old the next day that God didn't protect her daddy on the airplane, and she is never going to see her father again? How do you then explain to her that God loves her? God loves me? So how do you explain that to anyone who has gone through crisis, devastation, and loss? Where are those explanations?

Most people who go through a crisis of belief make the choice, out of anger and despair and desperation, to turn their backs on God. But then there are those who decide to look to God for comfort, love, and hope. Because if you turn your back on a God who says He loves us, you have no hope. Hope is gone.

I and the four other families who are in this room chose hope. We chose to look to God. We didn't have answers. To this day, we don't have answers. But we chose to go to our Lord for comfort.

So where are our answers? Our answers are found in four letters that spell *hope*.

And I went on to share my *H.O.P.E* acronym: *Hold* on to God's promises, *Open* your heart to others, *Position* yourself for obedience, and *Embrace* the past and face the future. I concluded my comments by reading Jon's last precious letter to me, ending with his phrase, "So life does go on."

And life did go on. And I did find a new future, as did the other widows of 603. We took one day at a time, and we continued to heal. And we embraced Jesus as we walked through the valleys.

I don't know what kind of flag has been handed to you today. I don't know what kind of grief you may be dealing with. But I ask you to embrace your faith and let Jesus cover your folded flag.

As I stepped down from the podium, I was thankful for that weekend, which was lovingly arranged by the Bear Ace family to help provide healing to the widows and surviving families of 603. But I'd like to think that we helped to provide promise to the former squadron mates of our husbands and brothers. We have healed. The process took time, but we have found joy, hope, life, peace, and purpose again. And that's the promise we held on to.

The families of Bear Ace 603 at the 25th Reunion of the mishap Norfolk, VA, March 26, 2018
L to R: Jordyn, Taylor, and Kris Rystrom Emmert;
Shelly Messier Hill; Paola Dyer McNeil and Christopher Dyer;
Katie Forwalder Riley and Sean Forwalder

Afterword

Over the Bear Ace Remembrance Weekend, my
sweet little granddaughter, Isabella, stole the show during our
naval tours, but her high point had to be the final and most significant tour. We began with a ship that represents the future of
the navy: USS *Gerald R. Ford*, the navy's most technologically advanced aircraft carrier. My granddaughter's inquisitive nature,
high-energy personality, and Rystrom sense of humor continued
to garner smiles the next day when we toured the Bear Ace
hangar and a working E-2C Hawkeye plane.

Bear Ace 25th anniversary reunion on
USS Gerald Ford aircraft carrier, Norfolk, VA

On March 26, 2018, twenty-five years to the day since Bear
Ace 603 was lost, our family and my coauthor and her husband
toured USS *Harry S. Truman*, a Nimitz class carrier—the same

class shared by both USS *Carl Vinson* and USS *Theodore Roosevelt*. The captain invited us to his cabin to warmly welcome us aboard. Our custom tour included the hangar bay, officer's mess, hospital ward, and ready room, including even the location of Jon's *TR* stateroom.

Isabella enjoyed climbing above the flight deck and up into the island and the bridge. While proudly sitting in the captain's chair, Isabella examined a map of the Ionian Sea provided by our gracious tour guides, who pointed out where Daddy Jon's plane went down on that fateful night. As always, Isabella was full of questions.

"Do these phones work?" Isabella inquired, looking up at the communications equipment surrounding the captain's chair.

One of our tour guides eagerly demonstrated, in a way a second-grader could understand, how they operated.

"Can you order some cookies on this thing?" she wondered, and the crew on the bridge laughed. Isabella shared Jon's sweet tooth, and she was remembering fondly the plates of chocolate chip cookies the staff of USS *Gerald R. Ford* had given us two days earlier. Isabella was always on the lookout for a yummy treat!

When our tour was complete, we stood outside on the pier at Norfolk Naval Station with patriotic red, white, and blue balloons and yellow roses in our hands. The twenty-fifth anniversary of Jon's death didn't fall on Father's Day, but we felt that a balloon launch in that meaningful location was an appropriate way to honor his memory. Perhaps Isabella couldn't use the phones on the ship to communicate, but a child's innocent prayer and a balloon released to heaven could bridge the gap between a precious granddaughter and her beloved grandfather.

With USS *Harry S. Truman* docked behind us on our right and USS *Gerald R. Ford* facing us to our left, Isabella and I said a quick prayer: "Dear Jesus, please tell Daddy Jon that we love him." With her back toward the past and her bright, hopeful face turned toward the future, Jon's granddaughter released her balloon of love toward the sky. The stiff, northeast wind propelled the shiny balloon over the water, above USS *Gerald R. Ford*, and out of sight, as Isabella raised her arms and waved goodbye. Smiling tenderly, she tossed her yellow roses into the harbor.

The Rystrom Emmert family on USS Gerald Ford, March 25, 2018; L to R: Cole Emmert, Taylor Rystrom Emmert, Kris Rystrom Emmert, Isabella Rystrom Emmert Collana, Jordyn Rystrom Emmert, Makenzie Emmert, and Joe Emmert

* * *

So now, Isabella, I have told you the story—the whole story—even the parts that, at your young age, you didn't know to ask. And now, I have a few more things that I want you to remember always. God is your Provider. He is the One who gives you promises. Cling to those promises every day of your life, on the good days and the bad days— especially on the bad days.

Remember that your freedom isn't free. Many brave men and women like Daddy Jon have paid the ultimate price so that you can live in liberty and safety. Remember and honor these heroes. And remember Jesus, who purchased your eternal freedom by laying down His life for you on the cross. Like you said, God never breaks His promise. *Never*!

God will always provide promise for you.

Jon Rystrom's girls today on the tarmac at the VAW-124 hangar during the Bear Ace 603 remembrance weekend; L to R: Isabella, Jordyn, Kris, and Taylor

Where Are They Now?

Frenchy's widow, Shelly Messier Hill, now lives in Marietta, Georgia, with her husband, State Senator Judson Hill. They have been married for over twenty years and have three children. At twenty-five years old when the mishap happened, Shelly was the youngest member of the Wids.

Billy Ray's widow, Paola Dyer McNeil, has been married for over twenty years to her husband Matt, a successful businessman from Midlothian, Virginia. Paola and Matt have three children, including Billy Ray's son, Christopher. Thanks to the VAW-VRC Memorial Scholarship Fund, Christopher Dyer graduated from Davidson College, where he also played baseball. He lives in Charlotte, North Carolina, and works as a financial services recruiter at Aerotek. Christopher also coaches nine-year-olds in AAU baseball.

Katie Forwalder Riley, Bob's widow, is married to her husband of twenty-two years, Captain Greg Riley, a retired U.S. Navy F-18 pilot, who now flies for American Airlines. Residing in Woodbridge, Virginia, Katie and Greg have four children, including Bob's son, Sean, who was born soon after the mishap. Sean Forwalder graduated from the Naval Academy in 2015 and was also a recipient of the VAW-VRC Memorial Scholarship Fund. Lt. j.g. Forwalder has been assigned to the helicopter squadron HSC-9, the Tridents, assigned to the aircraft carrier USS *George H. W. Bush,* out of Norfolk, Virginia. Sean is married to Kathleen Hawkins Forwalder.

Mrs. Ardaiz, the mother of Patrick "Aardvark" Ardaiz, is an active senior. Her family has a remarkable, positive outlook on Patrick's short life, and they actively honor his memory still today.

As for me, I married my amazing husband, Rev. Joe Emmert, in 1996 at the same church where, three years earlier, Jon's memorial service was held. Dr. Bob Reccord performed our ceremony. Joe adopted Jordyn and Taylor, and we had two children, Cole and Makenzie. We reside in Knoxville, Tennessee, where Joe is the senior pastor of North Knoxville Baptist Church.

My oldest daughter, Jordyn Rystrom Emmert, graduated with honors from Eastern University in Pennsylvania, thanks to the VAW-VRC Memorial Scholarship Fund. Jordyn received her juris doctorate from Thurgood Marshall School of Law, where she also graduated with honors. She is a practicing attorney in Houston, Texas, and is raising her daughter and our granddaughter, sweet Isabella—a bright, outgoing fourth grader.

Taylor Rystrom Emmert lives in East Tennessee. Thanks to the VAW-VRC Memorial Scholarship Fund, she graduated summa cum laude from Carson-Newman University in Tennessee in 2014, where she was awarded outstanding graduate as well as the presidential scholar award. She works as a systems coordinator for Two Roads and is married to Will Ford, a Citadel graduate.

My father, Chuck Windham, passed away several years ago, but my mother, Doris, is still going strong and joined us for the remembrance weekend. She resides at her beach home in coastal North Carolina.

Bear Ace 603 "Wids" today in the cockpit of an E-2C Hawkeye during the remembrance weekend.
L to R: Shelly Messier Hill, Kris Rystrom Emmert, Katie Forwalder Riley, and Paola Dyer McNeil.

A Place of Honor

26 MAR 2018
12:52 Eastern Daylight Time UTC-4
Arlington National Cemetery
Arlington, Virginia, USA
MH 657
38°87'83" N, 77°07'50" W

On the hallowed grounds where a grateful nation lays to rest those who have died in service to their country, there is also a place of honor for the ones whose bodies were never recovered. Down the hill from the Tomb of the Unknown Soldier lies a distinguished memorial section for those who never came home. These somber markers are placed near a wooded area, as these stones will not disturb the hidden roots as traditional graves do.

The warm, afternoon sun filters through the towering oak, hickory, and pine trees near grave marker MH 657. Etched in the white marble stone reads the words, Jon R. Rystrom CDR US Navy, Jan 21, 1955–March 26, 1993, VAW-124 Operation Provide Promise. Located near a newly planted dogwood tree, this monument—one of many arranged in neat, orderly rows—is found directly in front of another bearing the same date. Two navy brothers united in life and united in death in Bear Ace 603.

The solemn markers are a lasting testament to lives well-lived and costly sacrifices made. The sight of so many markers and the horrific losses they represent is sobering, but nothing is buried on this tranquil hillside. No coffins rest in repose under the surface. The bodies of those honored there lie concealed in foreign lands, were destroyed in unspeakable calamities, or were grimly lost at sea.

Tragically, many noble soldiers cannot be properly entombed. However, their successors can rest assured their soldiers' souls may live on regardless of their burials. When the Son appears, some things once buried will rise again: faith, hope, love, and the children of God.

That is a promise.

Jon A Rystrom
CDR
US Navy
Jan 21, 1955
Mar 26, 1993
VAW-124
Operation
Provide Promise

Discussion Questions

The following questions can be used for a small group, Bible study, book club, or an individual reader.

Chapter 1: Growing Up

1. Julie Voudrie talks of wreckage in "A Word from the Co-Author." Has there been a time in your life, now or in the past, when you were unexpectedly handed "wreckage"?

2. Was there a time in your life when you felt like you were living the "perfect life?" Read Matthew 6:19-21. Discuss what these verses say about achieving the possessions of this world.

3. Have you ever felt that because of your faith in God, life's calamities could not touch you?

4. Have you ever experienced being bullied by your peers, family members, or coworkers? What effect did that have on you?

Chapter 2: The Next Steps

1. Has there been a time in your life when you questioned your career path or felt like you were stuck in a dead-end job? What steps did you take to make your situation different?

2. Have you ever felt that no matter what awards you earned, achievements you accomplished, or compliments you received, it was never enough? Read Joshua 1:9 and John 16:33.

Chapter 3: The Hawkeye

1. Explain a time in your life when your hard work and determination to reach your goals helped you succeed? Read Colossians 3:23 and Proverbs 13:4. Was there a time when no matter how hard you worked, your life seemed to be filled with disappointments and failures?

2. How does Psalm 121:8 compare to the Hawkeye's mission? How does this verse make you feel?

Chapter 4: Freedom's Flagship

1. Have you or someone you know ever struggled with an eating disorder? Or have you ever been stuck in an addiction or struggle that consumed your thoughts and everyday activities? Read I Corinthians 6:19-20 and I Samuel 16:7. How do these scriptures help define how we are to look at our appearance?

2. What steps did you take to help yourself or friend overcome this struggle?

Chapter 5: Single and Searching

1. Has there been a time in your life when you had specific plans and goals for your life, but circumstances didn't work out right? Explain. Read Romans 15:13.

2. Jon went through the heartbreak of a divorce. Have you had to struggle through a heartbreak of your own? What

emotions did you feel? What areas of your life helped you get through those times? What advice would you give someone who is suffering with rejection, betrayal, or abandonment?

3. Have you ever used work as a substitute for personal fulfillment? Read Psalm 127:2. What does this verse say about work?

Chapter 6: Green-Eyed Lady

1. What part of the personal ad story and first meeting made you smile? Have you ever been on a blind date that turned into something special? Read 1 Corinthians 13:7.

2. How important is the approval of your family in your dating choices? Why do you think that is?

Chapter 7: Welcome to the Navy, Mrs. Rystrom

1. Have you or someone you know been engaged and married in less than a year of meeting one another? What are some of the challenges of a short courtship?

2. Have you ever attended a military wedding? The military tradition of the arch of swords demonstrates a pledge of fidelity from the military to the new couple. What is the symbolism between this tradition and the marriage covenant to God? Read Ephesians 5:25. Does this scripture have a personal meaning for you?

3. What is the irony of Jon's statement at the wedding of spending the next forty to fifty years with Kris? When looking back on your past, is there a memory, phrase, or gesture that foreshadows something in your future?

Chapter 8: Highway to the Danger Zone

1. Have you ever had to make a huge move to another state or country? What challenges did you have to face? Would this be harder or easier as a newlywed?

2. Has there ever been a time in your life when the only form of communication was letter writing? Did this make your relationship closer? How?

Chapter 9: Love Letters Across the Sea

1. Jon and I made a promise to write each other every day. Why is this promise significant in the story?

2. The apostle Paul wrote thirteen letters in Scripture. Our letters became an important part of our relationship. How are the New Testament letters an important part of our relationship with God?

3. Have you ever had a long-distance relationship? In what ways has the distance hurt or helped the relationship?

4. Assignment: Choose one person in your family or a close friend and make a promise that you will write a letter (not an email or a simple card) to that person every day for a week. After you do this, share how this exercise has changed how you feel toward this person. Has it made a difference in their life?

Chapter 10: Back at Sea

1. Why was July Fourth so meaningful to me? What does America's freedom mean to you?

Chapter 11: Hong Kong Homecoming

1. "When I looked at the image of the young widow holding the folded American flag on the front page of the local paper, I had the strange feeling that one day that would be me." Have you ever had a foreboding feeling or image that became true? Explain.

2. Read Daniel 7:1, Matthew 2:19-20, and Genesis 28:12. What is the common theme in these passages? Do you believe that God can speak to you in dreams?

Chapter 12: Go Big Red

1. Since most naval personnel are stationed on bases along coastlines, why was the move to an Air Force base in Nebraska significant to Jon and our family?

2. Has the birth of a child ever changed your career path/choices? How?

Chapter 13: Seagrass Reach

1. With every move we made, I was checking off the boxes in my life to see where I was at. What kind of boxes do you check off in your life?

2. I had a scare as a mom when my infant daughter, Taylor went into the hospital. Jon couldn't get home, and for the first time, I had the fear of single parenting. Have you been a single parent? What are your fears and challenges?

Chapter 14: Iron Grip

1. Do you find yourself dismissing the horrific news regarding conflicts in other parts of the world? After reading this chapter, how has your opinion changed toward the plight of refugees from war-torn countries?

2. There is much controversy over refugees in the United States. If you were the Bosniak mother trying to keep her children alive, how would your opinion change or not change?

3. Read Matthew 25: 35-40. Discuss how this relates to helping others in your community, in your country, around the world.

Chapter 15: Rosebushes and Goodbyes

1. The last few days leading up to Jon's deployment was filled with more "box checking." These were the types of boxes of a "honey-do list." If you knew that you were spending the last two weeks with your spouse or family member before they were leaving for six months, what "boxes" would you check?

2. What is the significance of Jon describing his survival gear in detail at the preschool presentation at Jordyn's career day?

3. Jordyn and I created the paper chain to countdown the days until Jon came home. Have you ever created a countdown chart for something special?

Chapter 16: Paper-Chain Prayers

1. Jon forgot to sign his new life insurance policy, but someone discovered that detail and was able to take care of it. Have you ever experienced times where you see God taking care of you in details that you almost missed?"

2. What is the significance of the storm of the century and the no-fly days? Do you believe there are any correlations between the lack of flight hours and the accident?

Chapter 17: Operation Provide Promise

1. Why do you think this operation was named Operation Provide Promise?

2. When Jon found out he had an extra hour to spare before his helo left for the JFK, what was the one thing he did that was important?

Chapter 18: No Horizon

1. Why is this chapter titled "No Horizon"? Pilots must fly by only their instruments when there is limited or no visibility. How does this relate to walking by faith when we can't see the path in front of us?

2. The initial approach of 603 to the flight deck was perfect, but due to the unexplained malfunction of an arresting wire, the ship had a foul flight deck and 603 was waved off. This resulted in the plane crashing into the water. Have there been times in your life when with your effort and work, everything was going as planned, but then a situation out of your control caused you to take an unexpected, and possibly detrimental, turn?

3. The recount of what the girls and I were doing at the time of the crash is accurate due to the preservation of the handwritten letters. Do you find a correlation between the peaceful evening the girls and I were spending and the horrific scene taking place at the same time in the Ionian Sea?

Chapter 19: Bear Ace 603

1. At the same time the girls and I were having a peaceful evening, a horrific scene was taking place in the Ionian Sea. Do you believe that God sometimes keeps us from being aware of tragic events happening around us for our emotional protection? How have you seen this in your life?

2. What do you think my first reaction was when I saw the men in stripes go by my dining room window? After my initial shock, I went into survival mode and started on the necessary tasks. Has there ever been a time when you continued with tasks after learning of a shock or trauma? Do you find that these are coping skills that you learn or are they from God to get you through the shock?

3. Have you ever experienced a deep loss? Have you ever had a time in your life when your life completely shattered and you felt like you could never breathe again? Share your experience. What are some verses that helped you? What is God's response to us when we ask why? How does He comfort us and meet us in those places?

4. How do you explain to someone who has lost their faith as a result of loss and death?

Chapter 20: Lost at Sea

1. What is God's response to us when we ask why those tragedies happen? How does He comfort us and meet us in those places? How do you explain why tragedy happens to someone who has lost their faith because of loss and death?

2. To this day, I am still haunted by the fact that Jon's body was never recovered and I have never received the answer to why that tragedy happened. Have you ever experienced a moment in your life where the hard questions were never answered? Have you had a loved one disappear from your life? How have you dealt with this tragic loss?

3. Despite the tragedy, the men on the ship had to continue their mission. Has there ever been a time when you had to continue with something even though you were deeply hurting inside? Have you ever been in situations where you had to compartmentalize your feelings just to survive? When and how did you eventually process?

Chapter 21: Love Letters from the Grave

1. When President Clinton addressed the nation about Jon's plane missing, it became a national tragedy. I was then considered "next of kin." Have you or your family ever been in a news spotlight for a tragic story? Do you feel that the circumstances of being on a national platform change how people react or feel?

2. When I received Jon's letter after I had been told he was gone, I felt heartache and comfort at the same time. Why do you think I felt this way? Is there a similarity of finding comfort in reading scripture?

3. What is the parallel between Jon's scuba picture underwater with his two thumbs up and where his final resting place is? Why do you think I found comfort in that picture?

4. The night of the accident, I rocked Taylor in her nursery alone in the dark and nursed her for the last time. Why do you think I made that decision?

5. During my first night alone in my bedroom after the accident, I found comfort in holding Jon's bathrobe. Is there an object or article of clothing that has deep meaning in your life?

6. Read Isaiah 43:2-4, which are the verses for my life. Describe the significance of these verses.

Chapter 22: Is My Daddy Happy?

1. Jon's letters are so special to me and our daughters. Do you have an item or items that mean a lot to you from someone special in your life?

2. How would you explain God's love to a child when prayers are not answered?

3. Read John 3:16-17. Why does this verse come to mean so much more after we lose someone? Read John 14:1-6. How are these verses comforting?

Chapter 23: My Folded Flag

1. The tradition of giving a serviceman/woman's family member a folded American flag at the time of their death means that this flag will no longer wave. It stands

for honor, service, and sacrifice. What are some words that would describe what my folded flag means to me?

2. When the missing-man formation flew overhead the church, why do you think I had a complete meltdown in front of everyone? Has there ever been a time where you thought you were holding yourself together and then something specific happened that caused you to lose it?"

3. What was the meaning of the last line in my dad's poem about Jon? Read Galatians 6: 9-10 and Colossians 3:23. How do these verses correlate to this last line of the poem?

Chapter 24: The Last Letter

1. Why was Jon's last letter to me so comforting? Jon always wrote to me at night before he went to bed. Do you find the significance of him writing to me the morning of his accident?

2. If you could write a letter to someone, knowing that this would be the last day of your life, who would you write and what would you say? Take time now to write that letter and mail it to that person.

3. Why was the crumpled box of Jon's ship belongings so impactful? Have you ever had an item bring you a painful memory? How did it make an impact on you and does it still today?

Chapter 25: Wreckage in My Hands

1. In this chapter, I was faced with the reality of Jon not returning with the squadron when I saw the fly-over

come by my hotel balcony. Was there ever a time when you felt like God put you into a situation you were trying to avoid, but you realized it was for your own good?

2. Has there ever been a time in your life when you tricked yourself into thinking that you are emotionally doing fine when you are not? Was there a defining moment when you faced reality?

3. Read Job 14:1-5 and Psalm 56:8. These scriptures describe grief and despair. What do these scriptures mean to you personally?

Chapter 26: How Do You Get Through?

1. Have you ever felt like God was "punishing" you with hurts or disappointments in your life? Explain.

2. Have you ever dealt with "pound-cake people"? What strategies did you find most effective? Who are the true blues in your life?

3. What part of this chapter was most helpful? Read Psalm 23. Write out verse 4. As you write it out, think about its meaning for you personally.

Chapter 27: From Triggers to Moving On

1. What are some triggers in your life?

2. What are some sprinkles of sunshine that have helped you get through a bad day or season in your life? Read Romans 15:13 and James 1:16-18. These scriptures speak of hope and joy. Do you find comfort from these verses?

3. The Wids were a huge support system for me. Has there been a time in your life when you have looked for a support group? Discuss the benefits or the problems you encountered.

Chapter 28: Hello, Mr. President

1. In the book by Dr. Dobson, *When God Doesn't Make Sense*, he states, "In your hour of crisis, don't demand explanation. Don't lean on your ability to understand. Don't turn loose of your faith. But do choose to trust Him ... The only other alternative is despair." What does this statement mean to you?

2. Dr. Dobson also states, "Pain and suffering do not cause the greatest damage. Confusion is the factor that shreds one's faith." Do you believe this statement? Why or why not? Read 1 Timothy 5:5. What does this scripture tell us about the widow, and how does it relate to my journey?

3. Has there been a time in your life when someone reached out to you when you least expected and it was a sprinkle of sunshine just when you needed it? How can you be a sprinkle of sunshine in someone's life today? Make a commitment to act on it.

Chapter 29: Balloons to Heaven

1. Have you or someone you know kept a tradition to remember someone who has died?

2. Dr. Reccord told me to "remember my legacy." What did he mean by that? What is your legacy, and why is it important? Read Psalm 78:4 and Psalm 145:4. What do

these scriptures tell you about teaching our children about God?

3. Has there been a time in your life when you cried out to God in despair and felt He didn't hear your prayers? Explain. Read Psalm 18:6. How does this scripture reassure you that God hears our prayers?

Chapter 30: My Letter from Heaven

1. When I found the balloon at my feet, I was in disbelief. Has there ever been a time in your life when God answered your prayers in an unexpected way?

2. My balloon said, "You're So Special!" Take time to meditate on how special you are in God's eyes. You are His masterpiece.

3. If you could write a love letter to God, what would it say? Take the time to write Him a letter. Be honest. After you have written it, pray it out loud. Make this a daily prayer for thirty days.

4. How is the Bible God's letter to His children?

Chapter 31: H.O.P.E.

1. *Hold on to the truth*: What steps can you take to hold on to the truth?

2. *Open your heart to others*: How can you reach out to others or allow others to help you in any way?

3. *Position yourself for obedience*: What areas of obedience do you struggle with? How can you take steps to obey what God is calling you to?

4. *Embrace the past—face the future*: Are you holding on to the past? How can you move forward in facing your future?

5. How has *Providing Promise* ministered to you? What three aspects of this book were helpful to you?

Works Cited

Chapman, Nancy. "Meeting Through the Personals." *Portfolio*. Vol. 5, No. 1. 06 May–12 May 1995. Print.

Department of the Navy. "Investigation into the Circumstances of E-2C Aircraft BUNO 161549 and Crew in the Ionian Sea on 26 March 1993." *JAG Investigation, 603 Mishap, BUNO 161549*.19 Apr. 1993. Norfolk, Virginia.

Dobson, Dr. James C. *When God Doesn't Make Sense*. Tyndale, 1993, ch. 1.

Shawshank Redemption. Dir. Frank Darabont. Perf. Tim Robbins, Morgan Freeman. Castle Rock, 2007. Film.

Woolley, John and Gerhard Peters. "The President's News Conference with Chancellor Helmut Kohl of Germany." *The American Presidency Project*, 26 Mar. 1993, presidency.ucsb.edu//ws/index.php?pid=46377.

Woolley, John and Gerhard Peters. "Remarks to the Crew of the USS *Theodore Roosevelt*." *The American Presidency Project*, 12 Mar. 1993, presidency.ucsb.edu//ws/index.php?pid=46330.

About the Authors

Kris Rystrom Emmert

Award-winning author and inspirational speaker **Kris Rystrom Emmert** impacts readers and audiences with her powerful message on having endured unspeakable tragedy and discovered unshakeable hope. With her contagious zest for life, she weaves her story of loss into a life-changing encounter that inspires others to experience their own healing and to uncover their God-given destinies.

A graduate of Wake Forest University and Regent University, Kris holds a master's degree in communications. In her writing and on stage, she combines her extensive education, military experience, challenges of single motherhood, talents as a businesswoman, and years of teaching at higher-education institutions to reach thousands with her motivating message. Topics include Hope after Heartache, God's Unfailing Love, Inner Beauty Discovered, Purpose in a Changing World, and Sanctity of Life.

Kris, a member of Gold Star Wives of America and Advanced Writers and Speakers Association, resides in East Tennessee and is a pastor's wife, mom to four children, a grandmother to one, and the founder of Providing Promise Ministries, a 501(c)3 non-profit ministry.

kris@providingpromise.com
www.providingpromise.com.
Twitter: @KristaEmmert
Facebook: Facebook.com/providingpromise
Instagram: @providingpromise

A portion of the proceeds from Providing Promise will be donated to the VAW-VRC Memorial Scholarship Fund.
For more information about this fund or to donate, visit www.vvosa.org.

Julie Voudrie

Julie Voudrie is a versatile storyteller, able to creatively capture hearts and minds in order to communicate compelling truths. As a mother of seven, grandmother, home educator, former missionary, public speaker, and entrepreneur, Julie has a passion for inspiring others to reach their potential and fulfill their God-given destiny. Julie and her husband live in the beautiful Appalachian Mountains of Northeast Tennessee.

Acknowledgments

To Our Families

Kris

To my loving husband, Joe, for being my "kinsman redeemer." You took a widow and her little girls and made us your family. You have always encouraged me to tell my story, and words cannot express how grateful I am. Jon was the love of my youth; you are the love of my life. 5-11-95.

To my daughter, Jordyn, for insisting that I finally write this book. I owe this project to your persistent but loving push. To my daughter, Taylor, for helping keep my focus on the prize—to God be the glory. To my younger children, Cole and Makenzie, for being patient as I spent hours in solitude writing and for putting up with all of Daddy Jon's unpacked boxes scattered all over the house.

To my precious Isabella, this story was written so you would know your other grandpa.

To my mom, Doris Windham, Dad would be so proud.

To my other mom, Faye Emmert, Richard would love this story.

To my Nebraska family, Barb and Gary Dean, Mike and Matt; Pat and Ken Everingham, Eric, Sara, and Joey; Jim and Laurie Parsley: Jon was proud to be a Rystrom, and he loved his hometown of Stromsburg.

To my Boston family, Martin and Maria Rystrom, Dan, Adam, and Nick: Jon loved playing with you boys in your pool and showing off his one-armed push-ups!

In memory of my other parents, Mervin and Josephine Rystrom: Jon loved them dearly.

Julie

To my beloved husband, Jeff, for patiently enduring the loss of your pool table for months while I used it for the spreading out of research material; for being understanding as I disappeared into another world and spent countless hours holed up at my desk day and night; for believing in me when I doubted myself; for being an objective sounding board; for assisting me any way you could and reassuring me as I pressed on to the finish. You are the wind in my sails, and you're still the song in me.

To my children, Jonathan, Danielle (and Bryan and Davona), Hannah, Josh, Aaron, Grace, and Leah: Thanks for your understanding as Mom was preoccupied for a season and for your encouragement as I labored away.

To my friend Kris for entrusting your story to me. Thank you for being brave—for opening your box and sharing your scars and your treasures with the rest of us. Your little acorn of an idea quickly grew into a massive project that transcended anything either of us expected. I have gained a faithful friend, and I am forever changed because of you.

To my Abba, Your timing is perfect. You are the God of the open door. Your grace is sufficient. Thank You for choosing me for this project but, most of all, for loving me above and beyond what I deserve or comprehend. Through my life, may the Lamb receive the reward for His suffering.

To My Military Family

Kris

To Lt. Cmdr. David E. Mullis, U.S. Navy, Retired; Maj. Ed Van Haute, USMC, retired; Cmdr. John "Waffle" Eggert, U.S. Navy,

Retired; Cmdr. Scott "Lenny" Bruce, U.S. Navy, Retired; Lt. Cmdr. Mike Purcell, U.S. Navy, Retired; Capt. Timothy R. Eichler, U.S. Navy, Retired; Capt. Steve Squires, U.S. Navy, Retired; and Capt. Randy "Bubba" Bannister, U.S. Navy, Retired; for your expertise in making the military scenes "navy ready." Without your help, this book would have been impossible to write.

USS *Gerald R. Ford:* Capt. Richard McCormack, commanding officer; Capt. Brent Gaut, executive officer; and crew.

USS *Harry S. Truman:* Capt. Nicholas Dienna, commanding officer; Capt. Cassidy Norman, executive officer; Lt. Cmdr. Laura Stegherr, public affairs officer; and crew.

David Adams Memorial Chapel: Chaplain Lt. Cmdr. Kimberly Cain, Vice Adm. Herman A. Shelanski, Naval Inspector General, and Rear Adm. Jesse A. Wilson, Jr., Cmdr., Naval Surface Force Atlantic

VAW-124 Bear Aces: Cmdr. Christian Goodman, commanding officer; Cmdr. Gregory Machi, executive officer; Lt. Cmdr. Blake "Sharpie" Baccigalopi; U.S. Navy retired Capt. Chris "Bolter" and Shelley Bolt; Rear Adm. John and Julie Lemmon; and the squadron.

A special thank you to my CACO officer, US Navy retired Capt. Rick Vanden Heuvel, who was my gentle companion through the darkest days of my life.

Julie

To Dave Mullis, who graciously opened his home and gave me a solid indoctrination into all things navy and to Randy Bannister, who willingly shared his immense knowledge and expertise, patiently answering many questions in detail without making me feel foolish in the least. Bravo Zulu!

To My Supportive Friends

Kris

To Dr. Bob Reccord, my pastor, for graciously writing my foreword. You and your sweet wife, Cheryl, have made an impact on my life like no other. Your ministering words each week helped awaken, for the first time, faith in Christ for me. Thank you for following your personal call to help widows and orphans. I will always call you *my* pastor.

To my publisher, Highbridge Books, and the incredible editorial talent of Sara Steindl. To Teresa Stanley, my editor and "seester." You have wanted me to write this book for years and believed in my calling before anyone else. Your brilliant mind and attention to detail kept me out of the grammar doghouse. I truly appreciate your talent and, most of all, our friendship.

To the Thrive Marketing team in Morristown, Tennessee: Leigh Sempkowski, Bobbi Odom, and Brittany Cross. You caught my vision from the start and encouraged me to be confident in my calling.

To Becca Perry. This dream became true because of you. Our trip to Arlington National Cemetery in April 2017 sparked the flame for this book. I am blessed to call you my friend.

To Premier Designs, Inc. and the Horner family for giving me the opportunity to tell my story to thousands of women across the country. I am thankful that yours is a company that stands on biblical principles.

To my photographers, Casey Lauren Townsend, Ashley Lodge, Leah Belcher, Ben Gibson, Scotty Bruce, Craig Moran, and Harry Gerwien. Each of you has an amazing craft, and I am thankful God brought you into my life to capture images that would help tell my story.

To my creative team, Robert and Amber Till, Tyton Rock. Your creative vision is a gift from God. Thank you for creating my website and using your artistic talents to enable others to experience my life story in print.

To Jamie Lewis, whom I love like a sister, praying for open doors as I tell my story and give hope.

To Rebecca Statzer, we will continue to look for our glimmers of hope every day.

To my coauthor and friend, Julie Voudrie, little did I know what God was going to do when He joined our lives together. You willingly took a vision and made it a dream come true. I cannot thank you enough for the hours, weeks, months, and, eventually, year that you poured your life into this project. My prayer is that you will be rewarded and blessed beyond measure. I have found a true sister in you, my friend. May you rest in our Provider as He blesses you with His promises. To God be the glory!

Notes

Printed in the USA
CPSIA information can be obtained
at www.ICGtesting.com
JSHW010004260124
55805JS00001B/1

9 781952 025631